PROTOCOLS of the ELDERS of ZION

BOOKS FROM CLEMENS & BLAIR
— www.clemensandblair.com —

The Riddle of the Jews' Success, by Theodor Fritsch
Triumph of the Truth, by Robert Penman
The Book of the Shulchan Aruch, by Erich Bischoff
For My Legionnaires, by Corneliu Codreanu
Myth and Sun, by Martin Friedrich
Unmasking Anne Frank, by Ikuo Suzuki
Pan-Judah! Political Cartoons of Der Stürmer, by Robert Penman
Passovers of Blood, by Ariel Toaff
The Poisonous Mushroom, by Ernst Hiemer
On the Jews and Their Lies, by Martin Luther
Mein Kampf, by Adolf Hitler
Mein Kampf (Dual English-German edition), by Adolf Hitler
The Essential Mein Kampf, by Adolf Hitler
The Myth of the 20th Century, by Alfred Rosenberg

BOOKS BY THOMAS DALTON
— www.thomasdaltonphd.com —

The Steep Climb: Essays on the Jewish Question
Classic Essays on the Jewish Question: 1850 to 1945
Debating the Holocaust
The Holocaust: An Introduction
The Jewish Hand in the World Wars
Eternal Strangers: Critical Views of Jews and Judaism
Hitler on the Jews
Goebbels on the Jews
Streicher, Rosenberg, and the Jews: The Nuremberg Transcripts

PROTOCOLS
of the
ELDERS of ZION

The Definitive English Edition

Edited and Translated
by
THOMAS DALTON

Clemens & Blair, LLC
— 2023 —

CLEMENS & BLAIR, LLC

Copyright © 2023, by Thomas Dalton, PhD

All rights reserved. No part of this publication may be reproduced, stored in a retrieval system, or transmitted, in any form or by any means, electronic, mechanical, photocopying, recording, or otherwise.

Clemens & Blair, LLC, is a non-profit educational publisher.
www.clemensandblair.com

Library of Congress Cataloging-in-Publication Data

Dalton, Thomas B. (ed.)
Protocols of the Elders of Zion: The Definitive English Edition

p. cm.
Includes bibliographical references

ISBN 979-8987-7263-27
(pbk.: alk. paper)

1. Jewish Question, the

Printing number: 9 8 7 6 5 4 3 2 1

Printed in the United States of America on acid-free paper.

CONTENTS

INTRODUCTION by Thomas Dalton 1

PART ONE: Overview and Early Commentaries

Summary, by the US Holocaust Memorial Museum 15
"The Jewish Peril," by Wickham Steed (8 May 1920) 19
On the *Protocols*, by Henry Ford (24 July to 14 August 1920) 25
"A Literary Forgery," by Philip Graves (16-18 August 1921) 57

PART TWO: The Protocols

Protocol No. 1: On liberalism, 'might means right,' Goyim vices, equality, power of money. 77
Protocol No. 2: On economic wars, the press. 83
Protocol No. 3: On rights, Goy aristocracy, liberalism. 85
Protocol No. 4: On liberty, financial speculation. 89
Protocol No. 5: On centralized government, power of gold, control of public opinion. 91
Protocol No. 6: On monopolies, trade, industry. 95
Protocol No. 7: On the military, social disruption, war. 97
Protocol No. 8: On new government, the role of Jews. 99
Protocol No. 9: On dictatorships, Jewish ambition, education. 100
Protocol No. 10: On Freemasonry, liberalism, legislative and executive government. 103
Protocol No. 11: On the new constitution, Goyim as animals. 108
Protocol No. 12: On liberty, the press, Freemasonry. 110
Protocol No. 13: On political problems, trade, diversion of the mob. 115
Protocol No. 14: On religion, pornography. 117
Protocol No. 15: On Freemasonry, civil disobedience, the judiciary, the power of the Sovereign. 119
Protocol No. 16: On universities, education. 126
Protocol No. 17: On law, religion, the virtue of spying. 128
Protocol No. 18: On open and secret defense of rulers. 131
Protocol No. 19: On sedition and political crimes. 133
Protocol No. 20: On financial matters, taxation, circulation of money, governmental loans. 134
Protocol No. 21: On domestic loans. 140
Protocol No. 22: On restoring social order. 142

Protocol No. 23: On the arising of the Sovereign. 143
Protocol No. 24: On the Sovereign, the King of Israel. 145

PART THREE: National Socialist Commentaries

Rosenberg on the *Protocols* (1923) 149
Hitler and Goebbels on the *Protocols* 177
"Introduction" to the *Protocols*, by the NSDAP (1938) 181
"Introduction" to the *Protocols*, by Julius Evola (1938) 209

PART FOUR: Contemporary Reflections

The Fake "Fake Protocols," by Carlo Mattogno 235
The *Protocols* in the 21st Century, by Thomas Dalton 259

BIBLIOGRAPHY 275

INDEX (PROTOCOLS ONLY) 277

PROTOCOLS of the ELDERS of ZION

INTRODUCTION
THOMAS DALTON

No study of the history of the Jewish Question is complete without a detailed look at the document known as the *Protocols of the Elders of Zion*. As mysterious as it is notorious, it has been called the most influential piece of anti-Semitic literature in history—perhaps comparable in importance only to Hitler's *Mein Kampf*. Nothing like it has ever been produced, before or since.

And yet, there is a remarkable irony here; the *Protocols* contains not a drop of Jew-hatred (in notable contrast to Hitler's famous book). Not even close: no criticism, no condemnation, no heated language. In fact, quite the opposite: the text lavishly praises Jews and Jewish cleverness and tenacity, and repeatedly celebrates Jewish successes. It acknowledges Jewish political and economic accomplishments of the past, and looks forward to yet greater achievements still, ultimately aiming at something that could loosely be called 'global Jewish superpower' status. For Jews and Judaism, the *Protocols* are a good-news story of the highest degree.

So—what's the problem? How can such a document as this be condemned and slandered as deeply anti-Semitic? Saying that Jews have been monumentally successful in economics and politics, and can look forward to much greater success in the near future? Is that bad? In what way? And why?

Only in the Jewish worldview can success be a bad thing—or rather, *publicity* about success, which is the real issue here. That the Jews, especially in the West, have prospered beyond all reasonable expectation is clear to anyone who has given even brief thought to the Jewish Question. But they have done so despite centuries, even millennia, of condemnation, attack, abuse, and yes, hatred. (That they have deserved this treatment is a story best left for another time.) A core element of the global Jewish strategy for interacting with the Gentiles—the non-Jews—is to play up the (historically valid) victimhood status, while at the same time hiding away the fact that they have simultaneously managed to acquire absurd amounts of wealth and power. Jews have been overly-influential for literally 2,000 years, and they have been detested, hated, and abused for just as long. They love playing the victim, but hate being exposed as the victor, the king, the tyrant.

Then around the turn of the 20th century comes along this little document—an extended essay, really, too short to be called a book—known today as the *Protocols of the Elders of Zion*, which seems to lay out, in clear and explicit terms, the nature of recent and phenomenal Jewish success, along with the plan to acquire more in the near future. The means for this success, however, is troubling: a suppression, manipulation, exploitation, and indeed virtual destruction of the detested non-Jews: the "Goyim" (or "Goy," singular).[1] So now we see the nature of the problem; the *Protocols* lay out a brutal plan of action by Jews to acquire effective global power over the Goyim by deceiving and exploiting them. But since it is cast in the form of a Jew talking to his fellow Jews, the language is benign, self-congratulatory, smug—but never 'anti-Semitic.' I am tempted to call it the nicest work of anti-Semitism known to man.

But even that would be to assume too much. As I alluded to above, the document truly is shrouded in mystery. Its origins are unknown, although a number of theories have been offered. The author likewise is unknown; we don't even know if he (or she) was a Jew or non-Jew. We know neither the year nor the country of writing, though we do have a few good clues to some of this. Here, in this Introduction, I will give just the basics of what we know; a number of entries to follow elaborate on various aspects of the story, so there is no need for me to repeat them here. By the end of this book, the reader will be well-informed on nearly all major aspects of the infamous *Protocols*.

The Preliminaries

The very first thing that one encounters about the *Protocols*, upon reading virtually any conventional source, is that they are "a forgery." All

---

[1] Technically, in Hebrew, 'goy' simply refers to a nation or ethnically-homogenous group of people. The Old Testament uses 'goy' or 'goyim' hundreds of times, referring both to Jews and non-Jews. However, since the first century AD, the term has been used by Jews to refer, negatively, to non-Jews. This is the sense that I employ here, and in the *Protocols*. I have also elected to capitalize the term, to emphasize the categorical importance.

orthodox sources—textbooks, news articles, encyclopedias, films, blogs—seem overly-anxious, desperately anxious, to impress upon the reader the idea that this document is bogus, fraudulent, nonsense, and utterly untrustworthy. For our present Jewish-inspired orthodoxy, this is Fact #1 about the *Protocols*. You, the reader, must first of all understand that they are totally and completely discredited; everything else then follows from this fact: that the document was written by anti-Semites, that it promotes Jew-hatred, that it has been unjustly famous, that it should never be taken seriously, and so on.

But before I can address this, we need to take a few steps back and look at the larger picture. First: what exactly are the "Protocols"? For that matter, what is a 'protocol'? The word itself derives from the Greek *protokollon*, meaning, 'the first' (*proto-*) 'sheets' (*kollema*)—that is, the initial sheets that were attached or even glued to a roll of papyrus writing, typically consisting of a kind of summary or 'table of contents' for the document itself. By the Middle Ages, the term came to be used as either a kind of draft or provisional statement of something, or as the formal record of a meeting or other important event. By the mid-1800s, the word acquired its modern connotation: "an official set of procedures for what actions to take in a certain situation."

And this, in fact, is what the "Protocols" are—a collection of 24 short writings that are written in the form of 'meeting minutes,' or 'lecture notes,' or perhaps a transcription of a series of talks, evidently given over a number of days.[2] They do in fact constitute "an official set of procedures for action"—toward the goal of world domination. Yet they are not extensive; the Protocols vary considerably in length, from around just 250 or 350 words (Protocols 8 and 19) to well over 2,400 words (Protocols 15 and 20).[3] They outline, in a general way, a Jewish plan to acquire increasing power over non-Jewish societies, growing from a present level of dominating influence to, in the future, something approaching total control. This gain in power will come at the expense of the Goyim, who will be degraded, exploited, and functionally enslaved to a Jewish world-leader called the 'Sovereign.'

---

[2] A few entries begin with "Today…"
[3] In total, the 24 Protocols contain about 23,400 words in English—an average of about 1,000 words per protocol.

Notably, there is virtually no context to the writings: as I mentioned above, no author, no introduction, no notes, no appendix—nothing to establish the actual setting of the document, and nothing to provide any elaboration. It is written in the first-person; the speaker (evidently) is addressing a group of fellow Jews, apparently quite skilled and knowledgeable already, although still in the final phases of their initiation into some kind of Jewish elite. The document reads as if a professor somewhere was addressing a group of graduate students, preparing them for their future leadership roles in society.

The outline is straightforward, but the text itself reads rather strangely. On the one hand, it is intelligent and sophisticated, addressing a number of subtleties of human nature and political economy. On the other, the organization of the text, even within a given Protocol, is abominable. The individual Protocols have no guiding theme at all—I have included rough 'titles' for each, but these are simply crude guides to the contents. Within each Protocol, the text jumps from one idea to the next, only rarely in a coherent manner. Even within individual paragraphs, there are no unifying ideas; two or three sentences will flow together, and then the text jumps to an entirely new theme, with no obvious connection.

There are other odd features. For much of the text, the reader has no confirmation that the speaker is a Jew or is speaking to other Jews. The lengthy Protocol No. 1 is generally neutral about the speaker's identity; only some half-dozen mentions of the term 'Goy' give away the Jewish nature of the talk.[4] Protocol No. 2 is similar. No. 3 becomes more explicit, mentioning the "symbolic serpent" as "the symbol of our people"—a reference to the snake eating its tail, an ancient image that, in some contexts, has been connected to the Jewish people. We also find there a rare reference to Zionism (the Jewish movement for a homeland in Palestine.) Not until Protocol 5 do we read of the speaker as one of the "Chosen People," which effectively gives it away. Notably, the word 'Jew' appears only twice in the entire document—both in the short Protocol 8. But there are other telling references: to Israel, anti-Semitism, the power of gold, and so on, that leave no question for the reader. By the final

---

[4] Some translations use the more neutral 'Gentile,' but this is still a referent of Jewish origin. If a translator were to use even more ambiguous terms like 'nation' or 'people,' there would be little indication of a Jewish speaker—at least, at first.

pages, we are reading of "the King of Israel" ruling the world, someone from "the seed of David." In the end, there is no doubt at all.

A final odd note about the *Protocols* is that, as a whole, it has virtually no progression. Most documents, stories, meeting minutes, lectures, etc. move along a logical and continuous path from start to finish; they begin with opening or introductory comments, follow a logical thread of discourse or argumentation, and arrive at a conclusion that typically summarizes or encapsulates the whole. But here, almost nothing like this occurs. The first three sentences are a kind of rough lead-in, but they say nothing of substance about what is to come; and then immediately afterward, the narrator jumps into his initial points. Similarly at the end: the final Protocol discusses the Sovereign, his plan of action, and how he will be viewed, but there is no attempt at any concluding thoughts. The last paragraph states how the Sovereign will rule with dispassionate calm—and then it ends. Very strange, to say the least.

Murky Origins

Adding to the above oddities is the story of how the *Protocols* came to light—and in particular, how little we actually know. Much of the claim of "forgery" rests on the confusion and obscurity of its origins. So, let me now give a short outline of what we do know about the creation of this most unusual document.

Apparently the first public mention of the document was in a Russian newspaper in St. Petersburg in April 1902, although none of the actual text was reproduced. Then in mid-1903, something like a rough early draft of the Protocols appeared in serial form, over nine issues of another Russian paper. The series was titled "The Jewish Plan to Conquer the World." It is likely that this was within two or three years of original composition, but no one really knows.

But it was, perhaps, this early version that caught the attention of a Russian author and fundamentalist Orthodox Christian named Sergei Nilus (1862-1929). In that same year (1903), he had just published a book titled *The Great within the Small* which dealt with Christian theology and the alleged coming of the Antichrist. It seems that Nilus was sufficiently impressed, such that, in 1905, as he was preparing to release a second edition of his book, he elected to include a new closing chapter:

the Protocols—now, and mysteriously, in an expanded form. Over the years, Nilus gave inconsistent accounts of how he came to acquire his version; allegedly they were stolen by a woman from the Jews, but later he stated that a friend "found them in a vault" at Zionist headquarters in Paris. Later still, Nilus claimed that they were written by prominent Zionist Theodor Herzl in 1897.

The obvious conclusion would be in favor of a Russian author, but there are many passing references in the document that suggest a French origin. One finds three or four mentions of the French Revolution and its slogan "liberty, equality, fraternity," and there is a brief mention, in Protocol 16, of French prime minister Leon Bourgeois. And a passing mention of Nietzsche (Protocol 2) would, at that time, be more likely in a French cultural context than a Russian one. But this is all speculation; if there ever were a 'French original' of the *Protocols*, it is now lost. In any case, the Protocols were now in print, in 1905, in the Russian language, in something like a final form.

It was a chaotic time in Russia. The first Russian Revolution of 1905 occurred at that time—essentially a civil war between the czar (Nicholas II) and a group of rebels headed by the Jew Leon Trotsky and the quarter-Jew Vladimir Lenin. After two years of fighting and some 20,000 dead, the revolutionary Jews retreated, only to regroup and later attack again, successfully, in 1917-1918.

Amidst the turmoil of 1905, Nilus' book and his Protocols apparently attracted little attention, even though radical, power-seeking Jews like Trotsky and Lenin were prominent at that time. But the Jewish hand in the 1905 revolution could certainly help to support a 'Russian source' theory of origin.

Then came World War One in 1914. The "German menace" raised its ugly head on the continent, and over the course of four years, was beaten down by the combined forces of England, France, Russia, and eventually the United States. For all this, Germany would likely have prevailed had it not been for substantial Jewish agitation in the German homeland that resulted in riots and general strikes at a key juncture in late 1918. The Jewish-led "stab in the back" caused the Kaiser to capitulate and allowed "the Jewish criminals" (Hitler's words) to take the reins of power and to promptly surrender.

From the standpoint of the Jewish Question, things got much worse in the third year of the war (1917), when the predominantly Jewish Bolsheviks in Russia succeeded in ousting the czar, eventually executing him and his family. Suddenly, Jews were in charge of a major nation and they were pressing a relentless, bloody war against many of the indigenous (Gentile) Russians. With the Bolshevik Revolution, the *Protocols* now seemed prescient, and more relevant than ever. Their popularity accelerated, first in Russia, then in Germany the following year, and eventually throughout Europe and beyond.

The English Editions

Some time in 1919, the British publisher Eyre & Spottiswoode hired a writer, George Shanks, to translate the *Protocols* into English. They appeared as a small booklet in early 1920, under the title *The Jewish Peril: Protocols of the Learned Elders of Zion* (Shanks was uncredited). For some unknown reason—though likely a result of Jewish pressure—Eyre quickly gave up publication rights; but owing to demand, the same Shanks translation was quickly republished as a 2nd edition, also in 1920, by a group called "The Britons"—presumably a small, impromptu publisher, possibly established just for that purpose.

Around the same time, the American publishing firm Small, Maynard, and Co. contracted with Natalie de Bogory and Boris Brasol to create another English translation, for the American market. They published their book, also in 1920, under the rather lengthy title *The Protocols and World Revolution: Including a translation of "The Protocols of the Meetings of the Zionist Men of Wisdom."*

But that's not all: apparently there was yet another effort at translation, this one performed by journalist Victor Marsden, in 1920. (It seems that Marsden, like Shanks, worked at the London paper *The Morning Post*; surely this was no coincidence.) Marden's version, though, fell into limbo for three years, eventually getting published in 1923 in England by "The Britons" under the title *Protocols of the Meetings of the Learned Elders of Zion*. Marsden died in October of 1920, and thus never lived to see his work appear in print.

In summary: To this day—prior to the present volume—there have existed *three distinct English translations*: (1) Shanks, (2) Borgory &

Brasol, and (3) Marsden. All were created in the same time frame: 1919/1920. All are now over 100 years old.

But most importantly: *all three are deficient*, from the perspective of a modern English reader. This is unsurprising, for several reasons: 100 years is long enough for literary styles to change significantly; two of the three are British, which imposes an extra burden for non-British English readers; and lastly, they are simply mediocre efforts. All three translations are, literally, painful to read. It is simply astonishing that the English-speaking world has had to tolerate such poor work, for over a century. Word choice, punctuation, grammar, sentence and paragraph structure—all aspects, it seems, of all three efforts are severely lacking.[5] The reader is invited to read through any of the three, and compare them to my new edition below. I think the contrast will be clear.

For sake of convenience, I compare below the first two sentences of the three old translations, along with the same text in my new edition. In this way, should the reader encounter a random version of the *Protocols* on the Internet or in print, simply by checking the leading words of Protocol No. 1, he will be able to instantly determine which translation he is reading:

> **Shanks**: "We will be plainspoken and discuss the significance of each reflection, and by comparisons and deductions, we will produce full explanations."
>
> **Borgory/Brasol**: "Let us put aside phraseology and discuss the inner meaning of every thought; by comparisons and deductions let us illuminate the situation."
>
> **Marsden**: "…Putting aside fine phrases we shall speak of the significance of each thought: by comparisons and deductions we shall throw light upon surrounding facts."

---

[5] Of the three, Borgory/Brasol is the best, and I have used this version as the basis for my own new edition. But that said, there is scarcely a sentence that remains unchanged.

Dalton (2023): "Let us set aside fine phrases and discuss the inner meaning of every thought. By comparisons and deductions, we will illuminate the situation."

These few words, of course, hardly scratch the surface of the differences in the (now) four versions. The reader is strongly urged to compare at least parts of the four. I am confident he will find my edition to be far clearer, much more concise, and highly reader-friendly—all while retaining (and hopefully enhancing) the meaning of the text.

A "Forgery" Exposed

For all this, the average British or American citizen of 1920 had little way to discover anything of the history, context, or even existence of the *Protocols*. In the UK, Eyre gave up on the small book soon after releasing it, and the obscure "Britons" had few means of promoting their edition. In the US, events in Europe or Russia were a world away, and meant little to the typical American reader; a translation of an odd and obscure Russian text was unlikely to get much attention.

Things began to change significantly in May 1920. At that time, an editor at the leading British paper *The London Times*, by the name of Wickham Steed, encountered the Eyre booklet, read it, and was sufficiently impressed to write a 1,700-word essay for his paper. Thus was published, on 8 May 1920 (p. 15), an article titled "'The Jewish Peril': A Disturbing Pamphlet: Call for Inquiry"; it is reprinted, in full, in the text below. Steed's essay is remarkably neutral, even laudatory, toward the *Protocols*. He asks for a clear-eyed reading by the public, and "an impartial investigation" on the part of authorities. Finally, for the first time, the English-speaking press acknowledged the existence and importance of this cryptic little book.

As it happens, at nearly the same time across the Atlantic, the Eyre edition came to the attention of automobile icon Henry Ford. He had long been predisposed to criticism toward Jewish involvement in political and world affairs—at least since the onset of World War One, which

Ford believed was largely instigated by Jews in England and France.[6] In order to promote public discussion about the Jewish Question, Ford purchased the small newspaper *The Dearborn Independent* in January 1919. For the first year of publication, the paper—under control of his aid William Cameron—covered conventional news, but by early 1920, Ford, with Cameron's supporting research, began to openly confront Jewish power. Thus, beginning with the 22 May 1920 edition, Ford and Cameron ran an astonishing 80 consecutive weekly issues dedicated to the Jewish Question; the series was titled "The International Jew." Ford's paper, with its circulation of nearly one million, brought the Jewish Question to a huge new American audience.

Just eight issues into the series, Ford made his first mention of the *Protocols*, which was then the central theme for six or seven subsequent issues.[7] Starting on June 26, the weekly paper presented the story of the *Protocols* and then summarized and critiqued its main themes. Ford's attack on the *Protocols* is simply astounding, and something, the likes of which, would be inconceivable today. Can we imagine any present-day industrialist or billionaire publishing an extended and detailed critique of Jewish power? It would be all but impossible.[8] And yet, for several months in 1920, the *Protocols* were front-and-center in the American public eye. Owing to their importance, extended passages from the "International Jew" series are included below.

Then in August of 1921 came something of a major breakthrough in the cryptic history of the *Protocols*. The Constantinople correspondent of the *London Times*, Philip Graves, managed, through various obscure means, to conclude that the Protocols were "a forgery." Apparently, an anonymous person contacted Graves and presented him with a ragged copy of an 1865 French book written by a French Jew, Maurice Joly, entitled *Dialogue in Hell, between Machiavelli and Montesquieu*. The

---

[6] The evidence suggests that Ford was largely correct. For details, see my book *The Jewish Hand in the World Wars* (2019).

[7] It seems likely that Cameron did the actual writing of the weekly essays, but certainly with Ford's oversight and blessing. Following tradition, I attribute the *Independent*'s writings to Ford.

[8] Although, something vaguely similar occurred in late 2022 with black rapper Ye (Kanye West), who declared open war on "the Jews." But little came of it, and of late he seems to have backed down from his early, aggressive stance.

book was a veiled attack against then-French "emperor" Napoleon III, using the character of Machiavelli as Napoleon's stand-in.[9] To the point, the book contained a number of passages that were strikingly similar—and in some cases, virtually identical—to phrases in the *Protocols*. Graves thus concluded that the Russian original was a "crude forgery" that drew upon and plagiarized Joly's obscure, 35-year-old book. He published his findings in a three-part series in the *London Times*, between 16 and 18 of August, 1921; the series is published below, in full.

To press his case, Graves included direct comparisons between passages in both books; and indeed, the degree of similarity is striking. There seems to be little doubt that the original *Protocols* author, whether French or Russian, had read, and lifted text from, Joly's book. The coincidences are simply too strong. But the key question is this: *What does this imply?* For Graves, it means that the *Protocols*, in sum and in whole, are fraudulent nonsense, literary trash, and something to be ignored and discarded with all due haste. And this has been the conclusion of our Jewish orthodoxy ever since. But of course, this is far from the case. The mere fact that the author borrowed, or "stole," phrases from an earlier work says, technically, *nothing at all about the truth-value of the Protocols*. The author is simply using words, phrases, and images taken from elsewhere to make his points. He is not fully "original"—hardly uncommon in the literary world, and arguably irrelevant here.

Let me be clear about what seems to be the two main hypotheses of the origins of the *Protocols*: One, they were spoken by some prominent Jewish leader (perhaps Herzl or a colleague) at a series of meetings with the Jewish elite, sometime around the year 1900. Someone else—a scribe or recording secretary—later encapsulated and summarized, in rough and "plagiarized" form, the talks, which included several main planks of the Zionist-Jewish platform for world power. This was a platform that, by 1920, had been realized in Russia and Germany, and was looming in other nations.

Two: A well-read French or Russian "anti-Semite," concerned about the growth in Jewish power and influence in Europe and the consequent undermining of White, Christian culture, adapted ideas from Joly and perhaps others into a new 'fictional' speech that, nonetheless, represented

---

[9] Napoleon III was the nephew of the more famous Napoleon I ('Bonaparte').

true facts about Jews, Zionism, and the Jewish power elite. These took the form of a series of "protocols" that, in themselves, never claimed to be the literal transcription of an actual Jewish presentation or talk. It was later individuals, such as Nilus, who put forth the assertion that they were the actual minutes of some actual meeting. Whether Nilus was told this, or invented the idea himself, we will likely never know.

But again, the larger point is that, in a sense, we don't care which theory is true. What we care is: *Are they true?* or perhaps, *Do they accurately reflect the present state of affairs?* or maybe, *Do they say something valid and meaningful about wealthy and powerful Jews?* These are the relevant questions; these are the points that merit discussion and inquiry. Whether Nilus or someone else "forged" the document by claiming something untruthful about its provenance is largely incidental. With respect to the relevant questions, the answer reached by many thoughtful and unbiased commentators over the years is that, yes, it is meaningful; yes, it is relevant; and yes, it does reflect the thought and action of wealthy and powerful Jews worldwide.

And what about in the present day, now 120 years after their composition? The *Protocols* are, in an odd way, still present with us, always there, hovering in the background, just out of sight. It doesn't garner much major publicity these days, at least in the West, but this is likely because (a) there have been no new developments regarding the *Protocols* in decades, and (b) the three standard English translations are so poor that few people bother to read them, or about them. As a text, it can be found in various places on the Internet, though most sources are of questionable integrity and virtually none offer solid academic analysis. And online booksellers like Amazon sell copies and analyses, but nearly all are anti-*Protocols* and many have Jewish authors; Amazon is well-known for censoring anything that is seriously anti-Jewish.

Historically, the prime event of the past century has been the Jewish-inspired Allied powers' victory over National Socialist Germany in WW2. Since that time, 80 years ago, global Jews have only increased their levels of wealth, power, and control. In a very real sense, the prophecy of the *Protocols* has been realized. There is no Jewish 'Sovereign,' no such 'world leader,' but there is a collective Jewish Lobby, globally interconnected, that, as a body, exercises dominating control over the US and Europe, at a minimum. This was clear 20 years ago when, upon initiation of the second US-Iraq war, Malaysian prime minister Mahathir Mohamad stated, "The Jews rule the world by proxy. They get others to fight and die for them".[10] He was referring specifically to Jewish control in the US which, as the sole global superpower, meant that Jews had *de facto* rule over the planet.

Today, Jewish ideals and Jewish values utterly dominate the US and throughout the West. Via Jewish Hollywood, Jewish-American media conglomerates, Jews in American academia, and Jewish money in US politics, the stranglehold is nearly complete. The rare dissident from the pro-Jewish line is quickly fired, slandered, 'cancelled,' sued, or imprisoned. The US military regularly implements pro-Jewish and pro-Israeli policies throughout the world, including assassinating troublesome individuals and fostering revolt and rebellion in any uncooperative countries. Such things are, in their own way, a fulfillment and confirmation of many of the basic themes of the *Protocols*. The intent, it would appear, has remained the same, even if the means and the mechanisms have changed with the times.

Plan of the Book

This book is organized in four parts. Rather than dive directly into the *Protocols*, I have elected to attempt to recreate, in a rough sense, the process by which a typical reader of 1920 might come across the document: by first reading an account of it in a newspaper. (Obviously, the reader is free to deviate from this little plan, as he sees fit.) Thus, Part One includes the three famous newspaper articles (or series) mentioned above, in chronological order: (1) Steed's initial and sympathetic essay from May 1920; (2) extended excerpts from Ford's *Dearborn Independent* of 1920; and (3) Graves' 1921 exposé in the *Times*, revealing the supposed "forgery." All this is preceded by a short "summary" of the conventional view, by Jewish researchers at the US Holocaust Memorial Museum, as posted in their online "Holocaust Encyclopedia."

Part Two contains the *Protocols* themselves, in my new translation. I have included explanatory footnotes (there were none in the original),

---

[10] See, for example, CNN: "Mahathir attack on Jews condemned" (17 Oct 2003).

Protocol 'titles' (also not in original), and section breaks ("*****"), as appropriate.

Part Three includes important commentaries by three leading National Socialists: Alfred Rosenberg, Joseph Goebbels, and Adolf Hitler (printed here chronologically). Rosenberg's text is an extract from his remarkable 1923 book *Die Protokolle der Weisen von Zion und die jüdische Weltpolitik* (The Protocols of the Wise Men of Zion and the Jewish World-Politic). This is the first time that this material has appeared in English translation. We then have a lengthy "Introduction" to the 22nd (!) edition, from 1938, of the official NSDAP version of the *Protocols*, entitled *Die Geheimnisse der Weisen von Zion*. Lastly, the intriguing and rather infamous "Introduction" to the Protocols by the Italian fascist sympathizer, Julius Evola.

Finally, Part Four includes two essays: a remarkably insightful analysis by Italian scholar Carlo Mattogno, and then some final reflections of my own—both intended to provide a contemporary look at the 120-year-old Protocols.

With this material, the reader will have, for the first time, a clear, unbiased, objective, and comprehensive account of the infamous *Protocols*, from the very beginning. The implications of all this for the future are surely the subject of books yet to come. For now, the *Protocols* remain as mysterious and compelling as ever.

PART ONE

OVERVIEW AND EARLY COMMENTARIES

Protocols of the Elders of Zion

SUMMARY
"PROTOCOLS OF THE ELDERS OF ZION"

HOLOCAUST ENCYCLOPEDIA (USHMM)[1]

> "If ever a piece of writing could produce mass hatred, it is this one… This book is about lies and slander."
> —Elie Wiesel, Nobel Peace Prize Laureate

The Protocols of the Elders of Zion is the most notorious and widely distributed antisemitic publication of modern times. Its lies about Jews, which have been repeatedly discredited, continue to circulate today, especially on the Internet. The individuals and groups who have used the *Protocols* are all linked by a common purpose: to spread hatred of Jews.

The *Protocols* is entirely a work of fiction, intentionally written to blame Jews for a variety of ills. Those who distribute it claim that it documents a Jewish conspiracy to dominate the world. The conspiracy and its alleged leaders, the so-called Elders of Zion, never existed.

The Origin of a Lie

In 1903, portions of *The Protocols of the Elders of Zion* were serialized in a Russian newspaper, *Znamya* (The Banner). The version of the *Protocols* that has endured and has been translated into dozens of languages, however, was first published in Russia in 1905 as an appendix to *The Great in the Small: The Coming of the Anti-Christ and the Rule of Satan on Earth,* by Russian writer and mystic Sergei Nilus.

Although the exact origin of the *Protocols* is unknown, its intent was to portray Jews as conspirators against the state. In 24 chapters, or protocols, allegedly minutes from meetings of Jewish leaders, the *Proto-*

---

[1] From the US Holocaust Memorial Museum (USHMM), "Holocaust Encyclopedia": https://encyclopedia.ushmm.org/content/en/article/protocols-of-the-elders-of-zion (accessed 1 April 2023).

cols "describes" the "secret plans" of Jews to rule the world by manipulating the economy, controlling the media, and fostering religious conflict.

Following the Russian Revolution of 1917, anti-Bolshevik émigrés brought the *Protocols* to the West. Soon after, editions circulated across Europe, the United States, South America, and Japan. An Arabic translation first appeared in the 1920s.

Beginning in 1920, auto magnate Henry Ford's newspaper, *The Dearborn Independent,* published a series of articles based in part on the *Protocols*. *The International Jew,* the book that included this series, was translated into at least 16 languages. Both Adolf Hitler and Joseph Goebbels, later head of the propaganda ministry, praised Ford and *The International Jew.*

Fraud Exposed

In 1921, the London *Times* presented conclusive proof that the *Protocols* was a "clumsy plagiarism." The *Times* confirmed that the *Protocols* had been copied in large part from a French political satire that never mentioned Jews—Maurice Joly's *Dialogue in Hell Between Machiavelli and Montesquieu* (1864). Other investigations revealed that one chapter of a Prussian novel, Hermann Goedsche's *Biarritz* (1868), also "inspired" the *Protocols.*

The Nazi Era

Nazi Party ideologue Alfred Rosenberg introduced Hitler to the *Protocols* during the early 1920s, as Hitler was developing his worldview. Hitler referred to the *Protocols* in some of his early political speeches, and, throughout his career, he exploited the myth that "Jewish-Bolshevists" were conspiring to control the world.

During the 1920s and 1930s, *The Protocols of the Elders of Zion* played an important part in the Nazis' propaganda arsenal. The Nazi party published at least 23 editions of the *Protocols* between 1919 and 1939. Following the Nazis' seizure of power in 1933, some schools used the *Protocols* to indoctrinate students.

Fraud Exposed

In 1935, a Swiss court fined two Nazi leaders for circulating a German-language edition of the *Protocols* in Berne, Switzerland. The presiding justice at the trial declared the *Protocols* "libelous," "obvious forgeries," and "ridiculous nonsense."

The US Senate issued a report in 1964 declaring that the *Protocols* were "fabricated." The Senate called the contents of the *Protocols* "gibberish" and criticized those who "peddled" the *Protocols* for using the same propaganda technique as Hitler.

In 1993, a Russian court ruled that Pamyat, a far-right nationalist organization, had committed an antisemitic act by publishing the *Protocols*.

Despite these repeated exposures of the *Protocols* as a fraud, it remains the most influential antisemitic text of the past one hundred years, and it continues to appeal to a variety of antisemitic individuals and groups.

The *Protocols* Today

According to the US Department of State's "Report on Global Anti-Semitism" (2004),

> "The clear purpose of the [*Protocols* is] to incite hatred of Jews and of Israel."

In the United States and Europe, neo-Nazis, white supremacists, and Holocaust deniers endorse and circulate the *Protocols*. Books based on the *Protocols* are available worldwide, even in countries with hardly any Jews such as Japan.

Many school textbooks throughout the Arab and Islamic world teach the *Protocols* as fact. Countless political speeches, editorials, and even children's cartoons are derived from the *Protocols*. In 2002, Egypt's government-sponsored television aired a miniseries based on the *Protocols*, an event condemned by the US State Department. The Palestinian organization Hamas draws in part on the *Protocols* to justify its terrorism against Israeli civilians.

The Internet has dramatically increased access to the *Protocols*. Even though many websites expose the *Protocols* as a fraud, the Internet has made it easy to use the *Protocols* to spread hatred of Jews. Today, a typical Internet search yields several hundred thousand sites that disseminate, sell, or debate the *Protocols* or expose them as a fraud.

"THE JEWISH PERIL"
WICKHAM STEED[1]

The Times has not as yet noticed this singular little book. Its diffusion is, however, increasing, and its reading is likely to perturb the thinking public. Never before have a race and a creed been accused of a more sinister conspiracy. We in this country, who live in good fellowship with numerous representatives of Jewry, may well ask that some authoritative criticism should deal with it, and either destroy the ugly "Semitic" bogy or assign their proper place to the insidious allegations of this kind of literature.

In spite of the urgency of impartial and exhaustive criticism, the pamphlet has been allowed, so far, to pass almost unchallenged. The Jewish Press announced, it is true, that the anti-Semitism of the "Jewish Peril" was going to be exposed. But save for an unsatisfactory article in the March 5 [1920] issue of the *Jewish Guardian* and for an almost equally unsatisfactory contribution to the Nation of March 27, this exposure is yet to come. The article of the *Jewish Guardian* is unsatisfactory, because it deals mainly with the personality of the author of the book in which the pamphlet is embodied, with Russian reactionary propaganda, and the Russian secret police. It does not touch the substance of the "Protocols of the Learned Elders of Zion".[2] The purely Russian side of the book and its fervid "Orthodoxy" is not its most interesting feature. Its author—Professor S. Nilus—who was a minor official in the Department of Foreign Religions at Moscow, had, in all likelihood, opportunities of access to many archives and unpublished documents.

On the other hand, the world-wide issue raised by the "Protocols" which he incorporated in his book and are now translated into English as "The Jewish Peril," cannot fail not only to interest, but to preoccupy.

---

[1] Reproduced from the *London Times*, 8 May 1920, p. 15.
[2] This has been a standard Jewish ploy for at least a century: to attack the author or the context of some anti-Jewish text or speech without addressing the truth-value of its contents. This strongly suggests that they have no good response and nothing to say to refute the assertions.

What are the theses of the "Protocols" with which, in the absence of public criticism, British readers have to grapple alone and unaided? They are, roughly:—

(1) There is, and has been for centuries, a secret international political organization of the Jews.

(2) The spirit of this organization appears to be an undying traditional hatred of the Christian world, and a titanic ambition for world domination.

(3) The goal relentlessly pursued through centuries is the destruction of the Christian national States, and the substitution for them of an international Jewish dominion.

(4) The method adopted for first weakening and then destroying existing bodies politic is the infusion of disintegrating political ideas of carefully measured progressive disruptive force, from liberalism to radicalism, and socialism to communism, culminating in anarchy as a *reductio ad absurdum* of egalitarian principles. Meanwhile Jewry remains immune from these corrosive doctrines. "We preach Liberalism to the Gentiles, but on the other hand we keep our own nation in entire subjection". Out of the welter of world anarchy, in response to the desperate clamour of distraught humanity, the stern, logical, wise, pitiless rule of "the King of the Seed of David" is to arise.

(5) Political dogmas evolved by Christian Europe, democratic statesmanship and politics, are all equally contemptible to the Elders of Zion. To them, statesmanship is an exalted secret art, acquired only by traditional training, and imparted to a select few in the secrecy of some occult sanctuary, "Political problems are not meant to be understood by ordinary people; they can only be comprehended, as I have said before, by rulers who have been directing affairs for many centuries."

(6) To this conception of statesmanship, the masses are contemptible cattle, and the political leaders of the Gentiles, "upstarts from its midst as rulers, are likewise blind in politics." They are puppets, pulled by the

hidden hand of the "Elders," puppets mostly corrupt, always inefficient, easily coaxed, or bullied, or blackmailed into submission, unconsciously furthering the advent of Jewish dominion.

(7) The Press, the theatre, stock exchange speculations, science, law itself, are, in the hands that hold all the gold, so many means of procuring a deliberate confusion and bewilderment of public opinion, demoralization of the young, and encouragement of the vices of the adult, eventually substituting, in the minds of the Gentiles, for the idealistic aspiration of Christian culture the "cash basis" and a neutrality of materialistic scepticism, or cynical lust for pleasure.

Such are the main theses of the "Protocols." They are not altogether new, and can be found scattered throughout anti-Semitic literature. The condensed form in which they are now presented lends them a new and weird force.

Incidentally, some of the features of the would-be Jewish programme bear an uncanny resemblance to situations and events now developing under our eyes. Professor Nilus' book was, undoubtedly, published in Russia in 1905. The copy of the original at the British Museum bears the stamp of August 10, 1906. This being so, some of the passages assume the aspect of fulfilled prophecies, unless one is inclined to attribute the prescience of the "Elders of Zion" to the fact that they really are the hidden instigators of these events. When one reads that "it is indispensible for our plans that wars should not produce any territorial alterations," one is most forcibly reminded of the cry, "Peace without annexations" raised by all the radical parties of the world, and especially in revolutionary Russia. And, again:—

> We will create a universal economic crisis, by all possible underhanded means and with the help of gold, which is all in our hands. Simultaneously we will throw on to the streets huge crowds of workmen throughout Europe. We will increase the wages, which will not help the workmen as, at the same time, we will raise the price of prime necessities... [I]t is essential for us at all costs to deprive the aristocracy of their lands. To attain this purpose the best method is

to force up rates and taxes. These methods will keep the landed interests at their lowest possible ebb.

Nor can one fail to recognize Soviet Russia in the following:—

> [I]n governing the world the best results are obtained by means of violence and intimidation. ... In politics, we must know how to confiscate property without any hesitation, if by so doing we can obtain subjection and power. Our State, following the way of peaceful conquest, has the right of substituting for the terrors of war, executions less apparent and more expedient, which are necessary to uphold terror, producing blind submission. ... By new laws we will regulate the political life of our subjects as though they were so many parts of a machine. Such laws will gradually restrict all freedom and liberties allowed by the Gentiles. ... It is essential for us to arrange that, besides ourselves, there should be in all countries nothing but a huge proletariat, so many soldiers and police loyal to our cause; in order to demonstrate our enslavement of the Gentile Governments of Europe, we will show our power to one of them by means of crime and violence, that is to say a reign of terror; our programme will induce a third part of the populace to watch the remainder from a pure sense of duty or from the principle of voluntary service.

Bearing in mind when this was published, we see, 15 years later, a government established in Russia of which a high percentage of the leaders are Jews, whose *modus operandi* follows the principles quoted, and whose mainstay is a Communist Party, which answers to the last quotation. We see this, and it seems uncanny. The trouble is that all this fosters indiscriminate anti-Semitism. That the latter is rampant in Eastern Europe is a fact. That its propaganda in France, England, and America is growing is a fact also. Do we want, and can we afford to add exacerbated race-hatred to all our political, social, and economic troubles? If not, the question of the "Jewish Peril" should be taken up and dealt with. It is far too interesting, the hypothesis it presents is far too ingenious, attractive, and sensational not to attract the attention of our none too happy and none too contented public. The average man thinks that there is something very fundamentally wrong with the world he lives in. He will eagerly grasp at a plausible "working hypothesis."

What are these "Protocols"? Are they authentic? If so, what malevolent assembly concocted these plans, and gloated over their exposition? Are they a forgery? If so, whence comes the uncanny note of prophecy, prophecy in parts fulfilled, in parts far gone in the way of fulfillment? Have we been struggling these tragic years to blow up and extirpate the secret organization of German world dominion only to find beneath it another more dangerous because more secret? Have we, by straining every fibre of our national body, escaped a "Pax Germanica" only to fall into a "Pax Judaica"? The "Elders of Zion," as represented in their "Protocols" are by no means kinder taskmasters than William II [Kaiser Wilhelm II], and his henchmen would have been.

All these questions, which are likely to obtrude themselves on the reader of the "Jewish Peril," cannot be dismissed by a shrug of the shoulders unless one wants to strengthen the hand of the typical anti-Semite and call forth his favorite accusation of the "conspiracy of silence." An impartial investigation of these would-be documents and of their history is most desirable. That history is by no means clear from the English translation. They would appear, from internal evidence, to have been written by Jews for Jews, or to be cast in the form of lectures, and notes for lectures, by Jews to Jews. If so, in what circumstances were they produced and to cope with what inter-Jewish emergency? Or are we to dismiss the whole matter without inquiry and to let the influence of such a book as this work unchecked?

ON THE *PROTOCOLS*
HENRY FORD[1]

Does a Definite Jewish World Program Exist?[2]

[I]n the *American Hebrew* of June 25, 1920, Herman Bernstein writes:

> About a year ago a representative of the Department of Justice submitted to me a copy of the manuscript of 'The Jewish Peril' by Professor Nilus, and asked for my opinion of the work. He said that the manuscript was a translation of a Russian book published in 1905 which was later suppressed. The manuscript was supposed to contain 'protocols' of the Wise Men of Zion and was supposed to have been read by Dr. Herzl at a secret conference of the Zionist Congress at Basle. He expressed the opinion that the work was probably that of Dr. Theodor Herzl... He said that some American Senators who had seen the manuscript were amazed to find that so many years ago a scheme had been elaborated by the Jews which is now being carried out, and that Bolshevism had been planned years ago by Jews who sought to destroy the world.

This quotation is made merely to put on record the fact that it was a representative of the Department of Justice of the United States Government, who introduced this document to Mr. Bernstein, and expressed a certain opinion upon it, namely, "that the work was probably that of Theodor Herzl." Also that "some American Senators" were amazed to note the comparison between what a publication of the year 1905 proposed and what the year 1920 revealed.

---

[1] Reproduced from the "International Jew" series in the *Dearborn Independent*. The actual author of these words was likely William Cameron, not Ford.
[2] Excerpted from 10 July 1920.

The incident is all the more preoccupying because it occurred by action of the representative of a government who today is very largely in the hands of, or under the influence of, Jewish interests. It is more than probable that as soon as the activity became known, the investigator was stopped. But it is equally probable that whatever orders may have been given and apparently obeyed, the investigation may not have stopped.

The United States Government was a little late in the matter, however. At least four other world powers had preceded it, some by many years. A copy of the Protocols was deposited in the British Museum and bears on it the stamp of that institution, "August 10, 1906." The notes themselves probably date from 1896, or the year of the utterances previously quoted from Dr. Herzl. The first Zionist Congress convened in 1897.

The document was published in England recently under auspices that challenged attention for it, in spite of the unfortunate title under which it appeared. Eyre and Spottiswoode are the appointed printers to the British Government, and it was they who brought out the pamphlet. It was as if the Government Printing Office at Washington should issue them in this country. While there was the usual outcry by the Jewish press, the *London Times* in a review pronounced all the Jewish counter-attacks as "unsatisfactory".[3]

The Times noticed what will probably be the case in this country also that the Jewish defenders leave the text of the protocols alone, while they lay heavy emphasis on the fact of their anonymity. When they refer to the substance of the document at all there is one form of words which recurs very often—"it is the work of a criminal or a madman."

The protocols, without name attached, appearing for the most part in manuscripts here and there, laboriously copied out from hand to hand, being sponsored by no authority that was willing to stand behind it, assiduously studied in the secret departments of the governments and passed from one to another among higher officials, have lived on and on, increasing in power and prestige by the sheer force of their contents. A marvelous achievement for either a criminal or a madman! The only evidence it has is that which it carries within it, and that internal evidence is, as the *London Times* points out, the point on which attention is to be

---

[3] See the chapter "The Jewish Peril" in the present volume.

focused. And the very point from which Jewish effort has been expended to draw us away.

The interest of the Protocols at this time is their bearing on the questions: Have the Jews an organized world system? What is its policy? How is it being worked?

These questions all receive full attention in the Protocols. Whosoever was the mind that conceived them possessed a knowledge of human nature, of history and of statecraft which is dazzling in its brilliant completeness, and terrible in the objects to which it turns its powers. Neither a madman nor an intentional criminal, but more likely a super-mind mastered by devotion to a people and a faith could be the author, if indeed one mind alone conceived them. It is too terribly real for fiction, too well-sustained for speculation, too deep in its knowledge of the secret springs of life for forgery.

Jewish attacks upon it thus far make much of the fact that it came out of Russia. That is hardly true. It came *by way of* Russia. It was incorporated in a Russian book published about 1905 by a Professor Nilus, who attempted to interpret the Protocols by events then going forward in Russia. This publication and interpretation gave it a Russian tinge which has been useful to Jewish propagandists in this country and England, because these same propagandists have been very successful in establishing in Anglo-Saxon mentalities a certain atmosphere of thought surrounding the idea of Russia and Russians. One of the biggest humbugs ever foisted on the world has been foisted by Jewish propagandists, principally on the American public, with regard to the temper and genius of the truly Russian people. So, to intimate that the Protocols are Russian, is partially to discredit them.[4]

The internal evidence makes it clear that the Protocols were not written by a Russian, nor originally in the Russian language, nor under the influence of Russian conditions. But they found their way to Russia and were first published there. They have been found by diplomatic officers in manuscript in all parts of the world. Wherever Jewish power is able to do so, it has suppressed them, sometimes under the supreme penalty.

---

[4] It was clear, even back then, that organized Jewry viewed Russia as an enemy. We should bear this in mind in the present day, as Jews continue to demonize and punish Russia, such as in the current war in Ukraine.

Their persistence is a fact which challenges the mind. Jewish apologists may explain that persistence on the ground that the Protocols feed the anti-Semitic temper, and therefore are preserved for that service. Certainly there was no wide nor deep anti-Semitic temper in the United States to be fed or that felt the greed for agreeable lies to keep itself alive. The progress of the Protocols in the United States can only be explained on the ground that they supply light and give meaning to certain previously observed facts, and that this light and meaning is so startling as to give a certain standing and importance to these otherwise unaccredited documents. Sheer lies do not live long, their power soon dies. These Protocols are more alive than ever. They have penetrated higher places than ever before. They have compelled a more serious attitude to them than ever before.

The Protocols would not be more worthy of study if they bore, say, the name of Theodor Herzl. Their anonymity does not decrease their power any more than the omission of a painter's signature detracts from the art value of a painting. Indeed, the Protocols are better without a known source. For if it were definitely known that in France or Switzerland in the year 1896, or thereabouts, a group of International Jews, assembled in conference, drew up a program of world conquest, it would still have to be shown that such a program was more than a mere vagary, that it was confirmed at large by efforts to fulfill it. The Protocols are a World Program—there is no doubt anywhere of that. Whose program, is stated within the articles themselves. But as for outer confirmation, which would be the more valuable—a signature, or six signatures, or 20 signatures, or a 25-year unbroken line of effort fulfilling that program?

The point of interest for this and other countries is not that a "criminal or a madman" conceived such a program, but that, when conceived, this program found means of getting itself fulfilled in its most important particulars. The document is comparatively unimportant; the conditions to which it calls attention are of a very high degree of importance.

An Introduction to the "Jewish Protocols"[5]

The documents most frequently mentioned by those who are interested in the theory of Jewish World Power rather than in the actual operation of that power in the world today, are those 24 documents known as "The Protocols of the Learned Elders of Zion."

The Protocols have attracted much attention in Europe, having become the center of an important storm of opinion in England only recently, but discussion of them in the United States has been limited. These are the documents concerning which the Department of Justice was making inquiries more than a year ago, and which were given publication in London by Eyre and Spottiswoode, the official printers to the British Government.

Who it was that first entitled these documents with the name of the "Elders of Zion" is not known. It would be possible without serious mutilation of the documents to remove all hint of Jewish authorship, and yet retain all the main points of the most comprehensive program for world subjugation that has ever come to public knowledge.

Yet it must be said that thus to eliminate all hint of Jewish authorship would be to bring out a number of contradictions which do not exist in the Protocols in their present form. The purpose of the plan revealed in the Protocols is to undermine all authority, in order that a new authority in the form of autocracy may be set up. Such a plan could not emanate from a ruling class which already possessed authority, although it might emanate from anarchists. But anarchists do not avow autocracy as the ultimate condition they seek. The authors might be conceived as a company of French Subversives such as existed at the time of the French Revolution and had the infamous Duc d'Orleans as their leader,[6] but this would involve a contradiction between the fact that those Subversives have passed away, and the fact that the program announced in these Protocols is being steadily carried out, not only in France, but throughout Europe and very noticeably in the United States.

---

[5] Excerpted from 24 July 1920.
[6] Louis-Philippe II was a notable member of the French nobility who supported the Revolution.

In their present form which bears evidence of being their original form, there is no contradiction. The allegation of Jewish authorship seems essential to the consistency of the plan.

If these documents were the forgeries which Jewish apologists claim them to be, the forgers would probably have taken pains to make Jewish authorship so clear that their anti-Semitic purpose could easily have been detected. But only twice is the term "Jew" used in them.[7] After one has read much further than the average reader usually cares to go into such matters, one comes upon the plans for the establishment of the World Autocrat, and only then it is made clear of what lineage he is to be.

But all through the documents, there is left no doubt as to the people against whom the plan is aimed. It is not aimed against aristocracy as such. It is not aimed against capital as such. It is not aimed against government as such. Very definite provisions are made for the enlistment of aristocracy, capital, and government for the execution of the plan. It is aimed against the people of the world who are called "Gentiles." It is the frequent mention of "Gentiles" that really decides the purpose of the documents.[8] Most of the destructive type of "liberal" plans aim at the enlistment of the people as helpers; this plan aims at the *degeneration* of the people in order that they may be reduced to confusion of mind and thus manipulated. Popular movements of a "liberal" kind are to be encouraged, all the disruptive philosophies in religion, economics, politics and domestic life are to be sown and watered, for the purpose of so disintegrating social solidarity that a definite plan, herein set forth, may be put through without notice, and the people then molded to it when the fallacy of these philosophies is shown.

The formula of speech is not, "We Jews will do this," but "The Gentiles will be made to think and do these things." With the exception of a few instances in the closing Protocols, the only distinctive racial term used is "Gentiles."

To illustrate: the first indication of this kind comes in the first Protocol in this way:

---

[7] In Protocol No. 8.
[8] Ford uses his own variant of the Shanks translation, substituting 'Gentile' for 'Goy.'

> The great qualities of the people—honesty and frankness—are essentially vices in politics, because they dethrone more surely and more certainly than does the strongest enemy. These qualities are attributes of Gentile rule; we certainly must not be guided by them.

And again:

> On the ruins of the hereditary aristocracy of the Gentiles we have set up the aristocracy of our educated class, and over all the aristocracy of money. We have established the basis of this new aristocracy on the basis of riches, which we control, and on the science guided by our wise men.

Again:

> We will force up wages, which however will be of no benefit to workers, for we at the same time will cause a rise in the prices of prime necessities, pretending that this is due to the decline of agriculture and of cattle raising. We will also artfully and deeply undermine the sources of production by instilling in the workmen ideas of anarchy and encourage them in the use of alcohol, at the same time taking measures to drive all the intellectual forces of the Gentiles from the land.

(A forger with anti-Semitic malice might have written this any time within the last five years, but these words were in print at least 14 years ago according to British evidence, a copy having been in the British Museum since 1906, and they were circulated in Russia a number of years prior.)

The above point continues:

> That the true situation shall not be noticed by the Gentiles prematurely, we will mask it by a pretended effort to serve the working classes and promote great economic principles, for which an active propaganda will be carried on through our economic theories.

These quotations will illustrate the style of the Protocols in making reference to the parties involved. It is "we" for the writers, and "Gentiles" for those who are being written about. This is brought out very clearly in the Fourteenth Protocol:

> In this divergence between Gentiles and ourselves in ability to think and reason is to be seen clearly the seal of our election as the chosen people, as higher human beings, in contrast with the Gentiles who have merely instinctive and animal minds. They observe, but they do not foresee, and they invent nothing (except perhaps material things). It is clear from this that nature herself predestined us to rule and guide the world.

This, of course, has been the Jewish method of dividing humanity from the earliest times. The world was only Jew and Gentile; all that was not Jew was Gentile.

The use of the word 'Jew' in the Protocol may be illustrated by this passage in the eighth section:

> For the time being, until it will be safe to give responsible government positions to our brother Jews, we shall entrust them to people whose past and whose characters are such that there is an abyss between them and the people.

This is the practice known as using "Gentile fronts," which is extensively practiced in the financial world today in order to cover up the evidences of Jewish control. How much progress has been made since these words were written is indicated by the occurrence at the San Francisco convention when the name of Judge Brandeis was proposed for President.[9] It is reasonably to be expected that the public mind will be made more and more familiar with the idea of Jewish occupancy—which will be really a short step from the present degree of influence which the Jews exercise—of the highest office in the government. There is no function of the

---

[9] Louis Brandeis (1856-1941) was a prominent Jewish lawyer who, at the time of this writing, was a justice of the US Supreme Court (the first Jew to serve). Certain compliant Democrats had promoted him for president.

American Presidency in which the Jews have not already secretly assisted in a very important degree. Actual occupancy of the office is not necessary to enhance their power, but to promote certain things which parallel very closely the plans outlined in the Protocols now before us.

Another point which the reader of the Protocols will notice is that the tone of exhortation is entirely absent from the documents. They are not propaganda. They are not efforts to stimulate the ambitions or activity of those to whom they are addressed. They are as cool as a legal paper and as matter-of-fact as a table of statistics. There is none of the "Let us rise, my brothers" stuff about them. There is no "Down with the Gentiles" hysteria. These Protocols, if indeed they were made by Jews and confided to Jews, or if they do contain certain principles of a Jewish World Program, were certainly not intended for the firebrands but for the carefully prepared and tested initiates of the higher groups.

Jewish apologists have asked, "Is it conceivable that if there were such a world program on the part of the Jews, they would reduce it to writing and publish it?" But there is no evidence that these Protocols were ever uttered otherwise than in spoken words by those who put them forth. The Protocols as we have them are apparently the notes of lectures which were made by someone who heard them. Some of them are lengthy; some of them are brief. The assertion which has always been made in connection with the Protocols since they have become known is that they are the notes of lectures delivered to Jewish students presumably somewhere in France or Switzerland. The attempt to make them appear to be of Russian origin is absolutely forestalled by the point of view, the reference to the times, and certain grammatical indications.

The tone certainly fits the supposition that they were originally lectures given to students, for their purpose is clearly not to get a program accepted but to give information concerning a program which is represented as being already in process of fulfillment. There is no invitation to join forces or to offer opinions. Indeed it is specifically announced that neither discussion nor opinions are desired. ("While preaching liberalism to the Gentiles, we shall hold our own people and our own agents in unquestioning obedience." "The scheme of administration must emanate from a single brain… Therefore, we may know the plan of action, but we must not discuss it, lest we destroy its unique character… The inspired work of our leader therefore must not be thrown before a crowd to be torn to pieces, or even before a limited group.")

Moreover, taking the Protocols at their face value, it is evident that the program outlined in these lecture notes was not a new one at the time the lectures were given. There is no evidence of its being of recent arrangement. There is almost the tone of a tradition, or a religion, in it all, as if it had been handed down from generation to generation through the medium of specially trusted and initiated men. There is no note of new discovery or fresh enthusiasm in it, but the certitude and calmness of facts long known and policies long confirmed by experiment.

This point of the age of the program is touched upon at least twice in the Protocols themselves. In the First Protocol this paragraph occurs:

> Already in ancient times we were the first to shout the words, 'Liberty, Equality, Fraternity,' among the people. These words have been repeated many times by unconscious poll-parrots, flocking from all sides to this bait, with which they have ruined the prosperity of the world and true personal freedom… The presumably clever and intellectual Gentiles did not understand the symbolism of the uttered words; did not observe their contradiction in meaning; did not notice that in nature there is no equality…

The other reference to the program's finality is found in the Thirteenth Protocol: "Questions of policy, however, are permitted to no one except those who have originated the policy and have directed it for many centuries." Can this be a reference to a secret Jewish Sanhedrin, self-perpetuating within a certain Jewish caste from generation to generation? Again, it must be said that the originators and directors here referred to cannot be at present any ruling caste, for all that the program contemplates is directly opposed to the interests of such a caste. It cannot refer to any national aristocratic group, like the Junkers of Germany, for the methods which are proposed are the very ones which would render powerless such a group. It cannot refer to any but a people who have no government, who have everything to gain and nothing to lose, and who can keep themselves intact amid a crumbling world. There is only one group that answers that description.

Again, a reading of the Protocols makes it clear that the speaker himself was not seeking for honor. There is a complete absence of personal ambition throughout the document. All plans and purposes and expectations are merged in the future of Israel, which future, it would seem, can only be secured by the subtle breaking down of certain world ideas held by the Gentiles.

The Protocols speak of what has been done, what was being done at the time these words were given, and what remained to be done. Nothing like them in completeness of detail, in breadth of plan and in deep grasp of the hidden springs of human action has ever been known. They are verily terrible in their mastery of the secrets of life, equally terrible in their consciousness of that mastery. Truly they would merit the opinion which Jews have recently cast upon them, that they were the work of an inspired madman, were it not that what is written in the Protocols in words is also written upon the life of today in deeds and tendencies.

The criticisms which these Protocols pass upon the Gentiles for their stupidity are just. It is impossible to disagree with a single item in the Protocols' description of Gentile mentality and veniality. Even the most astute of the Gentile thinkers have been fooled into receiving as the motions of progress what has only been insinuated into the common human mind by the most insidious systems of propaganda.

It is true that here and there a thinker has arisen to say that science so-called was not science at all. It is true that here and there a thinker has arisen to say that the so-called economic laws both of conservatives and radicals were not laws at all, but artificial inventions. It is true that occasionally a keen observer has asserted that the recent debauch of luxury and extravagance was not due to the natural impulses of the people at all, but was systematically stimulated, foisted upon them by design. It is true that a few have discerned that more than half of what passes for "public opinion" is mere hired applause and booing and has never impressed the public mind.

But even with these clues here and there, for the most part disregarded, there has never been enough continuity and collaboration between those who were awake, to follow all the clues to their source. The chief explanation of the hold which the Protocols have had on many of the leading statesmen of the world for several decades is that they explain whence all these false influences come and what their purpose is. They give a clue to the modern maze. It is now time for the people to know. And whether the Protocols are judged as proving anything concerning the Jews or not, they constitute an education in the way the masses are turned about like sheep by influences which they do not understand. It is almost certain that once the principles of the Protocols are known widely and understood by the people, the criticism which they now rightly make of the Gentile mind will no longer hold good.

It is the purpose of future articles in this series to study these documents and to answer out of their contents all the questions that may arise concerning them.

Before that work is begun, one question should be answered—"Is there likelihood of the program of the Protocols being carried through to success?" The program is successful *already*. In many of its most important phases it is already a reality. But this need not cause alarm, for the chief weapon to be used against such a program, both in its completed and uncompleted parts, is clear publicity. Let the people know. Arousing the people, alarming the people, appealing to the passions of the people is the method of the plan outlined in the Protocols. The antidote is merely enlightening the people.

That is the only purpose of these articles. Enlightenment dispels prejudice. It is as desirable to dispel the prejudice of the Jew as of the Gentile. Jewish writers too frequently assume that the prejudice is all on one side. The Protocols themselves ought to have the widest circulation among the Jewish people, in order that they may check those things which are bringing suspicion upon their name.

"Jewish" Estimate of Gentile Human Nature[10]

> Upon completing this program of our present and future actions, I will read to you the principles of these theories.—Protocol 16.

> In all that I have discussed with you hitherto, I have endeavored to indicate carefully the secrets of past and future events and of those momentous occurrences of the near future

---

[10] Excerpted from 31 July 1920.

toward which we are rushing in a stream of great crises, anticipating the hidden principles of future relationships with the Gentiles and of our financial operations.—Protocol 22.

The Protocols, which profess themselves to be an outline of the Jewish World Program, are found upon analysis to contain four main divisions. These, however, are not marked in the structure of the documents, but in the thought. There is a fifth, if the object of it all is included, but this object is assumed throughout the Protocols, being only here and there defined in terms. And the four main divisions are great trunks from which there are numerous branches.

There is first what is alleged to be the Jewish conception of human nature, by which is meant Gentile nature. It is inconceivable that such a plan as that which the Protocols set forth could have been evolved by a mind that had not previously based the probability of success on a certain estimate of the ignobility and corruptibility of human nature—which all through the Protocols is referred to as Gentile nature.

Then, secondly, there is the account of what has already been accomplished in the realization of the program—things actually done.

Thirdly, there is a complete instruction in the methods to be used to get the program still further fulfilled—methods which would themselves supply the estimate of human nature upon which the whole fabric is based, if there were nothing else to indicate it.

Fourth, the Protocols contain in detail some of the achievements which, at the time these words were uttered, were yet to be made. Some of these desired things have been achieved in the meantime, for it should be borne in mind that between the year 1905 and the year 1920 there has been time to set many influences in motion and attain many ends. As the second quotation at the head of this article would indicate, the speaker knew that events were "rushing in a stream of great crises," a knowledge which is amply attested by Jewish sources outside the Protocols.

If this series of articles represented a special pleading upon the Jewish Question, the present article would seek to win the reader's confidence by presenting first the set of facts which are described under "secondly" in the above list of main divisions. To begin with the estimate of human nature here disclosed is to court alienation of the reader's interest, especially if the reader be a Gentile. We know from abundant sources what the Jewish estimate of human nature is, and it tallies in all respects with what is disclosed in the Protocols, but it has always been one of the fallacies of Gentile thought that human nature is, now, full of dignity and nobility. There is little question, when the subject is considered in all its lights, that the Jewish conception is right. And so far as these Protocols are concerned, their low estimate of mankind, though harsh to human pride and conceit, are very largely true. [...]

The method is one of disintegration. Break up the people into parties and sects. Sow abroad the most promising and utopian of ideas and you will do two things: you will always find a group to cling to each idea you throw out; and you will find this partisanship dividing and estranging the various groups. The authors of the Protocols show in detail how this is to be done. Not one idea, but a mass of ideas are to be thrown out, and there is to be no unity among them. The purpose is not to get the people thinking one thing, but to think so diversely about so many different things that there will be no unity among them. The result of this will be vast disunity, vast unrest—and that is the result aimed for.

When once the solidarity of the Gentile society is broken up—and the name, "Gentile society" is perfectly correct, for human society is overwhelmingly Gentile—then this solid wedge of another idea which is not at all affected by the prevailing confusion can make its way unsuspectedly to the place of control. It is well enough known that a body of 20 trained police or soldiers can accomplish more than a disordered mob of a thousand persons. So the minority initiated into the plan can do more with a nation or a world broken into a thousand antagonistic parties, than any of the parties could do. "Divide and rule" is the motto of the Protocols.

The division of society is perfectly easy, according to the estimate of human nature made in these documents. It is human nature to take promises for acts. No one who considered the list of dreams and vagaries and theories that have swayed the people through the centuries can doubt this. The more utopian, the more butterfly-like the theory, the more it commands public adherence. Just as the Protocols say, Gentile society does not scrutinize the origin or the consequences of the theories it adopts. When a theory makes its appeal to the mind, the tendency is to believe that the mind which receives it always had it in essence, and therefore the experience has all the glow of original discovery.

In this manner, theory after theory has been exploited among the masses, theory after theory has been found to be impracticable and has been discarded, but the result is precisely that which the program of the Protocols aims for—with the discarding of each theory, society is a little more broken than it was before. It is a little more helpless before its exploiters. It is a little more confused as to where to look for leadership. As a consequence, society falls an easy victim again to a theory which promises it the good it seeks, and the failure of this theory leaves it still more broken. There is no longer any such thing as public opinion. Distrust and division are everywhere. And in the midst of the confusion everyone is dimly aware that there is a higher group that is not divided at all, but is getting exactly what it wants by means of the confusion that obtains all around. It will be shown, as claimed by the Protocols, that most of the disruptive theories abroad in the world today are of Jewish origin; it will also be shown that the one solid unbroken group in the world today, the group that knows where it wants to go and is going there regardless of the condition of society, is the Jewish group.

The most dangerous theory of all is that which explains the rise of theories and the social break-up which follows them. These are all "symptoms of progress" we are told. If so, then "progress" is toward dissolution. No one can predicate the fact of "progress" on the ground that, whereas our fathers made wheels to go round with the blowing wind or the running water, we make them go round by successive small explosions of gasoline. The question of "progress" is, Where are the wheels taking us? Was windmill and water wheel society better or worse than the present society? Was it more unified in its morality? Did it more highly respect law, did it produce a higher and sturdier type of character? The modern theory of "ferment," that out of all the unrest and change and transvaluation of values a new and better mankind is to be evolved is not borne out by any fact on the horizon. It is palpably a theory whose purpose is to make a seeming good out of that which is undeniable evil. The theories which cause the disruption and the theory which explains the disruption as good, come from the same source. The whole science of economics, conservative and radical, capitalistic and anarchistic, is of Jewish origin. This is another of the announcements of the Protocols which the facts confirm.

Now, all this is accomplished, not by acts, but by words. The word-brokers of the world, those who wish words to do duty for things, in their dealings with the world outside their class, are undoubtedly the Jewish group—the international Jews with which these articles deal—and their philosophy and practice are precisely set forth in the Protocols.

Take for illustration these passages: ... [T]his from the Thirteenth Protocol:

> [A]nd you may also notice that we seek approval, not for our acts, but for our words uttered in regard to one or another question. We always announce publicly that we are guided in all our measures by the hope and the conviction that we are serving the general good.
>
> To divert over-restless people from discussing political questions, we shall now bring forward new problems apparently connected with the people—problems of industry. In these, let them lose themselves as much as they like. Under such conditions we shall make them think that the new questions have also a political bearing.

(It is to be hoped that the reader, as his eye passes over these details of the Program, is also permitting his mind to pass over the trend of events, to see if he may detect for himself these very developments in the life and thought of the past few years.)

> To prevent them from really thinking out anything themselves, we shall deflect their attention to amusements, games, pastimes, excitements, and people's palaces. Such interests will distract their minds completely from questions on which we might be obliged to struggle with them. Becoming less and less accustomed to independent thinking, people will express themselves in unison with us because we alone offer new lines of thought—of course, through persons whom they do not consider as in any way connected with us.

In this same Protocol [13], it is plainly stated what is the purpose of the output of "liberal" theories, of which Jewish writers, poets, rabbis, societies and influences are the most prolific sources:

> The role of the liberal Utopians will be completely played out when our government is recognized. Until that time they will perform good service. For that reason, we will continue to direct thought into all the intricacies of fantastic theories, new and supposedly progressive. Surely we have been completely successful in turning the witless heads of the Gentiles by the word 'progress.'

Here is the whole program of confusing, enervating, and trivializing the mind of the world. And it would be the most outlandish thought to put into words, were it not possible to show that this is just what has been done, and is still being done, by agencies which are highly lauded and easy to be identified among us.

A recent writer in a prominent magazine has pointed out what he calls the impossibility of the Jewish ruling group being allied in one common World Program because, as he showed, there were Jews acting as leading minds in all the divisions of present-day opinion. There were Jews at the head of the capitalists, Jews at the head of the labor unions, and Jews at the head of those more radical organizations which find even the labor unions too tame. There is a Jew at the head of the judiciary of England and a Jew at the head of Sovietism in Russia. How can you say, he asked, that they are united, when they represent so many points of view?

The common unity, the possible common purpose of it all, is thus expressed in the Ninth Protocol:

> People of all opinions and of all doctrines are at our service, restorers of monarchy, demagogues, Socialists, communists, and other Utopians. We have put them all to work. Every one of them from his point of view is undermining the last remnant of authority, is trying to overthrow all existing order. All the governments have been tormented by these actions. But we will not give them peace until they recognize our super-government.

The function of the idea is referred to in the Tenth Protocol also: "When we introduced the poison of liberalism into the government organism, its entire political complexion changed."

The whole outlook of these Protocols upon the world is that the idea may be made a most potent poison. The authors of these documents do not believe in liberalism, they do not believe in democracy, but they lay plans for the constant preaching of these ideas because of their power to break up society, to divide it into groups, to destroy the power of collective opinion through a variety of convictions. The poison of an idea is their most relied-on weapon.

The plan of thus using ideas extends to education:

> We have misled, stupefied, and demoralized the youth of the Gentiles by means of education in principles and theories, patently false to us, but which we have inspired.—Protocol 9.

It extends also to family life:

> Having in this way inspired everybody with the thought of his own importance, we will break down the influence of family life among the Gentiles, and its educational importance.—Protocol 10.

And in a passage which might well provide the material for long examination and contemplation by the thoughtful reader, this is said:

> Until the time is ripe, let them amuse themselves... Let those theories of life which we have induced them to regard as the dictates of science play the most important role for them. To this end we shall endeavor to inspire blind confidence in these theories by means of our Press...
>
> Note the successes we have arranged in Darwinism, Marxism, and Nietzscheism. The demoralizing effect of these doctrines upon the minds of the Gentiles should be evident at least to us.—Protocol 2.

That this disintegration and division of Gentile society was proceeding at a favorable rate when the Protocols were uttered is evident from every line of them. For it must be remembered that the Protocols are not bidding for support for a proposed program, but are announcing progress on a program which has been in process of fulfillment for "centuries" and "from ancient times." They contain a series of statements regarding things accomplished, as well as a forelook at things yet to be accomplished. The split of Gentile society was very satisfactorily proceeding in 1896, or thereabouts, when these oracles were uttered.

It is to be noticed that the purpose is nowhere stated to be the extermination of the Gentiles, but their subjugation, at first under the invisible rule which is proposed in these documents, at length under the rule of one whom the invisible forces would be able to put in control of the world through political changes which would create an office of World President or Autocrat. The Gentiles are to be subdued, first intellectually, as here shown, and then economically. Nowhere is it hinted that they are to be deprived of the earth, but only of their independence of those whom the Protocols represent to be Jews. […]

As far as that concerns the dissensions of the Gentiles or Christian world, it is absolutely true. And we have seen in our own nation how "the antagonism between personal and national interests" have rested on "religious and race hatreds." But whoever suspected a common source for these? More amazing still, who would expect any man or group to avow themselves the source? Yet it is thus written in the Protocols—"we have created the antagonism—we thus assure ourselves against the possibility of a Gentile coalition against us." And whether these Protocols are of Jewish origin or not, whether they represent Jewish interests or not, this is exactly the state of the world, of the Gentile world, today.

But a still deeper division is aimed for, and there are signs of even this coming to pass. Indeed, in Russia it has already come to pass, the spectacle of a Gentile lower class led by Jewish leaders against a Gentile upper class! In the First Protocol, describing the effects of a speculative industrial system upon the people, it is said that this sort of economic folly—

> has already created and will continue to create a society which is disillusioned, cold, and heartless. Such a society is

completely estranged from politics and religion. Lust of gold will be the only guide of the people... THEN, not for the sake of good, nor even for the sake of riches, but solely on account of their hatred of the privileged classes, the lower classes of the Gentiles will follow us in the struggle against our rivals for power, the Gentiles of the intellectual classes.

The lower classes of the Gentiles will follow us... against... the Gentiles of the intellectual classes.

If that struggle were to occur today, the leaders of the Gentile insurgents against Gentile society would be Jewish leaders. They are in the leader's place now—not only in Russia, but also in the United States.

"Jewish Protocols" Claim Partial Fulfillment[11]

As a mere literary curiosity, these documents which are called "The Protocols of the Learned Elders of Zion" would exercise a fascination by reason of the terrible completeness of the World Plan which they disclose. But they discourage at every turn the view that they are literature; they purport to be statesmanship, and they provide within their own lines the clue by which their status may be determined. Besides the things they look forward to doing, they announce the things they have done and are doing. If, in looking about the world, it is possible to see both the established conditions and the strong tendencies to which these Protocols allude, it will not be strange if interest in a mere literary curiosity gives way to something like alertness, and it may be alarm.

A few general quotations will serve to illustrate the element of present achievement in the assertions of these documents, and in order that the point may be made clear to the reader the key words will be emphasized.

Take this from Protocol Nine:

> In reality there are no obstacles before us. Our super-government has such an extra-legal status that it may be called by the energetic and strong word—dictatorship. I can conscientiously say that, at the present time, we are the

---
[11] Excerpted from 7 August 1920.

3 — On the *Protocols* (Henry Ford) 45

> lawmakers. We create courts and jurisprudence. We rule with a strong will because we hold in our hands the remains of a once strong party, now subjugated by us.

And this from the Eighth Protocol:

> We will surround our government with a whole world of economists. It is for this reason that the science of economics is the chief subject of instruction taught by the Jews. We shall be surrounded by a whole galaxy of bankers, industrialists, capitalists, and especially by millionaires because, actually, everything will be decided by an appeal to figures.

These are strong claims, but not too strong for the facts that can be marshaled to illustrate them. They are, however, but an introduction to further claims that are made and equally paralleled by the facts. All through the Protocols, as in this quotation from the Eighth, the pre-eminence of the Jews in the teaching of political economy is insisted upon, and the facts bear that out. They are the chief authors of those vagaries which lead the mob after economic impossibilities, and they are also the chief teachers of political economy in our universities, the chief authors of those popular textbooks in the subject, which hold the conservative classes to the fiction that economic theories are economic laws. The idea, the theory, as instruments of social disintegration are common to both the university Jew and the Bolshevik Jew. When all this is shown in detail, public opinion upon the importance of academic and radical economics may undergo a change.

And, as claimed in the quotation just given from the Ninth Protocol, the Jewish world power does today constitute a super-government. It is the Protocol's own word, and none is more fitting. No nation can get all that it wants, but the Jewish World Power can get all that it wants, even though its demands exceed Gentile equality. "We are the lawmakers," say the Protocols, and Jewish influences have been lawmakers in a greater degree than any but the specialists realize. In the past ten years, Jewish international rule, or the power of the group of International Jews, has quite dominated the world. More than that, it has been powerful enough to prevent the passage of salutary laws, and where one law may have slipped through to a place on the statute books, it has been powerful enough to get it interpreted in a sense that rendered it useless for its purpose. This, too, can be illustrated by a large collection of facts.

Moreover, the method by which this is done was outlined long ago in the program of which the Protocols purport to be an outline. "We create courts," continues the quotation, and it is followed in other Protocols by numerous references to "our judges." There is a Jewish court sitting in a public building in the city of New York every week, and other courts, for the sole advantage and use of this people whose spokesmen deny that they are a "separate people," are in formation everywhere. The Zionist plan has already been used in some of the smaller European countries to confer an extra-citizenship upon Jews who already enjoy citizenship in the lands of their residence, and in addition to that a degree of self-rule under the very governments which they demand to protect them. Wherever Jewish tendencies are permitted to work unhindered, the result is not "Americanization," or "Anglicization" nor any other distinctive nationalism, but a strong and ruling reversion back to essential "Judaization."

The "agents" referred to in the first quotation will receive attention in another article. To resume the claims of the Protocols: This from the Seventeenth Protocol:

> We have taken good care long ago to discredit the Gentile clergy and thereby to destroy their mission, which at present might hamper us considerably. Their influence over the people diminishes daily. ... Freedom of conscience has been proclaimed everywhere. Consequently it is only a question of time when the complete crash of the Christian religion will occur. It will be easier to handle the other religions, but it is too early to discuss this phase of the subject.

This will be of considerable interest, perhaps, to those clergymen who are laboring with Jewish rabbis to bring about some kind of religious union. Such a union would of necessity dispose of Christ as a well-meaning but wholly mistaken Jewish prophet, and thus distinctive Christianity would cease to exist insofar as the "union" was effective. The principal religious aversion of the Protocols, however, so far as it is expressed, is against the Catholic church in general and the pontifical office in particular.

A curious paragraph in this Protocol claims for the Jewish race a particular skill in the art of insult:

> Our contemporary press will expose governmental and religious affairs and the incapacity of the Gentiles, always using expressions so derogatory as to approach insult, the faculty of employing which is so well known to our race.

This from the Fifth Protocol:

> Under our influence the execution of the laws of the Gentiles is reduced to a minimum. Respect for the law is undermined by the liberal interpretation we have introduced in this sphere. The courts decide as we dictate, even in the most important cases in which are involved fundamental principles or political issues, viewing them in the light in which we present them to the Gentile administration through agents with whom we have apparently nothing in common, through newspaper opinion and other avenues. ... In Gentile society where we have planted discord and Protestantism...

The word "protestantism" is evidently not used in the religious or sectarian sense, but to denote a temper of querulous fault-finding destructive of harmonious collective opinion.

This from the Fourteenth Protocol:

> In countries called advanced, we have created a senseless, filthy and disgusting literature. For a short time after our entrance into power we shall encourage its existence so that it may show in greater relief the contrast between it and the written and spoken announcements which will emanate from us.

Discussing in the Twelfth Protocol the control of the Press—a subject which must be treated more extensively in another article—the claim is made:

> We have attained this at the present time to the extent that all news is received through several agencies in which it is centralized from all parts of the world. These agencies will then be to all intents and purposes our own institutions and will publish only that which we permit.

This from the Seventh Protocol bears on the same subject:

> We must force the Gentile governments to adopt measures which will promote our broadly conceived plan, already approaching its triumphant goal, by bringing to bear the pressure of stimulated public opinion, which has been organized by us with the help of the so-called 'great power' of the press. With a few exceptions not worth considering, it is already in our hands.

To resume the Twelfth Protocol:

> If we have already managed to dominate the mind of Gentile society to such a point that almost all see world affairs through the colored lenses of the spectacles which we place before their eyes, and if now there is not one government with barriers erected against our access to that which by Gentile stupidity is called state secrets, what then will it be when we are the recognized masters of the world in the person of our universal ruler?

The Jewish nation is the only nation that possesses the secrets of all the rest. No nation long protects a secret which directly concerns another nation, but even so, no nation has all the secrets of all the other nations. Yet it is not too much to say that the International Jews have this knowledge. Much of it, of course, amounts to nothing and their possession of it does not materially add to their power, but the fact that they have the access, that they can get whatever they want when they want it is the important point—as many a secret paper could testify if it could talk, and many a custodian of secret papers could tell if he would. The real secret diplomacy of the world is that which hands over the world's so-called secrets to a few men who are members of one race. The surface of diplomacy, those activities which get written down in the memoirs of comfortably aging statesmen, those coups and treaties which are given high-sounding fame as if they really were important—that is incomparable with the diplomacy of Judah, and its matchless enginery for worming out the hidden knowledge of every ruling group. The United States is included in all these statements. Perhaps there is no government in the world so completely at their service as our own at present, their control having been gained during the past five or six years.[12]

The Protocols do not regard the dispersal of the Jews abroad upon the face of the earth as a calamity, but as a providential arrangement by which the World Plan can be more certainly executed, as see these words of the Eleventh Protocol:

> God gave to us, His Chosen People, as a blessing, the dispersal, and this which has appeared to all to be our weakness has been our whole strength. It has now brought us to the threshold of universal rule.

The claims to accomplishment which are put forth in the Ninth Protocol would be too massive for words were they too massive for concrete realization, but there is a point where the word and the actuality meet and tally.

> In order not to destroy prematurely the Gentile institutions, we have laid our efficient hands on them, and rasped the springs of their mechanism. They were formerly in strict and just order, but we have replaced them with a liberal disorganized and arbitrary administration. We have tampered with jurisprudence, the franchise, the press, freedom of the person, and, most important of all, education and culture, the corner stone of free existence.

---

[12] This is a remarkable statement—and already in 1920. In fact, American Jewry had demonstrated its power back in 1911, when they forced the US government to abrogate a long-standing US-Russia treaty. And in the century since this was written, things in the US have only gotten worse. For details, see my essays in *The Steep Climb* (2023).

> We have misled, stupefied and demoralized the youth of the Gentiles by means of education in principles and theories patently false to us, but which we have inspired.
>
> Above existing laws, without actual change but by distorting them through contradictory interpretations, we have created something stupendous in the way of results.

Everyone knows that, in spite of the fact that the air was never so full of theories of liberty and wild declarations of "rights," there has been a steady curtailment of "personal freedom." Instead of being socialized, the people, under a cover of socialistic phrases, are being brought under an unaccustomed bondage to the state. The Public Health is one plea. Various forms of Public Safety are other pleas. Children are hardly free to play nowadays except under play-masters appointed by the State, among whom, curiously enough, an astonishing proportion of Jews manage to find a place. The streets are no longer as free as they were; laws of every kind are hedging upon the harmless liberties of the people.

A steady tendency toward systemization, every phase of the tendency based upon some very learnedly stated "principle," has set in, and curiously enough, when the investigator pursues his way to the authoritative center of these movements for the regulation of people's life, he finds Jews in power. Children are being lured away from the "social center" of the home for other "centers"; they are being led away (and we are speaking of Gentile children—no Gentiles are ever allowed to regulate the lives of Jewish children) from their natural leaders in home, church and school, to institutionalized "centers" and scientific "play spots," under "trained leaders" whose whole effect, consciously or unconsciously, is to lead the modern child to look to the State, instead of its natural environment, for leadership. All this focuses up to the World Plan for the subjugation of the Gentiles, and if it is not the Jewish World Plan, it would be interesting to know why the material for it is so largely Gentile children and the leaders of it so often of the Jewish race.

Jewish liberties are the best safeguarded in the United States. Gentiles take their chance with public matters, but every Jewish community is surrounded by special protectors who gain special recognition by various devices—political and business threats not the least of them. No public-spirited Gentiles are welcomed to the task of regulating the lives of

Jewish children. The Jewish community in every city is all-sufficient in itself as far as such activities go. The most secret of all parochial schools are the Jewish schools, whose very locations are not all known to the officials of large cities. The Jew is almost anxious in his efforts to mold the Gentile mind; he insists on being permitted to tell the Gentile what to think, especially about the Jew; he is not averse to influencing general Gentile thought in a manner which, though it come about by wide circles, works ultimately into the Jewish scheme of things. The anxiety and the insistence, so well-known to all who have observed them, are only reflections of the Jew's conviction that his is the superior race and is capable of directing the inferior race—of which there is but one, including the whole non-Jewish world.

Every influence that leads to lightness and looseness in Gentile youth today heads up in a Jewish source. Did the young people of the world devise the "sport clothes" which have had so deleterious an effect on the youth of the times that every publicist has thought it worthy of mention? Those styles come out of Jewish clothing concerns, where certainly art is not the rule nor moral influence the main consideration. The moving picture is an interesting development of photography allied with the show business, but whose is the responsibility for its development along such lines as make it a menace to the minds of millions—so serious a menace that it has not escaped observation and condemnation everywhere? Who are the masters of musical jazz in the world? Who direct all the cheap jewelry houses, the bridge-head show parks, the "coney islands," the centers of nervous thrills and looseness? It is possible to take the showy young man and woman of trivial outlook and loose sense of responsibility, and tag them outwardly and inwardly from their clothing and ornaments to their hectic ideas and hopes, with the same tag, "Made, introduced, and exploited by a Jew."

There is, therefore, something most sinister in the light which events cast upon this paragraph:

> We have misled, stupefied, and demoralized the youth of the Gentiles by means of education in principles and theories, patently false to us but which we have inspired.

"Principles and theories" do not necessarily imply lofty or even modest intellectual qualities. The youngster who spends his noon hours and evenings at the movies is getting his "principles and theories" just as the more intellectual youngster from a higher grade of society who listens to a Jewish "liberal" expound "sex liberty" and the "control of population" is getting his. The looseness which inheres in these "principles and theories" does not emanate from the Gentile home, or the Gentile church, or from any line of money-making which is filled principally with Gentiles, but from theories, movements and lines of money-making mostly fancied by Jews. This line of accusation could be run much deeper, but it is preferred to restrict it to what is observable by decent eyes everywhere.

And that "the youth of the Gentiles" are the principal victims, and not the youth of the Jews, is also observable. While a certain percentage of Jewish youth itself is overcome by this social poison, the percentage is almost nothing compared with the results among the youth of the Gentiles. It is a significant fact that Jews who link this process of enervation of Gentiles with large profits are not themselves, nor are their sons and daughters, the victims of this enervation. Jewish youth comes through more proudly and more cleanly than the mass of Gentile youth.

Many a father and mother, many a sound-minded, uncorrupted young person, and thousands of teachers and publicists have cried out against *luxury*. Many a financier, observing the manner in which the people earned and flung away their money, has warned against luxury. Many an economist, knowing that the nonessential industries were consuming men and materials that were necessary to the stabilizing of essential industries; knowing that men are making knick-knacks who should be making steel; knowing that men are engaged in making gew-gaws who should be working on the farm; that materials are going into articles that are made only to sell and never to use, and that materials are thus diverted from the industries that support the people's life—every observer knowing this crazy insistence on luxurious nonessentials has lifted up a strong voice against it.

But, according to these Protocols, we have been starting at the wrong end. The people, it is true, buy these senseless nonessentials which are called luxuries. But the people do not devise them. And the people grow tired of them one by one. But the stream of varieties continues—always something else being thrust at the people, dangled before their eyes, set bobbing down the avenue on enough mannikins to give the impression that it is "style"; newspaper print and newspaper pictures; movie pictures; stage costumes enough to force the new thing into "fashion" with a kind of force and compulsion which no really worthy essential thing can command.

Where does it come from? What power exists whose long experience and deliberate intent enable it to frivolize the people's minds and tastes and compel them to pay most of their money for it too? Why this spasm of luxury and extravagance through which we have just passed? How did it occur that before luxury and extravagance were apparent, all the material to provoke and inflame them had been prepared beforehand and shipped beforehand, ready for the stampede which also had been prepared?

If the people of the United States would stop to consider, when the useless and expensive thing is offered them—if they would trace its origin, trace the course of the enormous profits made out of it, trace the whole movement to flood the market with uselessness and extravagance and thus demoralize the Gentile public financially, intellectually, and socially—if, in short, it could be made clear to them that Jewish financial interests are not only pandering to the loosest elements in human nature, but actually engaged in a calculated effort to render them loose in the first place and keep them loose—it would do more than anything else to stop this sixfold waste—the waste of material, the waste of labor, the waste of Gentile money, the waste of Gentile mind, the waste of Jewish talent, and the worse than waste of Israel's real usefulness to the world.

We say the Gentile public is the victim of this stimulated trade in useless luxuries. Did you ever see Jewish people so victimized? They might wear very noticeable clothing, but its price and its quality agree. They might wear rather large diamonds, but they are diamonds. The Jew is not the victim of the Jew, the craze for luxuries is just like the "coney island" crowd to him; he knows what attracts them and the worthlessness of it.

And it is not so much the financial loss that is to be mourned, nor yet the atrocities committed upon good taste, but the fact that the silly Gentile crowds walk into the net willingly, even gaily, supposing the change of the fashion to be as inevitable as the coming of spring, supposing the new demand on their earnings to be as necessary and as natural as

taxes. The crowds think that somehow they have part in it, when their only part is to pay, and then pay again for the new extravagance when the present one palls. There are men in this country who know two years ahead what the frivolities and extravagances of the people will be, because they decree what they shall be. These things are strictly business, demoralizing to the Gentile majority, enriching to the Jewish minority.
Look at the Sixth Protocol for a sidelight on all this:

This is an excerpt from a longer passage dealing with the plans by which the people's interest could be swung from political to industrial questions, how industry could be made insecure and unfair by the introduction of speculation into its management, and finally how against this condition the people could be rendered restless and helpless. Luxury was to be the instrument:

> To destroy Gentile industry, we shall, as an incentive to this speculation, encourage among the Gentiles a strong demand for luxuries—all enticing luxuries.

And in the First Protocol: "Surely we cannot allow our own people to come to this. The people of the Gentiles are stupefied with spirituous liquors..."—incidentally, the profits of spirituous liquors flow in large amounts to Jewish pockets. The history of the whiskey ring in this country will show this. Historically, the whole prohibition movement may be described as a contest between Gentile and Jewish capital, and in this instance, thanks to the Gentile majority, the Gentiles won.

The amusement, gambling, jazz song, scarlet fiction, side show, cheap-dear fashions, flashy jewelry, and every other activity that lived by reason of an invisible pressure upon the people, and that exchanged the most useless of commodities for the prices that would just exhaust the people's money surplus and no more—every such activity has been under the mastery of the Jews.

They may not be conscious of their participation in any wholesale demoralization of the people. They may only be conscious of "easy money." They may sometimes yield to surprise as they contrast the silly Gentiles with their own money-wise and fabric-wise and metal-wise Jews. But however this may be, there is the conception of a program by which a people may be deliberately devastated materially and spiritually, and yet kept pleasant all the time—and there also is the same program translated into terms of daily transactions and for the most part, perhaps altogether under control of the members of one race.

"A LITERARY FORGERY"
PHILIP GRAVES[1]

Preface

The so-called "Protocols of the Elders of Sion" were published in London in 1920 under the title of "The Jewish Peril."

This book is a translation of a book published in Russia, in 1905, by Sergei Nilus, a Government official, who professed to have received from a friend a copy of a summary of the minutes of a secret meeting, held in Paris by a Jewish organization that was plotting to overthrow civilization in order to establish a Jewish world state.

These Protocols attracted little attention until after the Russian Revolution of 1917, when the appearance of the Bolshevists, among whom were many Jews professing and practising political doctrines that in some points resembled those advocated in the "Protocols," led many to believe that Nilus's alleged discovery was genuine. The Protocols were widely discussed and translated into several European languages. Their authenticity has been frequently attacked and many arguments have been adduced for the theory that they are a forgery.

In the following three articles the Constantinople Correspondent of *The Times* presents for the first time conclusive proof that the document is in the main a clumsy plagiarism. He has forwarded to *The Times* a copy of the French book from which the plagiarism is made. The British Museum has a complete copy of the book, which is entitled *Dialogue aux Enfers entre Machiavel et Montesquieu, ou la Politique de Machiavel au XIX. Siècle. Par un Contemporain*, and was published at Brussels in 1865. Shortly after its publication the author, Maurice Joly, a Paris lawyer and publicist, was arrested by the police of Napoleon III. and sentenced to 15 months' imprisonment.

---

[1] Reproduced from the *London Times*, 16-18 August 1921.

I. A Literary Forgery

"There is one thing about Constantinople that is worth your while to remember," said a diplomatist to me in 1908. "If you only stay here long enough you will meet many men who matter, and you may find the key to many strange secrets." Yet I must confess that when the discovery which is the theme of these articles was communicated to me I was at first incredulous. Mr. X., who brought me the evidence, was convinced. "Read this book through," he said, "and you will find irrefutable proof that the 'Protocols of the Learned Elders of Sion' is a plagiarism."

Mr. X., who does not wish his real name to be known, is a Russian landowner with English connexions. Orthodox by religion, he is in political opinion a Constitutional Monarchist. He came here as a refugee after the final failure of the White cause in South Russia. He had long been interested in the Jewish question as far as it concerned Russia, had studied the "Protocols," and during the period of Denikin's ascendancy had made investigations with the object of discovering whether any occult "Masonic" organization, such as the Protocols speak of, existed in Southern Russia. The only such organization was a Monarchist one. The discovery of the key to the problem of the Protocols came to him by chance.

A few months ago he bought a number of old books from a former officer of the "Okhrana" (Russian Political Police) who had fled to Constantinople. Among these books was a small volume in French, lacking the title-page, with dimensions of 5½ in. by 3¾ in. It had been cheaply rebound. On the leather back is printed in Latin capitals the word 'Joli.' The preface, entitled *Simple avertissement*, is dated Geneva, October 15, 1864. The book contains 324 pages, of which numbers 315–322 inclusive follow page 24 in the only copy known to Mr. X, perhaps owing to a mistake when the book was rebound. Both the paper and the type are characteristic of the "sixties and seventies" of the last century. These details are given in the hope that they may lead to the discovery of the title of the book [See Preface]. Mr. X. believes it must be rare, since, had it not been so, the Protocols would have speedily been recognized as a plagiarism by anyone who had read the original.

That the latter is a "fake" could not be maintained for an instant by anyone who had seen it. Its original possessor, the old Okhrana officer, did not remember where he obtained it, and attached no importance to it.

Mr. X, glancing at it one day, was struck by a resemblance between a passage which had caught his eye and a phrase in the French edition of the Protocols (Edition de la Vieille France, 1920). He followed up the clue, and soon realized that the Protocols were to a very large extent as much a paraphrase of the Geneva original as the published version of a War Office or Foreign Office telegram is a paraphrase of the ciphered original.

Before receiving the book from Mr. X, I was, as I have said, incredulous. I did not believe that Sergei Nilus's "Protocols" were authentic; they explained too much by the theory of a vast Jewish conspiracy. Professor Nilus's account of how they were obtained was too melodramatic to be credible, and it was hard to believe that real "Learned Elders of Sion" would not have produced a more intelligent political scheme than the crude and theatrical subtilties of the Protocols. But I could not have believed, had I not seen, that the writer who supplied Nilus with his originals was a careless and shameless plagiarist.

The Geneva book is a very thinly-veiled attack on the despotism of Napoleon III. in the form of a series of 25 dialogues divided into four parts.[2] The speakers are Montesquieu and Machiavelli. In the brief preface to his book, the anonymous author points out that it contains passages which are applicable to all Governments, "but it particularly personifies a political system which has not varied in its application for a single day since the fatal and alas! too distant date when it was enthroned." Its references to the "Haussmannisation" of Paris,[3] to the repressive measures and policy of the French Emperor, to his wasteful financial system, to his foreign wars, to his use of secret societies in his foreign policy (cf., his notorious relations with the Carbonari) and his suppression of them in France, to his relations with the Vatican, and to his control of the Press are unmistakable.

The Geneva book, or as it will henceforth be called, the Geneva Dialogues, opens with the meeting of the spirits of Montesquieu and Machiavelli on a desolate beach in the world of shades.[4] After a lengthy exchange of civilities, Montesquieu asks Machiavelli to explain why from an ardent

---

[2] It is unclear how the "25 dialogues" converts to the "24 Protocols."
[3] Georges-Eugène Haussmann (1809-1891) redesigned large portions of central Paris in the 1850s and 1860s.
[4] "Shades" are souls of the deceased. The "world of shades" would be somewhere in the underworld.

Republican he had become the author of *The Prince* and "the founder of that sombre school of thought which has made all crowned heads your disciples, but which is well fitted to justify the worst crimes of tyranny." Machiavelli replies that he is a realist and proceeds to justify the teaching of *The Prince*, and to explain its applicability to the Western European States of 1864.

In the first six "Geneva Dialogues," Montesquieu is given a chance of argument of which he avails himself. In the seventh dialogue, which corresponds to the fifth, sixth, seventh, and part of the eighth "Protocols," he gives Machiavelli permission to describe at length how he would solve the problem of stabilizing political societies "incessantly disturbed by the spirit of anarchy and revolution." Henceforth Machiavelli, or in reality Napoleon III., speaking through Machiavelli, has the lion's share of the dialogue. Montesquieu's contributions thereto become more and more exclamatory; he is profoundly shocked by Machiavelli-Napoleon's defence of an able and ruthless dictatorship, but his counter-arguments grow briefer and weaker. At times, indeed, the author of *L'Esprit des Lois* is made to cut as poor a figure as—*parvum componere magno*[5]—does Dr. Watson when he attempts to talk criminology to Sherlock Holmes.

The Protocols follow almost the same order as the Dialogues. Dialogues 1-17 generally correspond with Protocols 1-19. There are a few exceptions to this. One is in the 18th "Protocol," where, together with paraphrases of passages from the 17th Dialogue ("Geneva Dialogues," pp. 216, 217), there is an echo of a passage in the 25th "Geneva Dialogue," viz.: "*Quand le malheureux est opprimé il dit 'Si le Roi le savait'; Quand on veut se venger, qu'on espère un secours, on dit 'le Roi le saura.'*" This appears on page 68 of the English edition of the Protocols (4th Edition, published by "The Britons") as "In order to exist, the prestige of power must occupy such a position that the people can say among themselves, 'If only the King knew about it,' or 'When the King knows about it.'"

The last five Protocols (Nos. 20-24 inclusive) do not contain so many paraphrases of the "Geneva Dialogues" as the first 19. Some of their resemblances and paraphrases are, however, very striking, e.g., the following:—

---

[5] 'To combine the great with the small.'

A loan is an issue of Government paper which entails an obligation to pay interest amounting to a percentage of the total sum of the borrowed money. If a loan is at 5 per cent., then in 20 years the Government will have unnecessarily paid out a sum equal to that of the loan in order to cover the percentage. In 40 years it will have paid twice, and in 60 thrice that amount, but the loan will still remain as an unpaid debt.— (Protocols, p. 77).

Montesquieu.— "How are loans made? By the issue of bonds entailing on the Government the obligation to pay interest proportionate to the capital it has been paid. Thus, if a loan is at 5 per cent., the State, after 20 years, has paid out a sum equal to the borrowed capital. When 40 years have expired it has paid double, after 60 years triple: yet it remains debtor for the entire capital sum."— (Geneva Dialogues, p. 250).

But generally speaking, Protocols 20 and 21, which deal (somewhat unconvincingly) with the financial programme of the Learned Elders, owe less to the "Geneva Dialogues," Nos. 18-21, than to the imagination of the plagiarist author who had for once, in a way, to show a little originality. This is natural enough since the "Dialogues" in question describe the actual financial policy of the French Imperial Government, while the Protocols deal with the future. Again in the last four "Geneva Dialogues," Machiavelli's apotheosis of the Second Empire, being based upon historical facts which took place between 1852 and 1864, obviously furnished scanty material for the plagiarist who wished to prove or, very possibly, had been ordered to prove in the Protocols that the ultimate aim of the leaders of Jewry was to give the world a ruler sprung from the House of David.

The scores of parallels between the two books and a theory concerning the methods of the plagiarist and the reasons for the publication of the Protocols in 1905 will be the subject of further articles [below]. Meanwhile it is amusing to find that the only subject with which the Protocols deal on lines quite contrary to those followed by Machiavelli in the "Dialogues" is the private life of the Sovereign. The last words of the Protocols are "Our Sovereign must be irreproachable." The Elders evidently propose to keep the King of Israel in good order. The historical Machiavelli was, we know, rather a scandalous old gentleman, and his shade insists that amorous adventures, so far from injuring a Sovereign's reputation, make him an object of interest and sympathy to "the fairest half of his subjects."

II. Plagiarism at Work

While the Geneva Dialogues open with an exchange of compliments between Montesquieu and Machiavelli, which covers seven pages, the author of the Protocols plunges at once *in medias res*.[6]

One can imagine him hastily turning over those first seven pages of the book which he has been ordered to paraphrase against time, and angrily ejaculating, "Nothing here." But on page 8 of the Dialogues he finds what he wants; the greater part of this page and the next are promptly paraphrased, thus:—

> Among mankind the evil instinct is mightier than the good. Man is more drawn to evil than to good. Fear and Force have more empire over him than reason… Every man aims at domination; not one but would be an oppressor if he could; all or almost all are ready to sacrifice the rights of others to their own interests… (Geneva Dialogues, p. 8)

> It must be noted that people with corrupt instincts are more numerous than those of noble instinct. Therefore in governing the world the best results are obtained by means of violence and intimidation, and not by academic discussions. Every man aims at power; every one would like to become a dictator if he only could do so, and rare indeed are the men who would not be disposed to sacrifice the welfare of others in order to attain their own personal aims. (Protocols, p. 1)

And again:

---

[6] 'Into the midst of things.'

> What restrains those beasts of prey which they call men from attacking one another? Brute unrestrained Force in the first stages of social life, then the Law, that is still force regulated by forms. You have consulted all historic sources; everywhere might precedes right. Political Liberty is merely a relative idea…

> What restrained the wild beasts of prey which we call men? What has ruled them up to now? In the first stages of social life they submitted to brute and blind force, then to law, which in reality is the same force, only masked. From this I am led to deduct that by the law of nature right lies in might. Political freedom is not a fact but an idea.

The gift of liberty, according to the Machiavelli of the Geneva Dialogues, of self-government according to the Protocols (page 2), leads speedily to civil and social strife, and the State is soon ruined by internal convulsions or by foreign intervention following on the heels of civil war. Then follows a singular parallel between the two books which deserves quotation:—

> What arms will they (States) employ in war against foreign enemies? Will the opposing generals communicate their plans of campaign to one another and thus be mutually in a position to defend themselves? Will they mutually ban night attacks, traps, ambushes, battles with inequality of force? Of course not; such combatants would court derision. Are you against the employment of these traps and tricks, of all the strategy indispensable to war against the enemy within, the revolutionary? (Dialogues, p. 9)

> I would ask the question why is it not immoral for a State which has two enemies, one external and one internal, to use different means of defence against the former to that which it would use against the latter, to make secret plans of defence, to attack him by night or with superior forces? (Protocols, p. 2)

Both "Machiavelli" and the author of the Protocols agree (Prot. p. 3, Dialogues, p. 11) almost in the same words that politics have nothing in common with morality. Right is described in the Protocols as "an abstract idea established by nothing," in the Dialogues as an "infinitely vague" expression. The end, say both, justifies the means. "I pay less attention," says Machiavelli, "to what is good and moral than to what is useful and necessary." The Protocols (p. 4) use the same formula, substituting "profitable" for "useful." According to the Protocols, he who would rule "must have recourse to cunningness (sic) and hypocrisy." In the second Dialogue (p. 15) Montesquieu reproaches Machiavelli for having "only two words to repeat—'Force' and 'guile.'" Both Machiavelli and the "Elders" of the Protocols preach despotism as the sole safeguard against anarchy. In the Protocols this despotism has to be Jewish and hereditary. Machiavelli's despotism is obviously Napoleonic.

There are scores of other parallels between the books. Fully 50 paragraphs in the Protocols are simply paraphrases of passages in the Dialogues. The quotation *"per me reges regnant,"* is rightly given in the Vieille France edition of the Protocols (p. 29), while 'regunt' is substituted for 'regnant' in the English version (p. 20), appears on p. 63 of the Geneva Dialogues. Sulla, whom the English version of the Protocols insists on calling "Silla," appears in both books.

> After covering Italy with blood, Sulla reappeared as a simple citizen in Borne: no one durst touch a hair of his head. (Geneva Dialogues, p. 159).

> Remember at the time when Italy was streaming with blood, she did not touch a hair of Silla's head, and he was the man who made her blood pour out. (Protocols, p. 51).

Sulla, who after the proscriptions stalked "in savage grandeur home," is one of the tyrants whom every schoolboy knows, and those who believe that Elders of the 33rd Degree are responsible for the Protocols, may say that this is a mere coincidence. But what about the exotic Vishnu, the hundred-armed Hindu deity who appears twice in each book? The following passages never were examples of "unconscious plagiarism."

> Machiavelli.— "Like the God Vishnu, my press will have a hundred arms, and these arms will give their hands to all the different shades of opinion throughout the country." (Dialogues, p. 141)

> These newspapers, like the Indian god Vishnu, will be possessed of hundreds of hands, each of which will be feeling the pulse of varying public opinion. (Protocols, p. 43)

And again:

> Montesquieu.— "Now I understand the figure of the god Vishnu; you have a hundred like the Indian idol, and each of your fingers touches a spring." (Dialogues, p. 207)

> Our Government will resemble the Hindu god Vishnu. Each of our hundred hands will hold one spring of the social machinery of State. (Protocols, p. 65)

Taxation of the Press

The Dialogues and the Protocols alike devote special attention to the Press, and their schemes for the muzzling and control thereof are almost identical—absolutely identical, indeed, in many details. Thus Machiavelli expounds the following ingenious scheme:—

> I shall extend the tax on newspapers to books, or rather I shall introduce a stamp duty on books having less than a certain number of pages. A book, for example, with less than 200 or 300 pages will not rank as a book, but as a brochure. I am sure you see the advantage of this scheme. On the one hand, I thin by taxation that cloud of short books which are the mere appendages of journalism; on the other, I force those who wish to escape stamp duty to throw themselves into long and costly compositions, which will hardly ever be sold and scarcely read in such a form. (Dialogues, pp. 135-136)

The Protocols has:—

> We will tax it [the book press] in the same manner as the newspaper Press—that is to say, by means of Excise stamps and deposits. But on books of less than 300 pages we will place a tax twice as heavy. These short books we will classify as pamphlets, which constitute the most virulent form of printed poison. These measures will also compel writers to publish such long works that they will be little read by the public and so chiefly on account of their high price. (p. 41)

Both have the same profound contempt for journalists.

> Machiavelli.— "You must know that journalism is a sort of Freemasonry; those who live by it are bound...to one another by the ties of professional discretion; like the augurs of old, they do not lightly divulge the secret of their oracles. They would gain nothing by betraying themselves, for they have mostly won more or less discreditable scars..." (Dialogues, pp. 145-146)

> Already there exists in French journalism a system of Masonic understanding for giving counter-signs. All organs of the Press are tied by mutual professional secrets in the manner of the ancient oracles. Not one of its members will betray his knowledge of the secret, if the secret has not been ordered to be made public. No single publisher will have the courage to betray the secret entrusted to him, the reason being that not one of them is admitted into the literary world without bearing the marks of some shady act in his past life. (Protocols, p. 44)

Contempt for the People

But this contempt is nothing compared to that which both Machiavelli and the Elders evince towards the masses whom tyranny is to reduce to a more-than-Oriental servitude.

> Machiavelli.— "You do not know the unbounded meanness of the peoples…grovelling before force, pitiless towards the weak, implacable to faults, indulgent to crimes, incapable of supporting the contradictions of a free régime, and patient to the point of martyrdom under the violence of an audacious despotism…giving themselves masters whom they pardon for deeds for the least of which they would have beheaded twenty constitutional kings." (Dialogues, p. 43)

> In their intense meanness the Christian peoples help our independence—when kneeling they crouch before power; when they are pitiless towards the weak; merciless in dealing with faults, and lenient to crimes; when they refuse to recognize the contradictions of freedom; when they are patient to the degree of martyrdom in bearing with the violence of an audacious despotism. At the hands of their present dictators, Premiers, and Ministers, they endure abuses for the smallest of which they would have murdered twenty kings. (Protocols, p. 15)

Both the Elders and Machiavelli propose to make political crime thoroughly unpopular by assimilating the treatment of the political criminal to that of the felon. Both devote not a little attention to police organization and espionage; the creator of Machiavelli had evidently studied Napoleon III.'s police methods and suffered at the hands of his agents. Each proposes to exercise a severe control over the Bar and the Bench. As regards the Vatican, Machiavelli-Napoleon, with recent Italian history in mind, aims at the complete control of the Papacy. After inflaming popular hatred against the Church of Rome and its clergy, he will intervene to protect the Holy See, as Napoleon III. did intervene, when "the *chasse-*

pôts worked wonders".[7] The learned Elders propose to follow a similar plan "when the people in their rage throw themselves on to the Vatican we shall appear as its protectors in order to stop bloodshed." Ultimately, of course, they mean to destroy the Church. The terrible chiefs of a Pan-Judaic conspiracy could hardly have any other plan of campaign. Machiavelli, naturally, does not go so far. Enough for him if the Pope is safely lodged in the Napoleonic pocket.

Is it necessary to produce further proofs that the majority of the Protocols are simply paraphrases of the Geneva Dialogues, with wicked Hebrew Elders, and finally an Israelite world ruler in the place of Machiavelli-Napoleon III., and the brutish goyim (Gentiles) substituted for the fickle masses, "gripped in a vice by poverty, ridden by sensuality, devoured by ambition," whom Machiavelli intends to win?

III. Some Conclusions

There is no evidence as to how the Geneva Dialogues reached Russia. The following theory may be suggested.

The Third Napoleon's secret police, many of whom were Corsicans, must have known the existence of the Dialogues and almost certainly obtained them from some of the many persons arrested on the charge of political conspiracy during the reign of Napoleon III. In the last two decades of the 19th century and in the early years of the 20th there were always a few Corsicans in the Palace Police of the Tsar, and in the Russian secret service. Combining courage with secretiveness, a high average of intelligence with fidelity to his chief, the Corsican makes a first-class secret agent or bodyguard. It is not improbable that Corsicans who had been in the service of Napoleon III., or who had had kinsmen in his secret service, brought the Geneva Dialogues to Russia, where some member of the Okhrana or some Court official obtained possession of them. But this is only a theory.

As to the Protocols, they were first published in 1905 at Tsarskoye Selo in the second edition of a book entitled *The Great Within the Small*, the author of which was Professor Sergei Nilus. Professor Nilus has been described to the writer as a learned, pious, credulous Conservative, who

---

[7] A *chassepôt* was a French rifle of the era.

combined much theological and some historical erudition with a singular lack of knowledge of the world. In January, 1917, Nilus, according to the introduction to the French version of the Protocols, published a book, entitled *It is Here, at Our Doors!!* in which he republished the Protocols. In this latter work, according to the French version, Professor Nilus stated that the manuscript of the Protocols was given him by Alexis Nicolaievich Sukhotin, a noble who afterwards became Vice-Governor of Stavropol.

According to the 1905 edition of the Protocols, they were obtained by a woman who stole them from

> one of the most influential and most highly initiated leaders of Freemasonry. The theft was accomplished at the close of the secret meeting of the 'initiated' in France, that nest of Jewish conspiracy.

But in the epilogue to the English version of the Protocols, Professor Nilus says, "My friend found them in the safes at the headquarters of the Society of Zion which are at present situated in France." According to the French version of the Protocols, Nilus in his book of 1917 states that the Protocols were notes of a plan submitted to the "Council of Elders" by Theodor Herzl at the first Zionist Congress which was held at Basle, in August, 1897, and that Herzl afterwards complained to the Zionist Committee of Action of the indiscreet publication of confidential information. The Protocols were signed by "Zionist representatives of the 33rd Degree" in Orient Freemasonry and were secretly removed from the complete file of the proceedings of the aforesaid Zionist Congress, which was hidden in the "Chief Zionist office, which is situated in French territory."

Such are Professor Nilus's rather contradictory accounts of the origin of the Protocols. Not a very convincing story! Theodor Herzl is dead; Sukhotin is dead; and where are the signatures of the Zionist representatives of the 33rd Degree?

*****

Turning to the text of the Protocols, and comparing it with that of the Geneva Dialogues, one is struck by the absence of any effort on the part of the plagiarist to conceal his plagiarisms. The paraphrasing has been very careless; parts of sentences, whole phrases at times, are identical: the development of the thought is the same; there has been no attempt worth mentioning to alter the order of the Geneva Dialogues. The plagiarist has introduced Darwin, Marx, and Nietzsche in one passage in order to be "up to date"; he has given a Jewish colour to "Machiavelli's" schemes for dictatorship, but he has utterly failed to conceal his indebtedness to the Geneva Dialogues. This gives the impression that the real writer of the Protocols, who does not seem to have had anything to do with Nilus and may have been some quite unimportant *précis* writer employed by the Court or by the Okhrana, was obliged to paraphrase the original at short notice. A proof of Jewish conspiracy was required at once as a weapon for the Conservatives against the Liberal elements in Russia.

Mr. X, the discoverer of the plagiarism, informs me that the Protocols, shortly after their discovery in 1901, four years before their publication by Professor Nilus, served a subsidiary purpose, namely, the first defeat of Monsieur Philippe, a French hypnotist and thought-reader, who acquired considerable influence over the Tsar and the Tsaritsa at the beginning of the present century.[8] The Court favourite was disliked by certain great personages, and incurred the natural jealousy of the monks, thaumaturgists, and similar adventurers who hoped to capture the Tsar through the Empress in their own interest, or in that of various cliques. Philippe was not a Jew, but it was easy to represent a Frenchman from "that nest of Jewish conspiracy" as a Zionist agent. Philippe fell from favour, to return to Russia and find himself once more in the Court's good graces at a later date.

But the principal importance of the Protocols was their use during the first Russian Revolution [of 1905-1906]. This revolution was supported by the Jewish element in Russia, notably by the Jewish Bund. The Okhrana organization knew this perfectly well; it had its Jewish and crypto-Jewish agents, one of whom afterwards assassinated M. Stolypin[9]; it was in league with the powerful Conservative faction; with its allies it sought to gain the Tsar's ear. For many years before the Russian

---

[8] Nizier Anthelme Philippe (1849-1905) was a reputed healer and miracle worker.

[9] Pyotr Stolypin (1862-1911) was Russian prime minister until assassinated by a Jew, Dmitry Bogrov.

revolution of 1905-1906 there had been a tale of a secret council of Rabbis who plotted ceaselessly against the Orthodox. The publication of the Protocols in 1905 certainly came at an opportune moment for the Conservatives. It is said by some Russians that the manuscript of the Protocols was communicated to the Tsar early in 1905, and that its communication contributed to the fall of the Liberal Prince Sviatopolk-Mirski in that year and the subsequent strong reactionary movement. However that may be, the date and place of publication of Nilus's first edition of the Protocols are most significant now that we know that the originals which were given him were simply paraphrases.

The following conclusions are, therefore, forced upon any reader of the two books who has studied Nilus's account of the origin of the Protocols and has some acquaintance with Russian history in the years preceding the revolution of 1905-6:—

1. The Protocols are largely a paraphrase of the book here provisionally called the "Geneva Dialogues."

2. They were designed to foster the belief among Russian Conservatives, and especially in Court circles, that the prime cause of discontent among the politically minded elements in Russia was not the repressive policy of the bureaucracy, but a worldwide Jewish conspiracy. They thus served as a weapon against the Russian Liberals, who urged the Tsar to make certain, concessions to the intelligentsia.

3. The Protocols were paraphrased very hastily and carelessly.

4. Such portions of the Protocols as were not derived from the Geneva Dialogues were probably supplied by the Okhrana, which organization very possibly obtained them from the many Jews it employed to spy on their coreligionists.

So much for the Protocols. They have done harm not so much, in this writer's opinion, by arousing anti-Jewish feeling, which is older than the Protocols and will persist in all countries where there is a Jewish problem until that problem is solved; rather, they have done harm by persuading all sorts of mostly well-to-do people that every recent manifestation of discontent on the part of the poor is an unnatural phenomenon, a factitious agitation caused by a secret society of Jews.

Epilogue (Editors of *The Times*)

We publish today [18 August 1921] the last of the articles on the so-called "Protocols of the Elders of Zion," from our Constantinople Correspondent [Philip Graves], who has effectively exposed a remarkable forgery. We have, of course, no political object in making this discovery known. On the general aspects of the Jewish problem our attitude is known to be impartial, and we have no intention of taking sides in those political controversies on this question which too frequently engender excessive passion and obscure its real character. In the interests of objective truth, however, it was of great importance that a legend like that so long connected with the "Protocols of the Elders of Zion" should be exposed at the earliest possible opportunity.

Briefly summarized, the facts of this curious historical incident are as follows. A Russian book, published in 1905 by an official named Sergei Nilus, contained a document described as "The Protocols of the Elders of Zion," and purported to be a summary of the proceedings of a secret meeting of a Jewish organization that was plotting in France to overthrow Gentile civilization and establish a Jewish world State.

The document attracted little attention until after the [second] Russian Revolution in 1917, when the astounding collapse of a great country through the action of the Bolshevists and the presence of a large number of Jews in the Bolshevist ranks caused many to search for some simplified explanation of the catastrophe. The Protocols appeared to provide such an explanation, more particularly since the tactics of the Bolshevists in many respects resembled those advocated in the "Protocols." The book was translated into several European languages and made the basis for impassioned dissertations on an alleged Jewish world peril. There was a certain plausibility about this thesis that attracted many; but the authenticity of the Protocols was very vigorously called in question, and the whole matter was shrouded in doubt until our Correspondent made his remarkable discovery. A Russian in Constantinople, who had bought some books from an ex-officer of the Russian Secret Police, found among them one in which many passages struck him by their resemblance to the "Protocols."

Our Correspondent, whose attention was called to the matter, found on examination that the Protocols consisted in the main of clumsy plagiarisms from this little French book, which he has forwarded to us. The book had no title-page, but we identified it in the British Museum as a political pamphlet directed against Napoleon III. and published in Brussels in 1865 by a [Jewish] French lawyer named Maurice Joly, and entitled *Dialogue aux Enfers entre Machiavel et Montesquieu*. The book was published anonymously, but the author was immediately seized by Napoleon's police and sentenced to a term of imprisonment. A second edition was published in Brussels in 1868, with the author's name and a note on his imprisonment.

The author of the Protocols simply copied from the "Dialogues" a number of passages in which Machiavelli is made to enunciate the doctrines and tactics of despotism as they were at that time practised by Napoleon, and put them into the mouth of an imaginary Jewish Elder. There can be little doubt that the forgery was perpetrated by some member of the Russian Secret Police.[10] Nilus, who may have acted in good faith, declared that the manuscript of the Protocols had been given him by an official named Alexander Sukhotin, who professed to have received it from a woman who had stolen it from an Elder of Zion. On the leather back of the copy of the "Dialogues" sent us by our Correspondent we notice the letters A. S., and, seeing that the book was bought from an ex-officer of the Secret Police, it seems possible that this copy belonged at one time to Sukhotin, and that it was the copy actually used in the compilation of the "Protocols." For many years there was a close connexion between the Russian and the French police, and one of the confiscated copies of Joly's book may easily have fallen into the hands of a Russian agent—such as Rachkovsky, at one time head of the Russian Secret Police in Paris, to whom other and more clumsy forgeries have been traced—and may have inspired him to invent a weapon for use against Jewish revolutionaries.

At any rate, the fact of the plagiarism has now been conclusively established, and the legend may be allowed to pass into oblivion. The

---

[10] Actually, such a conclusion is highly disputed, even today. A French origin seems equally likely.

historical interest of the discovery is considerable, though, as we have indicated, it does not, in our opinion, affect the Jewish problem, which happily, in this country, cannot be said to exist in its Continental form.

PART TWO

THE PROTOCOLS OF THE ELDERS OF ZION

THE PROTOCOLS OF THE ELDERS OF ZION

Protocol No. 1

On liberalism, "might makes right," Goy vices, "Liberty, Equality, Fraternity," the power of money

Let us set aside fine phrases and discuss the inner meaning of every thought. By comparisons and deductions, we will illuminate the situation. In this way, I will describe our system, both from our own viewpoint and from that of the Goyim.

It must be remembered that people with base instincts are more numerous than those with noble ones; therefore, the best results in governing are achieved through violence and intimidation, and not through academic discourse.

*****

Every man seeks power; everyone would like to become a dictator if he possibly could; and rare indeed are those who would not sacrifice the common good in order to attain personal advantage.

What has thus far restrained the wild beasts that we call men? What has influenced them until now? In the early stages of social life, they submitted to brute and blind force; afterwards, to the law, which is the same force in disguised form. I therefore deduce from this that, according to the laws of nature, might makes right.

Political freedom is not a fact but an idea. One must know how to employ this idea when it becomes necessary to attract the masses to one's party, if the party plans to crush those in power. This task becomes easier if the ruler himself has embraced the idea of freedom, of 'liberalism,' and for the sake of this idea, yields some of his power.

It is precisely here that our theory triumphs: the relinquished aspects of power are, according to the laws of nature, immediately seized by a new hand because the blind force of the people cannot remain without a leader even for one day; and the new power merely replaces the old, weakened by liberalism.

*****

In our day, the power of gold has replaced liberal rulers. There was a time when faith ruled. But today, the idea of freedom cannot be realized because no one knows how to make reasonable use of it. Give the people self-government for a short time and it will become corrupted. From that very moment, conflict emerges and soon develops into social struggles; these will eventually set the state aflame, reducing its authority to ashes. Whether the state is exhausted by internal strife or whether civil war delivers it into the hands of its enemies, either way, the state is hopelessly lost; it is in our power. The despotism of capital, which is entirely in our hands, is the only lifeline for the state, and so it grasps it, even against its will, simply to avoid falling into an abyss.

To the liberally-inclined man who may feel that such arguments are immoral, I ask him: If a state has two enemies—one external and one internal—and if against the external enemy it is morally permitted to use all methods of warfare, and to keep the plans of attack a secret, then why should the same methods be regarded as immoral when applied to a worse foe, a transgressor against social order and prosperity?

I ask: How can a sound and logical mind hope to successfully guide the masses by means of reasonable persuasion or by arguments if there is a chance of contradiction by opposing arguments, even though they are unreasonable, but which may appear more attractive to the superficially-thinking masses? Guided entirely by shallow passions, superstitions, customs, traditions, and sentimental theories, the mob becomes embroiled in party dissensions that prevent all possibility of reaching an agreement, even one based on perfectly sound reasoning. Every decision of the mob depends upon an accidental or prearranged majority, which, owing to its ignorance of political secrets, reaches absurd decisions and thus introduces the seeds of anarchy into the government.

Politics have nothing in common with morals. The ruler guided by morality is not a skilled politician, and consequently his control is infirm. He who desires to rule must resort to cunning and hypocrisy. Noble and popular qualities—like honesty and frankness—become vices in politics, as they will defeat a leader more rapidly than the most powerful enemy. These are qualities of the Goyim nations; but by no means should we be guided by them.

Our right lies in might. In any case, the word 'right' is an abstract idea, not amenable to proof. This word means nothing more than: 'Give me what I want, so that I can prove that I'm stronger than you.'

Where does right begin? Where does it end? In a state with a poorly organized government and where the laws are weak, and where the ruler has lost his dignity thanks to liberalism, I find a new right: namely, the right of might to destroy all existing order and institutions, to lay hands on the law, to alter all institutions, and to become the ruler of those who have voluntarily and liberally renounced the rights to their own power.

Given the present instability of all authority, our power will be more unassailable than any other because it will be invisible until it is so well-rooted that no cunning can undermine it.

Out of the temporary evil to which we are now obliged, there will emerge the good of an unshakable governance that will reinstate the mechanism of a natural order that was interrupted by liberalism. The end justifies the means.

*****

In laying out our plans, we must turn our attention not so much to the good and moral as to the necessary and useful. Before us lies a plan in which a strategic path is put forth, from which we must not deviate—on pain of risking the collapse of many centuries of work.

In working out an expedient plan of action, it is necessary to take into consideration the crudity, the vacillation, and the changeability of the mob—its inability to appreciate and respect the conditions of its own existence and of its own well-being. It is necessary to realize that the power of the masses is blind, unreasoning, and void of discrimination, prone to listening to right and left. The blind man cannot lead the blind without bringing them both to the abyss; consequently, members of the crowd, upstarts from the people, even if they were geniuses, cannot step forward as leaders of the mob without ruining the entire nation.

Only a person raised from childhood to autocracy can understand the language of politics. The people left to themselves will be ruined by party strife caused by greed for power and honors, which must result in chaos and disorder. Is it possible for the masses to direct the national affairs without rivalry, and without interjecting personal interests? Are they capable of protecting themselves against external enemies? No, this is impossible, since any plan divided into as many parts as there are individuals in a mob loses its unity, and consequently, becomes incomprehensible and unworkable.

Only an autocrat can outline clear and visionary plans that can activate all the parts of the mechanism of the government machinery in an orderly way. Therefore, a government that most efficiently benefits a country must be concentrated in the hands of one responsible person. Civilization cannot exist without absolute despotism, because government is conducted not by the masses but by their leader, whoever he may be. A barbarous crowd shows its barbarism on every occasion. The moment that the mob grasps liberty in its hands, it quickly devolves to virtual anarchy, which is in itself the height of barbarism.

Look at those beasts, steeped in alcohol, stupefied by wine—such is the result of 'freedom.' Surely we cannot allow our own people to come to this. The Goy Christians are stupefied by alcohol; their youth are driven crazy by years of debauchery and vice, instigated by our agents—tutors, valets, governesses in rich houses, by clerks, and so forth, and by our women in their places of pleasure. Among the latter I include the so-called "society women"—their voluntary followers in vice and luxury.

*****

Our motto is 'Power and Hypocrisy.' Only power can conquer in politics, especially if it is concealed in the talents that are necessary for statesmen. Violence must be the principle; hypocrisy and cunning must be the rule of those governments that do not wish to lay down their crowns at the feet of some new power. This evil is the sole means of attaining the good. For this reason, we must not hesitate at bribery, fraud, and treason when these can help us to reach our end. In politics, it is necessary to seize the property of others without hesitation if, in so doing, we attain submission and power.

Our government, following the line of peaceful conquest, has the right to substitute unobtrusive and efficient executions in place of the horrors of war; these things are necessary to maintain a terror that induces blind submission. A just but inexorable strictness is the greatest factor of governmental power. We must follow a program of violence and hypocrisy, not only for the sake of profit, but also as a duty and for the sake of victory.

Our principles are as powerful as the means by which we put them into effect. That is why, not only by these very means, but by the severity of our doctrines shall we triumph and enslave all governments under our super-government.

*****

Even in olden times, we shouted the words "liberty, equality, and fraternity" among the people. These words have been repeated many times by unconscious parrots, which, flocking from all sides to the bait, have ruined the prosperity of the world and true individual freedom, formerly so well protected from the pressure of the mob. The supposedly clever and intelligent Goyim did not grasp the symbolism of the uttered words; they did not notice the contradiction in the meaning and the connection between them; they did not notice that there is no 'equality' in nature; that there can be no 'liberty,' since nature herself has established inequality of mind, character, and ability, as well as complete subjection to her laws. They did not reason that the power of the mob is blind; that the upstarts selected for government are just as blind in politics as is the mob itself, whereas the initiated man, even though a fool, is capable of ruling, while the uninitiated, even if a genius, will understand nothing of politics. All this has been overlooked by the Goyim.

Meanwhile, monarchic government has been based upon this, that the father passes along a knowledge of the course of political evolution to his son, so that no one except the members of the dynasty could possess this knowledge, and no one could disclose the secrets to the governed people. Over time, the meaning of the dynastic transmission of a true understanding of politics has been lost, thus contributing to the success of our cause.

In all parts of the world, the words "liberty, equality, and fraternity" have brought whole legions into our ranks through our blind agents, carrying our banners with delight. Meanwhile, these words were maggots that ruined Goy prosperity, everywhere destroying peace, calm, and solidarity, undermining all the foundations of their states. In what follows, you will see that this aided our triumph because it also gave us, among other things, the opportunity to grasp the trump card—the abolition of royal privileges. This was the very essence of the aristocracy of the Goyim, and it was their only protection against us.

On the ruins of natural and hereditary aristocracy, we built an aristocracy of our intellectual class—a monied aristocracy. We have established this new aristocracy on the basis of wealth, which is dependent upon us, and also upon science, which is promoted by our wise men.

Our triumph was also made easier because, through our connections with people who were indispensable to us, we always played upon the most susceptible parts of the human mind—namely, greed and the insatiable selfish desires of man. Each of these human weaknesses, taken separately, is capable of killing initiative and of placing the will of the people at the disposal of he who would deprive them of their own initiative.

The abstract concept of 'liberty' offered the opportunity for convincing the masses that government is nothing but a manager representing the owner of the country, namely, the people; and that this manager can be discarded like a pair of worn-out gloves. The fact that the representatives of the nation can be replaced, delivers them into our power and practically places their appointment in our hands.

Protocol No. 2

On economic wars, the press

It is necessary for us that, whenever possible, wars should bring no territorial advantages; this will shift war to an economic basis and force nations to realize the strength of our predominance. Such a situation will put both sides at the mercy of our million-eyed international agency, which will be unhampered by any frontiers. Then our international rights will do away with national rights, in a limited sense, and will rule the peoples in the same way that individual governments rule their subjects

The administrators chosen by us from among the people in accordance with their capacity for servility will be inexperienced in the art of government; consequently, they will easily become pawns in our game, in the hands of our scientists and wise counselors, who are specialists trained from early childhood for governing the world. As you are aware, these specialists have obtained the knowledge necessary for government from our political plans, from the study of history, and from the observation of current events. The Goyim are not guided by the practice of impartial historical observation, but by theoretical principles without any critical regard for results. Therefore, we can ignore them. Until the time comes, let them amuse themselves, or live in the hope of new amusements or in the memories of those past. Let them think that these laws of theory, with which we have inspired them, are of supreme importance to them.

For this purpose, by means of our press, we will increase their blind faith in these laws. Intelligent Goyim will boast of their knowledge, and verifying it logically, they will put into practice all scientific information compiled by our agents for the purpose of educating their minds in the direction that we demand.

Do not think that our assertions are baseless. Note the successes of Darwin, Marx, and Nietzsche, engineered by us.[1] The demoralizing effects of these doctrines upon the Goy minds should already be obvious.

---

[1] In a Christian context, these three thinkers are indeed "demoralizing": Darwin for his theory of evolution, Marx for his atheism, and Nietzsche for his radical critique of Christianity and Christian values. For the non-Christian, however, neither Darwin nor Nietzsche pose any threat, and on the contrary, offer hopeful and visionary ideas. Only the Jewish-"engineered"

It is essential that we take into account the modern ideas, temperaments, and tendencies of peoples in order that no mistakes are made in politics and in guiding administrative affairs. The triumph of our theory is its adaptability to the temperament of the nations with which we come into contact. Our theory can only succeed if its practical application is based on the experience of the past, in conjunction with observations of the present.

There is one great force in the hands of modern states that arouses thought movements among the people: the press. The press' role is to indicate necessary demands, to register complaints of the people, and to express and promote dissatisfaction. The triumph of free speech is incarnated in the press; but governments have been unable to profit by this power, and it has fallen into our hands. Through it, we have attained influence, while remaining in the background. Thanks to the press, we have gathered gold in our hands, although it cost us rivers of blood and tears. It cost us the sacrifice of many of our own people. But every sacrifice on our part is worth a thousand Goyim before God.

Marxism presents a universal threat to Gentile society; neither Darwin nor Nietzsche were "engineered" by the Jews. This, incidentally, is a remarkably early reference to Nietzsche, who was still largely unknown in 1905 (let alone 1901 or 1896), if in fact this was the date of original construction of the *Protocols*.

Protocol No. 3

On rights, Goy aristocracy, liberalism

Today I can tell you that our goal is close at hand. Only a small distance remains, and the cycle of the Symbolic Serpent—the symbol of our people—will be complete. When this circle is completed, then all the European states will be enclosed in it, as in unbreakable chains.

The modern constitutional scales will soon tip, for we have set them inaccurately, thus ensuring an unsteady balance that will wear out their holder. The Goyim thought it was strong enough and hoped that the scales would regain their equilibrium, but the holder—the ruler—is screened from the people by his representatives, who fritter away their time with their uncontrolled and irresponsible authority. Their power, moreover, has been built upon terrorism spread through the halls of government.

Unable to reach the hearts of their people, the rulers cannot draw strength from them in order to fend off the usurpers of power. The visible power of royalty and the blind power of the masses, separated by us, have both lost significance—for, thus separated, they are as helpless as a blind man without a stick.

To induce the lovers of authority to abuse their power, we have placed all forces in opposition to each other, having developed their liberal tendencies towards independence. We have encouraged every undertaking in this direction; we have placed formidable weapons in the hands of all parties, and made power the goal of every ambition. We turned governments into arenas in which party wars are fought out. Soon, chaos and bankruptcy will appear everywhere.

Unrestrained babblers have converted parliamentary sessions and bureaucratic meetings into oratorical contests. Daring journalists and impudent scribblers make daily attacks on the administrative personnel. The abuse of power is definitely preparing the downfall of all institutions, and everything will be overturned by the blows of the infuriated mobs.

The people are shackled by poverty to hard labor more surely than they were by slavery and serfdom. They could liberate themselves from the latter in one way or another, whereas nothing will liberate them from the tyranny of poverty.

We have included "rights" in their constitutions, but for regular people, these are fictitious. All the so-called "rights of the people" exist only in the abstract and can never be realized in practice. What difference does it make to the toiling proletarian, bent double by heavy toil, oppressed by his fate, that the babblers receive the "right" to speech, and journalists the "right" to mix nonsense with reason in their writings, if the proletariat has no other benefit from the constitution than the miserable crumbs that we throw them, in return for their vote for our agents? Republican rights are bitter irony to the poor man; the necessity of almost daily labor prevents him from using them, and at the same time deprives him of his guarantee of a permanent and certain livelihood by making him dependent upon labor strikes, organized either by his masters or by his comrades.

Under our guidance, the people have exterminated the aristocracy that was their natural protector and guardian; the aristocracy's well-being was inseparable from that of the people. Now, however, with the destruction of this aristocracy, the masses have fallen under the power of profiteers and cunning upstarts, who have set upon the workers as a merciless burden. We will present ourselves as saviors of the workers from this oppression when we suggest that they enter our army of socialists, anarchists, and communists, to whom we always extend our help, under the principle of brotherhood demanded by the humanitarianism of our socialistic masonry. The aristocracy benefited by the peoples' labor and was naturally interested that the workers should be well fed, healthy, and strong.

We, on the contrary, are concerned with the opposite—with the degeneration of the Goyim. Our power lies in the chronic malnutrition and weakness of the worker, because through this he falls under our power and is unable to find either strength or energy to combat it. Hunger gives capital a greater power over the worker than any sovereign legal authority under an aristocracy. Through misery, jealousy, and hatred, we manipulate the mob and crush those who stand in our way. When the time comes for our universal ruler to be crowned, the same hands will sweep away everything that stands in our way.

The Goyim are no longer able to think without our scientific advice. Consequently, they do not see the imperative of upholding that which we will sustain by all means when our kingdom is established: namely, the teaching in schools of the only true science, the first of all sciences—*the science of human life*, of social existence, which requires the division of labor and, consequently, the separation of people into classes and castes. It is necessary for all to know that true equality cannot exist, owing to the different nature of various kinds of work; that one whose actions compromise an entire class cannot have the same legal responsibility as one whose actions affect only himself.

The correct social science—the secrets of which we do not admit to the Goyim—would demonstrate to all that occupation and labor must be differentiated so as not to cause suffering by the discrepancy between education and work. The study of this science will lead the masses to a voluntary submission to authorities and to the governmental system. Whereas, under the present state of science, and due to our active guidance, the people, in their ignorance, blindly believing the printed word, and owing to the misconceptions that have been fostered by us, feel a hatred towards all classes that they consider superior to themselves, since they do not understand the importance of each class.

This hatred will be still more accentuated by an economic crisis, which will stop financial transactions and all industrial life. Having organized a general economic crisis by all possible underhanded means, and with the help of the gold that is all in our hands, we will throw great crowds of workmen into the street, simultaneously, in all nations. These simple-minded and ignorant masses will gladly shed the blood of those of whom they have hated since childhood and whose property they will then be able to loot. They will not harm our people because we will know the time of the attack and will take measures to protect ourselves.

We have persuaded the Goyim that liberalism would lead them into a rational paradise. Our despotism will be of such a nature that it will be in a position to pacify all revolts by wise restrictions, and it will eliminate liberalism from all institutions.

When the people saw that they obtained concessions and rights in the name of liberty, they imagined that they were the masters, and rushed to take power; but like every blind person, they encountered innumerable obstacles. Fearing a return to the old regime, they laid power at our feet. Remember the French Revolution, which we have called "great"; the secrets of its preparation are well known to us, for it was the work of our hands.[2]

Since that time, we have carried the masses from one disappointment to another, so that they will renounce even us in favor of a despotic Sovereign of Zionist blood, whom we are preparing for the world.

As things stand, as an international force, we are invulnerable; if we are attacked by one state, we are supported by others. The unlimited baseness of the Goyim aid our independence; they kneel before power, are pitiless toward the weak, merciless when dealing with faults, and patient to the point of martyrdom when suffering the violence of an outrageous despotism. At the hands of their present dictators, premiers, and ministers, they endure great abuses—for the smallest of which they would have, in times past, beheaded 20 kings.

How can such a phenomenon be explained? Why are the masses so illogical in their conception of events? The answer is explained by the fact that the despotic rulers, through their agents, whisper to their people that these abuses serve a supreme purpose: namely, prosperity and happiness, along with universal fraternity, solidarity, and equality. Of course, they are not told that this unification will be achieved only under our rule. Thus, the people condemn the just and acquit the unjust, always convinced that they can do what they please. Owing to this, the people destroy all stability and create disorder on every occasion.

The word 'liberty' brings all society into conflict with all authority, whether it be natural or divine. This is why, at the moment of our enthronement, we shall strike this word from the dictionary as being the symbol of a brute power that turns the masses into bloodthirsty beasts. It is true, however, that these beasts will sleep as soon as they have tasted blood, and then it is easy to shackle them; but if they don't get their blood, they will not sleep but rather struggle and fight.

---

[2] French Jews notably gained the rights of citizenship soon after the Revolution—the first such enfranchisement anywhere in Europe.

Protocol No. 4

On liberty, financial speculation

Every republic passes through several stages. The first stage is an early period like the insane ravings of a blind man who throws himself right and left. The second is a demagogy that breeds anarchy, which inevitably leads to despotism. This despotism is not of a legal and open nature and, therefore, it is irresponsible; it is an unseen and unknown despotism, no less effective because it is controlled by some secret organization, thus acting even less ceremoniously because it is hidden under cover and behind the backs of different agents. Who or what can overthrow an unseen power?

Such is the character of our power. Global Masonry acts as a mask for it and its aims, but the plan of action of this power, and its very headquarters, will always remain unknown to the people.

In theory, liberty could be harmless and remain on the state program without detriment to the well-being of the people, but only if it retained the ideas of a belief in God and human fraternity, and was freed from the conception of equality, for such an idea is contradicted by the laws of nature that establish subordination. With such a religious faith, the people would be governed by the guardians of the parish and would thrive quietly and obediently under the guidance of their spiritual leader, accepting God's dispensation on Earth. It is for this reason that we must undermine faith, tearing the very principles of God and soul from the minds of the Goyim, and substituting mathematical formulas and material needs.

In order to ensure that the Goy minds have no time to think and notice things, it is necessary to occupy them with industry and commerce. Thus, all nations will seek their own profit, and while engaged in the struggle, they will not notice their common enemy.

But to guarantee that liberty should finally undermine and ruin the Goy's society, it is necessary to put industry on a basis of speculation. The result of this will be that the wealth of the land obtained by production will not remain in Goy hands but will be directed towards speculation; that is, it will come to us.

The intense struggle for supremacy and the continuous economic speculations will create—and have already created—demoralized, selfish, and heartless societies. These societies will have complete disgust for high politics and religion. Their only guide will be a love of gold, for which they will have a real cult because of the material delights that it can supply. At this stage, the lower-class Goyim—not for the sake of doing good, nor even for the sake of wealth, but solely because of their hatred towards the privileged—will join us in the struggle against our competitors for power: the privileged and intelligent Goyim.

Protocol No. 5

On centralized government, the power of gold, control of public opinion

What form of government can be given to societies in which bribery has penetrated everywhere, where riches are obtained only by clever tricks and semi-fraudulent means, where corruption reigns, where morality is sustained by punitive measures and strict laws rather than by voluntary acceptance of moral principles, and where cosmopolitan convictions have eliminated patriotic feelings and religion? What form of government can be given to such societies, other than despotism, as I shall describe?

We will create a strong centralized government, so as to collect social forces under our power. We will implement new laws to mechanically regulate all the functions of the political life of our subjects. These laws will gradually eliminate all the concessions and liberties permitted by the Goyim. Our kingdom will be crowned by such a majestic despotism that it will be able, at all times and in all places, to crush both antagonistic and discontented Goyim.

One might say that this despotism is inconsistent with modern progress, but I will prove to you that the contrary is the case.

At a time when people considered rulers as an incarnation of the will of God, they subjected themselves unconditionally to the autocracy of the Sovereigns; but as soon as we inspired them with thoughts of personal rights, they began to regard the rulers as ordinary mortals. The holy anointment fell from the heads of Sovereigns, in the opinion of the people. And when we deprived them of their belief in God, authority was thrown into the street, where it became public property—and was seized by us.

Moreover, the art of governing masses and individuals by means of cunningly-constructed theories and fine phrases, by rulers of social life, and other devices not understood by the Goyim, belongs, among other faculties, to our administrative mind. We are educated in analysis and observation, and are also strong in skillful reasoning in which we have no competitors, just as we have none in the preparation of plans for political action and solidarity. Only the Jesuits could be compared to us; but we were able to discredit them in the mind of the senseless mob as a visible organization, whereas we, with our secret organization, remained in the dark. After all, does the world really care who will be its master—whether it be the head of Catholicism or our despot of Zionist blood? To us, however, the Chosen People, it is by no means a matter of indifference.

Temporarily, a world coalition of the Goyim would be able to hold us in check, but we are insured against this by roots of dissension so deep among them that they cannot now be extracted. We have set at odds the personal and national interests of the Goyim; we have incited religious and race hatred, nurtured by us in their hearts for 20 centuries.[3] Due to all this, no state will obtain aid from any side because each nation will think that a coalition against us will be disadvantageous to it. We are too powerful—we must be taken into account. No country can reach even an insignificant private understanding without our being secret parties to it.

Per me reges regnant—"By me, kings reign".[4] The prophets have told us that we were chosen by God himself to reign over the world. God endowed us with genius to enable us to cope with this work. Were there a genius in the opposing camp, he would struggle against us, but a newcomer is not equal to an old inhabitant. The struggle between us would be of such a merciless nature as the world has never seen before.[5]

Moreover, it is already too late. All the wheels of government mechanism move by the action of the motor that is in our hands, and that motor is *gold*. The science of political economy, invented by our wise men, has long ago demonstrated the royal prestige of capital. To attain freedom of action, capital must obtain freedom to monopolize industry and trade; this is already being done by an unseen hand in all parts of the world. Such liberty will give political power to traders, and will aid in subjugating the people.

At present, it is more important to disarm peoples than to lead them to war; it is more important to utilize flaming passions for our purposes

---

[3] Jews have indeed been known for race-hatred of others, and have long been accused of misanthropy—a hatred of the (non-Jewish) human race. This has been documented as far back as 300 BC; see the book *Eternal Strangers* (T. Dalton, 2020).
[4] Latin translation of Proverbs 8:15, where the "me" speaking is the Jewish God, Jehovah.
[5] A remarkable anticipation of the coming of Hitler and World War Two.

than to extinguish them; more important to grasp and interpret the thoughts of others in our own way than to discard them.

The most important problem of our government is to weaken the popular mind by criticism; to disaccustom it to thought, which creates opposition; and to deflect the power of thought into mere empty eloquence.

At all times, both peoples and individuals have mistaken words for deeds, as they are satisfied with the visible, rarely noticing whether the promise is performed in social life. Therefore, we will organize ostensible institutions that will eloquently prove their good work in the direction of "progress." We will appropriate to ourselves the liberal aspect of all parties, of all shades of opinion, and we will provide our orators with the same aspect, and they will talk so much that they will exhaust the people by their speeches and cause them to turn away from orators in disgust.

To control public opinion, it is necessary to perplex it by the expression of numerous contradictory opinions until the Goyim become lost in the labyrinth, and come to believe that it is best to have no opinion at all on political questions. Such questions are not intended to be understood by the people, since only the ruler knows them. This is the first secret.

The second secret necessary for the success of governing consists in multiplying popular failings, habits, passions, and conventional laws to such a degree that no one will be able to disentangle himself in the chaos; consequently, people will cease to understand each other. This measure would help us to sow dissension within all parties, to disintegrate all those collective forces that still seek to remain independent, and to discourage all individual initiative that might hamper our work in any way.

There is nothing more dangerous than individual initiative. If it has even a touch of genius, it can accomplish more than a million people among whom we have sown dissensions. We must direct the education of the Goy societies so that their arms will drop hopelessly at their side whenever they face any task where initiative is required. The intensity of action resulting from individual freedom of action dissipates its force when it encounters another person's freedom. This strikes a heavy blow against morale, yielding disappointments and failures.

We will so exhaust the Goyim by all this that we will force them to offer us global power, which will conveniently enable us to absorb all governmental forces of the world and thus to form a super-government. In lieu of modern rulers, we will place a monstrosity—a monstrosity called the Super-Governmental Administration. Its hands will be stretched out like pincers in every direction, so that this colossal organization cannot fail to conquer all peoples.

Protocol No. 6

On monopolies, trade, industry

We will soon begin to establish great monopolies—reservoirs of huge wealth, upon which even the large fortunes of the Goyim will be so dependent that they will sink, together with the credibility of the government, on the day following political catastrophe. You economists, present here, please carefully weigh the significance of this scheme!

We must promote, by all means, the importance of our super-government by representing it as the protector and compensator of all those who willingly submit to us.

The aristocracy of the Goyim as a political force is dead. We do not need to take it into consideration; but as land-owners, they are harmful to us because they can be independent in their necessities of life. For this reason, we must deprive them of their land at any cost. To attain this object, the best method is to increase real estate taxes—the indebtedness of the land. These measures will keep land ownership in subjection. The Goy aristocracy, which, as a matter of heredity, are dissatisfied with small gains, will soon be ruined.

At the same time, it is necessary to vigorously promote trade and industry, and more important, to encourage speculation, whose function is to act as a counterbalance to industry. Without speculation, industry will increase private capital and tend to the amelioration of land ownership by freeing it from indebtedness created by the loans granted by agricultural banks. It is necessary that industry should suck both labor and capital out of the land, and through speculation, deliver the world's money into our hands, thus casting all the Goyim into the ranks of the proletarians. Then the Goyim will bow before us, in order to obtain the mere right of existence.

To further destroy Goy industry, we will create a strong demand for boundless luxury among them, which we have already developed. We will raise wages—which, however, will be of no benefit to the workers, for we will simultaneously cause a rise in prices of basic necessities, under the pretext that this is due to the decline of agriculture. We will also artfully and deeply undermine the sources of production by promoting among the workers anarchy and the use of alcohol, while at the same time taking measures to expel all intelligent Goyim from the land.

So that the true situation remains unnoticed by the Goyim until the proper time, we will conceal it by an apparent desire to help the working classes in solving great economic problems—and which the propaganda of our economic theories is assisting in every possible way.

Protocol No. 7

On the military, social disruption, war

The intensification of the military and an increase in the police force are essential to the realization of the above-mentioned plans. It is necessary that there should be, besides ourselves, in all countries, nothing but a huge proletariat, along with a few millionaires devoted to us, policemen, and soldiers.

We must create unrest, dissension, and hatred throughout Europe, as well as on other continents. This gives us a twofold advantage: First, we will hold all countries under our influence, since they will realize that we have the power to create disorder or to restore order, as we wish. All countries will look to us to provide the necessary pressure, as required. Second, through various intrigues, we will entangle all governmental bodies with our strings, by means of politics, economic treaties, or financial obligations.

To attain these ends, we will worm our way into meetings and negotiations, armed with cunning; but in so-called "official language" we will assume the opposite tactics of seeming honest and reasonable. In this way, the peoples and the governments of the Goyim, taught by us to consider only superficial impressions, will look upon us as benefactors and saviors of mankind.

We must be able to overcome all opposition by provoking a war with the neighbors of any country that dares to oppose us. Should, however, those neighbors, in turn, decide to unite against us, we must respond by creating a world war.[6]

Chief success in politics lies in secrecy. There must also be inconsistency between the words and actions of diplomats. We must influence the Goy governments to act in accordance with our broadly conceived plan, which is now approaching its triumphant goal, by creating the impression that such action is demanded by public opinion. And this public opinion is, in reality, secretly organized by us, with the help of the so-

---

[6] Again, this is a remarkable anticipation, in 1905, of the coming two World Wars.

called "great power," namely, the press—but this is not a concern, given that the press is already largely in our hands.

In short, to sum up our system of enslaving the Goy governments of Europe, we will demonstrate our power to them by assassinations and terrorism. And should there be a possibility of all of them rising up against us, we will answer them with American, Chinese, or Japanese guns.

Protocol No. 8

On new government, the role of Jews

We must provide ourselves with the same arms that our enemies deploy against us. We must seek the most subtle expressions and evasions of the legal lexicon in order to justify those cases in which we will be forced to announce decisions that may seem unnecessarily bold and unjust. It is important that these decisions be expressed in such forcible terms that they will appear as the highest moral and legal rules.

Our government must be surrounded by all the forces of civilization, amongst which it will have to function. It will surround itself with publicists, experienced lawyers, administrators, diplomats, and, finally, people educated along special lines in our advanced schools. These people will know all the secrets of social existence; they will know the language of politics; they will be familiar with the reverse side of human nature, with all its sensitive chords, upon which they must know how to play. These chords are the structure of the Goy intellects: their tendencies, their failings, their vices and virtues, the peculiarities of classes and castes.

It is obvious that the highly talented members of our government, to which I refer, will not be recruited from the ranks of the Goyim, who are accustomed to performing their administrative duties without questioning their aim and without thinking why they are necessary. The Goy administrators sign papers without reading them and work for profit or ambition. We will surround our government by a whole host of economists. It is for this reason that economics is the chief science taught to the Jews. We will be surrounded by a crowd of bankers, traders, capitalists, and most important of all, by millionaires, because in essence everything will be decided by money.

Meanwhile, as it is not yet safe to give the responsible government posts directly to our brother Jews, we will give them to people whose record and whose character are so terrible that there is a vast gulf between them and the people. Such leaders would face nothing but condemnation and imprisonment, should they disobey our orders. This fact will force them to protect our interests, to their dying day.

Protocol No. 9

On dictatorships, Jewish ambition, education

In applying our principles, pay attention to the character of the people in whose countries you reside and among whom you will act. Do not expect to be successful until the people in question have been reeducated by our doctrines. But by proceeding carefully in their application, you will see that, within ten years, even the most obstinate character will have changed, and we can then count yet another people among those who have already submitted to us.

When we are enthroned, we will replace the liberal words of our Masonic slogan, "liberty, equality, and fraternity," with another group of words expressing simply *ideas*: namely, "the *right* of liberty, the *duty* of equality, the *ideal* of fraternity." Then we will have the bull by the horns.

We have already effectively destroyed all governments but our own, even though, nominally, many still remain. At present, if any government protests against us, it is done only as a matter of course, and at our desire, and by our order; this is because their anti-Semitism is necessary to enable us to control our lesser brethren. I will not explain this any further, as it has already been the object of numerous discussions.

In reality, there are no serious obstacles before us. Our super-government exists under such extra-legal conditions that we may call it a dictatorship. I can honestly state that, at the present time, we are lawmakers; we are the judges and inflict punishment; we execute and pardon; we are, as it were, the chief of all armies, riding at their head. We rule by indomitable will because we hold in our hands the fragments of a once-strong party, now subject to us.

We possess boundless ambition, burning greed for merciless revenge, and bitter hatred. From us emanates an all-embracing terror. People of all opinions and of all doctrines are in our service: monarchists, demagogues, socialists, communists, and other idealists. We have put all of them to work; every one of them is undermining the last remnant of authority, is trying to overthrow all existing order. All governments have been tortured by this procedure; they beg for peace, and for the sake of peace they are prepared to make any sacrifice. But we will not give them peace until they humbly recognize our international super-government.

The masses have begun to demand a solution to social problems by means of an international agreement. And party strife has delivered all such means to us because, in order to conduct a party struggle, money is required, and we have it all.

Theoretically, we might have to worry about a union of intelligent Goy leaders with the blind power of the masses; but we have taken all measures against such a possibility. Between these two forces, we have raised a wall in the form of mutual terror; thus, the blind power of the people continues to be our support, and we alone will act as its leader and, naturally, we will direct it towards our goal. In order that the blind masses not free themselves from our grip, we must regularly stay connected to them—if not through personal contact, then through our most devoted brethren. When we become a recognized power, we will personally and openly address the masses, and we will instruct them in political matters in whichever way we desire.

How can we control what is taught in rural schools? That which the representative of the government or the ruler himself states will be immediately known to the entire nation, for it will rapidly spread by the people's own voice.

In order to not prematurely destroy Goy institutions, we have grasped them with our experienced hands and control the springs of their mechanism. Formerly, these springs were rigid but fair; now, we have changed them to a liberal, disorderly, and arbitrary lawlessness. We have affected legal procedure, electoral law, the press, personal freedom—and most important of all, *education*: the cornerstone of free existence. We have misled, corrupted, deceived, and demoralized the Goy youth by education along principles and theories known by us to be false but which we ourselves have inspired.

Without substantially changing existing laws, we have created extraordinary results by distorting the laws through contradictory interpretations. These results first manifested themselves by the fact that 'interpretation' has concealed the law itself; thereafter, it has completely hidden it from the eyes of the governments by the impossibility of understanding such complicated jurisprudence.

You may say that there will be an armed rising against us if our plans are discovered prematurely; but in anticipation of this, we have such terrorizing maneuvers in the West that even the bravest soul will shudder. Hidden passages will be established in all the capitals, from where they can be destroyed, together with all their institutions and national documents.

Protocol No. 10

On Freemasonry, liberalism, legislative and executive government

Today I will begin by reiterating what has already been stated. Please keep in mind that the government and the masses are satisfied with visible results in politics. How can they examine the inner meaning of things when their representatives think only of amusement and distraction? It is important to know this one detail of our policy. It will help us when discussing such things as division of authority, freedom of speech, of the press, of religion (faith), the right of assembly, equality before the law, inviolability of property and of the home, indirect taxes, and the retrospective force of law. All such questions should never be directly and openly discussed in front of the masses. When we must discuss them, they should not be elaborated but merely mentioned, without going into details, pointing out that we accept modern legal principles. The significance of this reticence lies in the fact that a principle that has not been openly declared gives us freedom of action, whereas, if elaborated, the principle becomes as good as fixed.

The people feel a particular love and admiration towards the clever politician, and they always react to their criminal acts as follows: "Yes, of course it is villainy, but how clever! It is a swindle, but cleverly done! So majestic! So impudent!"

We count on attracting all nations to the construction of the foundations of the new edifice that we have planned. It is for this reason that it is necessary for us, first of all, to acquire that spirit of daring, enterprise, and force which, through our agents, will enable us to overcome all obstacles in our path.

When we accomplish our coup d'état, we will say to the people:

> "Everything went badly; all of you have suffered. We will abolish the cause of your sufferings, that is to say, nationalities, frontiers, and national currencies. Of course, you are free to condemn us, but would your judgment be fair if you were to pronounce it before trying what we will give you?"

Thereafter they will exalt us with a sentiment of unanimous delight and hope. The voting system that we have used as a tool for our enthronement, and to which we have accustomed even the humblest members of humanity by organizing meetings and prearranged agreements, will have performed its final service; voting will make its last appearance in the expression of a unanimous desire to become more closely acquainted with us before having pronounced a judgment.

To attain this, we must force all to vote, without class distinction; that is, to establish *an autocracy of the majority*, which cannot be obtained from the intellectual classes alone. Through this method of accustoming everyone to the idea of self-determination, we will shatter the Goy family and its educational importance. We will not allow the formation of individual minds, because the mob, under our guidance, will prevent them from distinguishing themselves or even expressing themselves. The mob has become accustomed to listen only to us, who reward it for obedience and attention. We will thus create such a blind power that it will be unable to move without the guidance of our agents, sent by us to replace Goy leaders. The masses will submit to this regime because they will understand that their earnings, wages, and other benefits depend upon these agents.

The plan of government must emanate fully-formed from one head, since it would be impossible to put it together if it were broken into small pieces by many minds. That's why only we are allowed to know the plan of action; but we must not discuss it openly, in order not to destroy its efficacy, the functions of its separate parts, and the practical meaning of each point. Were such a plan to be discussed and altered by frequent voting, it would reflect the stamp of the misconceptions of all those who have not penetrated its depth and the correlation of its aims. For this reason, our plans must be strongly and clearly conceived. Consequently, the inspired work of our leader must not be thrown to the mercy of the mob or even of a limited group.

These plans will not immediately upset contemporary institutions. They will only alter their organization and hence the entire combination of their development, which will thus be redirected according to our plans.

*****

Generally, the same institutions exist in different countries under different names, such as representative bodies, ministries, senate, state council, and legislative and executive bodies. It is unnecessary for me to explain to you the connecting mechanism of these different institutions, as you know it well. I only call to your attention that all of the aforesaid institutions fulfill some important governmental function; and moreover, I beg you to notice that the word 'important' refers not to the institution but to the function. Consequently, it is not the institutions that are important but their functions. Such institutions have divided among themselves all the functions of government—namely, administrative, legislative, and executive powers; therefore, their functions in the state organism have become similar to those in a human body. If one part of the governmental machine is injured, the state itself falls ill, just like the human body, and eventually it dies.

When we injected the poison of liberalism into the state organism, its entire political complexion changed; the states became infected with a mortal disease, namely, *the decomposition of the blood*.[7] It is only necessary to await the end of their agony.

Constitutional governments were born of liberalism, which replaced the autocracy (monarchy) that was the salvation of the Goyim. The constitution, as you well know, is nothing more than a school for dispute, discussion, disagreement, fruitless party agitation, dissension, and party tendencies—in other words, a school for everything that weakens governmental efficiency. The press condemned the authorities to inaction and impotency, thereby rendering them useless and superfluous, for which reason they were overthrown in many countries. The rise of the republican era then became possible; and then we substituted for the ruler a caricature of government—a president chosen from the mob, from among our creatures, our slaves. This was the kind of bomb we laid under the Goyim, or, more correctly, under the Goy nations.

In the near future, we will make the president a 'responsible' officer, whereupon we will have no hesitation in carrying out the things for which our dupe will be responsible. What difference does it make to us that the ranks of those aiming at authority will thin out, and that confusion

---

[7] By which they mean, racially 'diversified' and race-mixed, thereby ruining the original racial and ethnic homogeneity of traditional nations. Evidently, 'racial liberalism' is the worst form of poison.

will result from an inability to find real presidents—a confusion that will definitely disorganize the country?

To accomplish our plan, we will engineer the election of presidents whose past record contains some hidden scandal—then they will be faithful executors of our orders, for fear of exposure, and from a natural desire to retain the privileges, advantages, and dignity connected with the position of president. Parliaments will elect, protect, and screen presidents, but we will deprive parliament of the right of initiating laws or of amending them, for this right will be granted by us to the responsible president, a puppet in our hands.

Of course, the power of the president will then become the target of numerous attacks, but we will give him the means of self-protection by giving him the right of appeal directly to the people, for their decision, over the heads of their representatives. In other words, he will turn to the same blind slave—to the majority of the mob. Moreover, we will empower the president to proclaim martial law. We will justify this prerogative under the pretext that the president, as chief of the national army, must control it in order to protect the new republican constitution, which he, as a responsible representative, is bound to defend.

It is obvious that, under such conditions, the keys to the shrine will be in our hands, and no one except ourselves will be able to guide the legislative power.

*****

Moreover, when we introduce the new republican constitution, we will, under pretext of state secrecy, deprive the house of its right to question the desirability of measures taken by the government. With the aid of this new constitution, we will reduce the number of representatives to a minimum, thus also reducing to the same extent political passions. If, despite this, those remaining are recalcitrant, we will abolish them completely by appealing to the majority of the people.

The appointment of the chairmen and vice chairmen of the House and Senate will be the prerogative of the president. Instead of continuous parliamentary sessions, we will shorten them to a few months. Moreover, the president, as chief executive, will have the right to convene or dissolve parliament; and in the case of dissolution, defer the appointment of a new parliament.

But to prevent the president from being held responsible before our plans are matured, and before the results of all these essentially illegal actions inaugurated by us, we will give the ministers and other high administrative officials the idea of circumventing his orders by issuing instructions of their own. Consequently, they will be made responsible instead of him.

We recommend that the execution of this plan be given especially to the Senate, State Council, or Council of Ministers, and not to individuals. Under our guidance, the president will interpret in ambiguous ways such existing laws as it is possible to interpret. Moreover, he will annul them when demanded by us; he will also have the right to propose temporary laws and even modifications in the constitutional work of government, alleging as the motive for so doing the exigencies of the national welfare.

By such measures, we will be able to gradually destroy, step by step, everything that we were obliged to introduce into government constitutions, as a transition to the imperceptible abolition of all constitutions. This will occur when the time comes to convert all government into our autocracy.

The recognition of our autocrat may come even before the abolition of the constitutions. The moment for this recognition will come when the people, tormented by dissension and the incompetency of their rulers, incited by us, will exclaim: "Depose them, and give us one universal Sovereign who will unite us and abolish the causes of dissension—national frontiers, religion, state indebtedness—and who will give us the peace and quiet that we cannot find with our rulers and representatives!"

But you know well that to realize such a universal expression of desire, it is necessary to continuously disturb the relationship between the people and the government in all countries. We must exhaust everyone by dissension, hostility, struggle, hatred, and even martyrdom, hunger, inoculation of diseases, and misery, so as to make the Goyim see no other solution than an appeal to our money and our total rule.

If we give the people even a moment's rest, however, the longed-for day will likely never arrive.

Protocol No. 11

On the new constitution, Goyim as animals

The Council of State will tend to accentuate the power of the ruler; as an ostensibly legislative body, it will act as a committee for the drawing-up of laws and statutes on behalf of the ruler.

The following is the program of the new constitution that we are preparing. We will make laws and control the courts in the following manner:

1. By edicts of the legislative chamber, suggested by the president.

2. By means of general orders and orders of the Senate and State Council, and by means of decisions of the cabinet.

3. And when the opportune moment arrives—in the form of a coup d'état.

Having thus roughly outlined the *modus agendi*, we will now take up in detail those measures by which we will complete the development of the governmental mechanism in the above direction. By these measures, I mean the *freedom of the press, the right of assembly, religious freedom, electoral rights*, and many other things that must disappear from the human repertoire, or must be fundamentally altered on the day following the declaration of the new constitution.

Only at this moment will it become possible for us to announce all our decrees. At any time in the future, every perceptible change would be dangerous, for the following reasons: If these changes should be introduced and rigidly enforced, it might cause despair by creating the fear of further changes in a similar direction; if, however, they are made with a tendency to subsequent leniency, then it might be said that we have recognized our mistakes, which would undermine the faith in the infallibility of the new authority. It might also be said that we were frightened, and that we were forced to make concessions that no one would appreciate since they would be considered as legitimately due.

Any of these impressions would be detrimental to the prestige of the new constitution. It is necessary for us that, from the first moment of its proclamation, when the people are still dumbfounded by the accomplished revolution and are in a state of terror and surprise, they should realize that we are so strong, so invulnerable, and so mighty that we can safely ignore them. And not only will we ignore their opinions and desires, but we will be ready to, and capable of, suppressing, at any moment, any sign of opposition to our indisputable authority. We shall want the people to realize that we have taken at once everything we wanted, and that under no circumstances will we share our power with them. Then they will close their eyes to everything out of fear, and will await further developments.

The Goyim are like a flock of sheep—we are wolves. Do you know what happens to sheep when wolves get into the fold?

They will also close their eyes to everything because we will promise to return all their liberties to them, but only after the enemies of peace have been subjugated and all parties have been pacified. Need we add how long they will have to wait?

Why have we conceived and inspired this policy for the Goyim without giving them an opportunity to examine its inner meaning? It was for the purpose of attaining, by a circuitous method, that which was unattainable for our scattered race by direct means.

This was the real cause and origin of our organization of secret Masonry, which is unknown to and unfathomed by these cattle, the Goyim. They have been decoyed by us into our numerous ostensible organizations that appear to be Masonic lodges, so as to divert the attention of their comrades.

God has scattered us, his Chosen People, and in this dispersal, which seemed to the world to be our weakness, has proved to be our strength. This has now brought us to the threshold of universal rule. Little remains to be built on these foundations.

Protocol No. 12

On liberty, the press, Freemasonry

The word 'liberty' can be differently interpreted. We will define it as follows: "Liberty is the right to do that which is permitted by law." Such a definition of this word will eventually serve us, because liberty will be in our power; and also because the laws will either destroy or construct only what we desire, in accordance with the above-mentioned program.

We will deal with the press in the following manner: What is the present role of the press? It serves to arouse furious passions or egotistic party dissensions that may be necessary for our purpose. It is empty, unjust, and inaccurate, and most people do not understand what end it serves. We will shackle it and keep a tight rein on it. We will also do the same with other printed matter—for what use would it be for us to rid ourselves of attacks by periodicals if we remain open to criticism through pamphlets and books? We will convert the products of publicity, now so expensive, owing to the need for censorship, into a source of income for our state. We will impose a special stamp tax. When a new newspaper printing shop is begun, bonds will have to be deposited, which will protect our government from all attacks by the press. In case of an attack, we will mercilessly impose fines. Such measures as stamp taxes, bonds, and fines—the payment of which is guaranteed by the bonds—will bring a huge income to the government.

It is true that party papers might not fear the loss of money, but after a second attack on us, we would suppress them completely. No one will question the prestige of our political infallibility and remain unpunished.

The pretext for halting a publication will be that the publication in question excites public opinion without cause or reason. I ask you to bear in mind that, among those who attack us, there will be also organs established by us, but they will attack exclusively those points that we plan to change. Not one bit of information will be made public without our control. This is already being done by us, since the news from all parts of the world is received through a few agencies, in which it is centralized. These agencies will then be completely in our power and they will publish only such news as we permit.

If we have already managed to subjugate the minds of the Goyim to such an extent that almost all of them see world-events through colored glasses that we put over their eyes; if, even at present, there is not one state that bars our access to 'state secrets' (so termed by the stupid Goyim), then what will it be called when we, in the person of our universal Sovereign, are the acknowledged rulers of the world?

*****

Let us return to the future of the press. Anyone who wishes to become an editor, a librarian, or a printer, will be obliged to obtain a certification, which, in case of disobedience, will be immediately revoked. With such measures, thought will become an educational tool in the hands of our government; it will not allow the people to be led astray into realms of fancy and dreams about beneficent progress. Who of us does not know that these fantastic blessings are a direct road to baseless hopes that lead to anarchistic relations between the people and the government?

Progress, or better still the idea of progress, has led to the creation of different modes of emancipation without setting any limit to it. All so-called liberals are essentially anarchists in thought, if not in action. Each one of them pursues the phantom of liberty, becoming self-willed—that is to say, falling into a state of anarchy by protesting for the mere sake of protesting.

We will now again refer to the question of the press. We will place stamp taxes secured by bonds on each page of all printed matter; while on books of less than 300 pages, we will place a double tax. We will classify them as 'pamphlets,' so as to lessen the number of magazines, which represent the worst printed poison—and on the other hand, to force writers to prepare such long works that they will be little read, especially as they will be expensive. Our own publications, guiding public opinion in the direction we desire, will be cheap and rapidly bought. The tax will discourage the writing of mere leisure literature, whereas punishment will make writers dependent upon us.

Even if there were writers who would like to attack us, they would find no publishers for their works.[8] Before printing any work, the editor

---

[8] A remarkable anticipation of events in recent decades, in which books critical of Jews and the Jewish Lobby have become censored, 'cancelled,' and almost literally unpublishable.

or printer will have to apply to the authorities for permission. We will then know beforehand of the attacks that are being prepared against us, and we will destroy them by coming out with advance statements on the subject.

Literature and journalism are the two most important educational forces. For this reason, our government will become the owner of most of the periodicals.[9] This will neutralize the injurious influence of the private press and have great influence on the people. If we permit ten periodicals, we ourselves will print 30, and so forth. But the public must not suspect any of this. All the periodicals published by us will seem to be of contradictory views and opinions, inviting trust in us, and thus appearing attractive to our unsuspecting enemies; in this way, they will be caught in our trap and made harmless.[10]

Dominant position will be held by periodicals of an official character. They will always stand guard over our interests and consequently their influence will be comparatively benign. In a second class, we will place semi-official organs, whose aim will be to attract the indifferent and the lukewarm. The third category will be our ostensible opposition, which, at least in one of its publications, will represent the opposition to us. Our real enemies will mistake this seeming opposition as belonging to their own group, and thus will show us their cards.[11]

All our newspapers will represent different tendencies—namely, aristocratic, republican, revolutionary, even anarchistic, as long as the constitution lasts. Like the Indian God Vishnu, these periodicals will have 100 arms, each of which will feel the pulse of every group of public opinion. When the pulse beats faster, these arms will guide opinion toward our aims, since an excited person loses his power of reasoning and is easily led. Those fools who believe that they repeat the opinions expressed by 'their' newspapers will be repeating our opinions or those that

---

[9] Indeed—Jews today own or control most of the media organizations in the US, Europe, and the West generally.

[10] Modern-day Jews dominate both 'left' and 'right' media, both 'conservative' and 'liberal.' As a result, we have the appearance of free and open discussion, when in fact all media serves Jewish interests.

[11] A striking anticipation of the current notion of 'controlled opposition,' in which ostensible critics of Jewish power are themselves controlled by Jewish interests.

we desire them to have. Imagining that they are following their own press, they will follow the flag that we fly for them.

In order that our newspaper militia may carry out our program, we must organize the press with great care. Under the title of the Central Department of the Press, we will organize literary meetings at which our agents, unnoticed, will give passwords and countersigns. Discussing and contradicting our policies, although always superficially, and without touching their essence, our press will conduct empty debates against official newspapers, serving only to give us an opportunity to express ourselves in greater detail than we were able in our preliminary declarations. This, of course, will be done when it is useful to us.

These attacks against us will also convince the people that complete freedom of the press still exists; it will give our agents the opportunity to declare that the papers opposing us are mere wind-bags, since they are unable to find any real ground to refute our orders.

Such measures, which will escape the notice of public attention, will be the most successful means of guiding the public mind and of inspiring confidence in our government. Thanks to them, we will excite or pacify the public mind on political questions. We will be able to persuade or confuse them, sometimes printing the truth, sometimes lies, referring to facts or contradicting them, according to the way they are received by the public, and always carefully testing the ground before stepping on it. We will surely conquer our enemies because they will not have the press at their disposal in which to fully express themselves. Moreover, with the above-mentioned plans against the press, we will not even need to refute them seriously.

The trial balloons thrown out by us in the third category of our press will be energetically denied, as needed, by our semi-official organs.

In French journalism, there already exists the Masonic solidarity of a password. All organs of the press are bound by professional secrecy; like the ancient augurs, not one member will disclose his secret if he is not ordered to do so. Not one journalist will dare to disclose this secret, because none of them is admitted to the literary world unless he has a disgraceful action in his past record. That fact would immediately be made public. While these disgraceful actions are known only to a few, the prestige of the journalist attracts opinion throughout the country—he is followed and admired.

Our plans must extend chiefly to the rural districts. It is essential for us to create such ideas and inspire such opinions there, that we could, at any time, launch them on the capital city as the 'neutral views' of the rural regions. Of course, the source and origin of the idea would be the same; namely, it would be ours. It is necessary for us, while we are not yet in full power, that the capital should be under the influence of rural public opinion—that is, under the influence of the majority prearranged by our agents. It is necessary for us that, at the critical psychological moment, the capitals should not discuss a *fait accompli*, for the mere reason that it has already been accepted by the rural masses.

When we reach the phase of the new regime, which is transitory to our accession to power, we must not allow the press to expose social corruption. It must be thought that the new regime has satisfied everyone to such an extent that even criminality has stopped. Cases of criminal activity must only be known to their victims or their accidental witnesses, and to these alone.

Protocol No. 13

On political problems, trade, diversion of the masses

The need for daily bread silences the Goyim and compels them to remain our obedient servants. Agents taken from among them for our press will discuss only the facts that they are ordered to publish, when it is inconvenient for us to publish statements openly in official documents. While discussion and debate are taking place, we will simply pass the measures we desire and present them to the public as an accomplished fact. No one will dare to demand the rejection of measures thus passed—and even more, since they will be interpreted as an improvement. At this point, the press will divert the people's thoughts to new problems (we have always manipulated them via new emotions). Brainless political commentators will hasten to discuss the new problems; such people do not understand what they are talking about. Political questions are meant to be understood only by those who have created them and have been directing them for many centuries.

From all this, you will realize that by aiming to control the mob's opinion, we will only facilitate the functioning of our machinery; and you will also notice that we seek approval for the various questions not by deeds, but by words. We always declare that we are guided, in all our policies, by the hope and certainty of serving the general good.

To divert restless people from discussing political problems, we now make it appear that we provide them with new problems—namely, those pertaining to trade and commerce. Let them become excited by this subject as much as they like. The masses will consent to abstain from so-called political activity only if we can give them some new amusements—that is to say, commerce, which we make them believe is also a political question. We ourselves induced the masses to participate in politics in order to secure their support in our campaign against the Goy governments.

To prevent them from reaching any independent decisions, we will divert their minds with amusements, games, hobbies, passions, and public cultural centers. We will soon begin to offer prize contests through the press, and sports of all kinds. Such attractions will definitely deflect the mind from problems that we would otherwise have to fight with the people. By becoming less accustomed to independent thought, they will begin to talk in unison with us, because we alone will provide new lines of thinking by using only those persons that no one would suspect were allied with us.

The role of liberal idealists will definitely be terminated when our government is recognized. Until that time, they will benefit us. For this reason, we will still direct thought towards different idealistic theories that will appear to be progressive. For it was by the word 'progress' that we have successfully turned the heads of the stupid Goyim toward socialism. The brainless Goyim don't realize that progress is but a cover for digression from the truth, unless it is applied to scientific inventions; there is but one truth, and thus there is no room for progress. Progress, being a false conception, serves to conceal the truth, so that no one may know it except ourselves, God's Chosen, who are its guardians.

When our kingdom is established, our orators will discuss the great problems that have convulsed humanity in order to bring mankind under our blessed rule. Who will then suspect that all these problems were instigated by us, according to a political plan that has not been disclosed by anyone during so many centuries?

Protocol No. 14

On religion, pornography

When we become rulers, we will not tolerate the existence of any other religion except our own; it proclaims one God, with whom our fate is bound up because we are the Chosen People, and our fate has determined the fate of the world. For this reason, we must destroy all other religions. If the result of this produces modern atheists, as a transitory step, this will not interfere with our plans but will act as an example to those generations that will listen to our teaching of the religion of Moses—which, owing to its solid and thoughtful system, will eventually lead to our domination of all nations. We will also lay stress on the mystical truth of Masonic teaching which, we will assert, is the foundation of its whole instructive power.

On every possible occasion, we will publish articles in which we will compare our beneficial rule with that of the past. The benefits of peace, although attained through centuries of unrest, will serve to demonstrate the beneficial character of our rule. The mistakes made by the Goyim during their administration will be painted by us in the most vivid colors. We will cause such disgust towards the Goy administration that the masses will prefer the peace of serfdom to the rights of the much-lauded liberty that has so cruelly tortured them and drained the very source of human existence from them, and by which they were exploited by a mass of adventurers, ignorant of what they were doing.

The pointless changes of government—to which we ourselves prompted the Goyim, when we were undermining their governmental apparatus—will become such a nuisance to the people that they will prefer to endure anything from us rather than risk a repetition of former difficulties. We will, moreover, lay particular stress on the historical mistakes made by the Goy governments, which caused humanity to suffer for many centuries for lack of understanding of all matters pertaining to its true welfare, and because of their search for idealistic schemes of social welfare. The Goyim did not notice that such schemes, instead of improving the human relations that form the basis of social existence, have only made them worse.

The whole force of our principles and measures will lie in the fact that they are put forward and interpreted by us as being in sharp contrast to the decayed social order of former times. Our philosophers will discuss all the shortcomings of the Goy religion, but no one will ever discuss our religion in the light of its true aspect, and no one will ever thoroughly understand it, except our own people, who will never dare to disclose its secrets.[12]

In the so-called advanced countries, we have created senseless, dirty, and disgusting literature.[13] For a short time after our entrance into power, we will encourage its publication, so as to emphasize the contrast between it and our own lofty speeches and programs. Our wise men, trained to guide the Goyim, will prepare speeches, plans, memoranda, and articles by which we will influence their minds and direct them towards the conceptions and the knowledge that we want them to have.

---

[12] It is true that there are very few intelligent, critical studies of Judaism. The prime documents of this religion—the Old Testament, the Talmud, and the *Shulchan Aruch*—are rarely critiqued in a detailed and careful manner. Of importance here is the work of Erich Bischoff, a German scholar active in the 1920s and 1930s. See, for example, the recent translation of his *The Book of the Shulchan Aruch* (2023; Clemens and Blair).

[13] That is, pornographic—i.e. sexually exploitive and obscene—material.

Protocol No. 15

On Freemasonry, civil disobedience, the judiciary, the power of the Sovereign

We will finally become rulers by means of revolutions. These revolutions will be arranged so that they shall take place simultaneously in all countries and immediately after all existing governments have been officially declared incompetent—which may not happen soon, perhaps not for a century.[14]

When this happens, we will see to it that no plots are hatched against us. To effect this, we will ruthlessly kill all who take up arms against our rule. The establishment of any new secret society will be met by the death penalty, and those societies that now exist and are known to us will be disbanded, and their members exiled to continents far removed from Europe.

We will deal in the same manner with those Goy Masons who know too much. The Masons whom we may pardon for any reason will be kept under continual fear of exile. We will pass a law whereby all members of secret organizations will be exiled from Europe, the center of our government. The decisions of our government will be final and there will be no right of appeal.

In the Goy society, where we have planted such deep roots of dissension and protest, order can only be restored by merciless measures that will serve as proof that our power cannot be infringed. There is no need to worry about the victims sacrificed for the future good. To attain the good, even though by the sacrifice of life, is the duty of every government that realizes that its existence depends not upon privileges alone, but also upon the exercise of its duties.

The most important means for erecting a stable government is to strengthen the prestige of authority. This is only obtained by its majestic and unshakable power, which will convey the impression that it is

---

[14] Of course, this would have been a century from roughly 1900, and thus the projected date has passed. The predicted mass of revolutions seems not to have happened, and yet, Jews, via their influence in the US and Europe, do hold sway over much of the planet. And perhaps we need only wait another decade or two to see the full process play out.

inviolable because of its mystical nature—namely, because it is chosen by God. Until recently, this has been the case with the Russian Autocracy[15]—our only dangerous enemy in the world, with the exception of the Pope. Remember Italy drowning in blood; she did not touch a hair on the head of Sulla who had shed that blood. Sulla became powerful in the eyes of the people, although they were tortured by him; his manly return to Italy placed him beyond persecution.[16] The people do not touch those who hypnotize them by bravery and steadfastness of spirit.

Meanwhile, until our rule is established, we, on the contrary, will organize and multiply Free Masonic lodges in all the countries of the world. They will attract all those who are public-spirited, because these lodges will contain the chief source of information, and our influence will emanate from them. All these lodges will be centralized under one management, known only to us and unknown to all others; these lodges will be administered by our wise men. The lodges will have their own representatives in this management, in order to shield the abovementioned Masonic government; they will give the password and elaborate the program. We will tie the knot of all socialistic and revolutionary classes of society. The most secret political plans will be known to us and will fall under our leadership on the very day of their origination.

Nearly all agents of the national and international police will be members of these lodges. Their work is indispensable for us, inasmuch as the police not only are able to take independent measures against rebels, but they may also serve to mask our actions, to provoke discontent, and so forth.

Most people who become members of secret societies are adventurers, career-makers, and irresponsible people in general; we will have no difficulty in dealing with such people, and they will help us to set in motion the mechanism of the machine planned by us. If this world becomes perturbed, it will only prove that it was necessary for us to disorganize it, so as to destroy its overwhelming solidarity.

If a plot is laid, it must be headed by one of our most trustworthy servants. It is only natural that we want no one but ourselves to guide the

---

[15] Meaning, rule by the czars—specifically, Alexander II, Alexander III, and Nicholas II. They were notably hostile to their Jewish populations.

[16] Lucius Sulla (138-78 BC) was a Roman general and dictator who fought in two civil wars, eventually restoring peace through ruthless military action.

work of the Masons, for we know where we are heading; we know the final aim of every action. The Goyim, however, understand nothing, not even the immediate results. They are usually concerned about the momentary satisfaction of their ambitions. They do not notice, however, that their intentions were not initiated by them, but rather given to them by us.

The Goyim join the lodges out of pure curiosity, or hoping to receive their share of public funds. There are others who come for the opportunity to promote their impossible and baseless hopes. They long for a feeling of success and for the applause that we lavishly give to them. *We create their success* in order to utilize the self-deception that is born with it, and by which people, without noticing it, begin to follow our suggestions without suspecting them—being fully convinced of their own infallibility and, therefore, having no need of others.

You have no idea how easy it is to bring even the most intelligent Goyim to a state of unconscious gullibility, and, on the other hand, how easy it is to discourage them by the smallest failure—or merely by ceasing to applaud them, thus enslaving them for the sake of achieving new success. To the same extent as our people ignore success for the sake of carrying out their plans, so are the Goyim ready to sacrifice all their plans for the sake of success. Their psychology makes the problem of direction easier for us. Those who appear to be tigers are as stupid as sheep; nonsense filters through their heads.

As a side effect, we have given the Goyim the dream of subverting human individualism to the symbolic idea of collectivism. They have not yet discovered and will not discover that this dream is a clear infringement on the principal law of nature, which, from the beginning of the world, created each being unlike all others, precisely for the sake of expressing one's individuality. If we were able to lead them to such insane and blind beliefs, does it not obviously prove the low level of development of the Goy mind as compared to our own? It is precisely the thing that guarantees our success.

Our wise men of old were far-sighted when they said that, to attain a serious object, one must not stop at the means, nor should one count the victims sacrificed to the cause. We have not counted the victims from among the Goyim, those offspring of cattle. Although we have sacrificed many of our own people, we have already given them in return a formerly undreamed-of position on Earth. The comparatively few victims from among our own people have saved our race from destruction.

Death is the unavoidable end of all. It would be better to accelerate this end for those who interfere with our cause than for those who promote it. We kill Masons in such a way that none but the brothers suspect, not even the victims; they all die when necessary, apparently from a natural death. Knowing this, even the brotherhood, in their turn, dare not protest. It is through such measures that we have uprooted the heart of protest against our orders from among the Masons.

We preach liberalism to the Goyim, while at the same time we hold our people and our agents under strict discipline. Through our influence, enforcement of Goy laws has been reduced to a minimum. The prestige of the law has been undermined by liberal interpretations that we have introduced. The most important questions, both political and moral, are decided by the courts in whatever manner we prescribe. The Goy administrators of justice look upon cases in whatever light we choose to expose them.

We accomplish this naturally through agents that have no obvious connection to us—namely, through the press or otherwise. Even senators and high officials blindly follow our advice. The Goy's purely animal mind is incapable of analysis and observation, and even less so of foreseeing the results to which a given principle may lead.

It is through this difference in the process of reasoning between us and the Goyim that it becomes possible to clearly see the stamp of God's elect, as compared to the instinctive and bestial mentality of the Goyim. They see, but they cannot foresee; they cannot invent anything except material things. It is clear, therefore, that nature herself intended us to rule and guide the world.

When the time comes for our open rule, then will be the time to show its benefits, and we will change all the laws. Our laws will be short, clear, irrevocable, and require no interpretation, so that everyone will be able to thoroughly understand them. The chief point emphasized in them will be a highly developed obedience to authority, which will eliminate all abuses; everyone, without exception, will be responsible before the supreme power vested in the highest authority.

Abuse of power by minor officials will then disappear because it will be punished so mercilessly that they will lose the desire to experiment with their power. We will closely watch every action of the administration, which is in fact the action of the machinery of government; corruption there creates corruption everywhere. Not a single violation of law or act of corruption will remain unpunished. Acts of concealment and willful neglect on the part of governmental officials will disappear after they have seen the first example of severe punishment. The prestige of power demands that appropriate—that is to say, severe—punishments should be inflicted even for the smallest violations of the sanctity of the supreme authority, when committed for the sake of personal gain. The guilty, if punished severely, will be like a soldier who falls on the battlefield of administration for the sake of authority, principle, and law.

These principles do not allow any digression from their social function for a personal motive, even on the part of those who rule. For instance: Our judges will know that by attempting to show thoughtless mercy, they overstep the law of justice, which was created solely for exemplary punishment of crimes and not for the manifestation of moral qualities on the part of the judge. Such qualities are commendable in private, but not in public life, which constitutes the educational forum of society.

Our judges will not remain in office after the age of 55. First, because old people adhere more persistently to prejudiced opinions and are less capable of submitting to new commands; and secondly, because that enables us to achieve a certain flexibility of change in the personnel, which will bend more easily under our pressure. He who wishes to retain his position will have to blindly obey.

In general, our judges will be selected only from among those who will clearly understand that they must punish people and enforce the laws, and not indulge in dreams of liberalism at the expense of the government's educational plan, as is now imagined by the Goyim. The method of changing personnel will also serve to undermine the collective solidarity of governmental officials and will attach them to the government's cause, which decides their fate. The younger generation of judges will be so educated as to prevent any criminal activity that might interfere with the inter-relationship that we have established for our subjects.

At present, the Goy judges, lacking a clear conception of the nature of their duties, make exceptions to all kinds of crimes. This occurs because the present rulers, when appointing judges, do not take the trouble to encourage a sense of duty and conscientiousness in what they do. Just as an animal sends out its young in search of prey, so the Goyim are giving their subjects responsible offices without taking the time to explain their functions. Due to this, their rule is undermined by their own efforts and by the actions of their own administration. Let us use the result of such actions as one more example of the advantage of our own rule.

We will eliminate liberalism from all important strategic positions in our administration, upon which depend the training of our subjects for our social order. These positions will be given only to those who have been trained by us for governmental work.

In answer to a possible remark—that putting old officials on the retired list may prove expensive for the treasury—I can state, first, that, prior to their dismissal, some private work will be found for them to replace what they are losing; and secondly, all the world's money will be concentrated in our hands. Consequently, our government need not fear expense.

Our autocracy will be consistent in every respect, and consequently every manifestation of our great power will be respected and unconditionally obeyed. We will ignore grumbling and discontent, and any active manifestations of this will be suppressed by punishment, which will serve as an example to the rest of the people.

We will abolish the right of appellate courts to annul judicial decisions, which will become the exclusive prerogative of the Sovereign; we cannot permit the people to think that our judges could possibly render an incorrect decision. If, however, such an error happens, we ourselves will annul the decision. But the punishment that we will impose upon the judge for his mistake will be so severe that it will eliminate the possibility of recurrence. I repeat that we will watch every step taken by our administration, in order to enable us to satisfy the people, for they have a right to demand a good appointee from a good administration.

In the person of our Sovereign, our government will bear the appearance of a patriarchy or fatherly tutelage. The people, our subjects, will see him as a father who takes care of every need, of every action, and who is concerned with every relationship, both among the subjects themselves and between them and the Sovereign. Thus, they will become imbued with the idea that it is impossible for them to do without this guardian and leader, if they wish to live in a world of peace and quiet. They will recognize the autocracy of our Sovereign, whom they will respect and almost deify, especially when they realize that our agents do not usurp his power, but merely execute his orders blindly. They will be glad that everything is regulated in their lives, as is done by wise parents who wish to educate their children to a sense of duty and obedience. Regarding the secrets of our political plans, both the masses and their administration are like little children.

As you can see for yourselves, I base our despotism upon *right* and *duty*: the right of compelling the exercise of duty is the direct function of a government that acts as a father to its subjects. It is the right of the strong to utilize his power in order to lead humanity towards a social order established by the law of nature—namely, obedience. Everything in the world is subject, if not to some other persons, then to circumstances, or to its own nature; but in any case, to something stronger than itself. Consequently, let us be the strongest for the common good.

We must unhesitatingly sacrifice those individuals who violate the existing order, for in exemplary punishment of evil there lies a great educational value.

When the King of Israel places the crown offered to him by Europe on his sacred head, he will become the Patriarch of the World. The necessary sacrifices made by him will never equal the number of victims sacrificed to the mania of greatness during the centuries of rivalry between the Goy governments.

Our Sovereign will be in constant communication with the people, delivering addresses that will be spread to all parts of the world.

Protocol No. 16

On universities, education

For the purpose of destroying all collective forces except our own, we will transform the universities—the first stage of collectivism—by reconstructing them along new lines. Their directors and professors will be trained for their work through detailed secret programs of action, from which they will not be able to deviate in the least. They will be appointed with special care and will be so placed as to be completely dependent upon the government.

We will exclude civic law from the curriculum, as well as all that touches upon political questions. These subjects will be taught only to a few dozen, selected for their conspicuous ability from among the initiated. Universities must not allow inexperienced youths to graduate, who concoct plans of constitutions as they do comedies or tragedies, or who meddle with political matters that even their fathers do not understand.

Poorly-directed study of political questions by a great number of people creates utopians and poor citizens, as you can judge by the universal education created by the Goyim along those lines. It was necessary for us to interject principles into their educational system that have successfully broken down their social order. When we are in power, we will eliminate all disruptive subjects from educational systems and will make young people obedient children of their superiors, loving the Sovereign who promises them hope, peace, and quiet.

In place of the study of the classics and ancient history, which contain more bad examples than good, we will substitute a program dealing with the future. We will obliterate from the people's memory all those historical facts that are not to our advantage, leaving only those that emphasize the mistakes of the Goy governments. The educational program will be focused on the study of practical life, of obligatory social order, of the inter-relationship of human beings, of the avoidance of evil, and other questions of a pedagogical nature.

This program will differ for each caste, never allowing education to be of a uniform character. Such a system is of special importance. Each caste must be educated with strict limitations, according to its particular occupation and the nature of its work. The occasional genius has always been able to rise to a higher caste; but apart from this rare exception, it would be crazy to open the higher ranks to those below. You yourselves know what happened to the Goyim when they yielded to this nonsense.

In order to implant the Sovereign firmly in the hearts and minds of his subjects, it is necessary to acquaint the people with the importance of his activity and the benevolence of his enterprises, both in schools and in public places.

We will abolish all private education. Students will have the right to gather, with their relatives, in their colleges as if in clubs. During these gatherings, which will occur on holidays, the professors will read supposedly unbiased lectures on problems of human relationship, on the law, on the cruelty of unrestricted competition, and finally, on new philosophical theories that have not yet been disclosed to the world. We will promote these new theories into dogmatic beliefs, using them as stepping-stones to our faith.

After having presented our program of action for the present and for the future, I will read to you the principles of these theories.

We know from the experience of many centuries that men live and are guided by ideas, and take inspiration from them, only by means of education. This education can be given to men of all ages, but of course by different methods, and yet yield the same result. We will absorb and appropriate to our own advantage the last traces of independent thought, which for a long time have been directed to the ideas and the goal of our choosing. The system of enslaving thought has already been put into action, through so-called visual education. This system tends to turn the Goyim into thoughtless, obedient animals, who expect to *see* in order to understand. In France, one of our best agents, Bourgeois, has already announced a new program of visual education.[17]

---

[17] Leon Bourgeois (1851-1925) was a French statesman, who served as prime minister from late 1895 to mid-1896. He was also a prominent Freemason. He was the only living individual specifically named in the *Protocols*.

Protocol No. 17

On law, religion, the virtue of spying

The legal profession makes people grow cold, cruel, stubborn, and unprincipled. It compels lawyers to always take an abstract or purely legal viewpoint. They have learned to consider solely the personal gain derived from every case they handle and not the possibility of any resulting social benefit. They rarely refuse to take a case and always strive for acquittal at all cost, clinging to minor technical points of a legal nature. In this way, they demoralize the courts.

Therefore, we will limit this profession, converting it into an executive public office. Lawyers will be deprived of the right of contact with their clients, on the same basis as are the judges. They will receive their cases only from the court, preparing them on the strength of written reports and documents, and defending their clients after they have been examined in court on the basis of the facts obtained during the trial. They will receive a salary, regardless of whether the defense has succeeded or not. They will act as simple exponents of the case on behalf of the defense, in counterbalance to the public prosecutor, who will act as exponent on behalf of the prosecution. This will shorten legal procedures and establish an honest and impartial defense, conducted not for the sake of personal gain but based on the personal conviction of the lawyer. This will also eliminate the existing bribery among fellow lawyers, in which one side pays the other to win.

*****

We have already taken care to discredit the Goy clergy and thus to undermine their function, which at the present time could have been very much in our way. Their influence over the people diminishes daily.

Today, freedom of religion has been proclaimed everywhere; consequently, it is only a matter of a few years before Christianity completely collapses. It will be easier to deal with other religions, but it is too early to discuss this problem. We will restrict the clergy and their teachings to such a narrow field that their influence will have an effect opposite to what it used to have.

When the moment comes to completely annihilate the Papal court, an invisible hand, pointing towards this court, will guide the masses in their assault. When the masses attack, however, we will come forward as defenders to prevent too much bloodshed. By this method, we will penetrate to the very heart of this court and will not leave it until we have undermined its power.

The King of Israel will become the real Pope of the World—the Patriarch of the International Church.

But until we have accomplished the re-education of the youth to new transitional religions and finally to our own, we will not openly attack the existing churches; rather, we will fight them by means of criticism, thus creating dissension. In general, our press will denounce governmental activities and religion, and will expose the Goy institutions in the most unscrupulous terms, so as to humiliate them in such a way as only our ingenious race can do.

Our rule will simulate the God Vishnu, who resembles us physically; each of our hundred hands will hold one of the levers of the social machine. We will see everything without the aid of the official police; in its present organization, however, which we have worked out for the Goyim, the police prevent the government from seeing anything. According to our program, one-third of our subjects will watch the others from a pure sense of duty, as volunteers for the government. Then it will not be considered disgraceful to be a spy and an informer; on the contrary, it will be regarded as praiseworthy. Unfounded reports, however, will be severely punished to prevent abuse of this privilege.

Our agents will be recruited from among both the highest and the lowest ranks of society. They will be selected from among the pleasure-loving governmental officials, editors, printers, booksellers, salesmen, workmen, drivers, butlers, etc. This 'police force' will have no official rights or credentials that might present the opportunity for an abuse of power; consequently, it will be powerless. It will merely act as observer and will make reports. The verification of such reports and the issue of arrest warrants will rest with a responsible group of police controllers. The actual arrests, however, will be made by a 'gendarme corps' or city police. In case of a failure to report any political matter that has been observed or rumored, the guilty party may be brought to trial for concealment of crime, if he is proven guilty.

In the same way that our brethren are now under obligation to report all apostates on their own initiative, or on any person marked as being opposed to the Kahal, so in our Universal Kingdom it will be obligatory for all subjects to serve the state in that direction.[18]

Such an organization will eliminate all abuse of power and various kinds of coercion and corruption—in fact, the very things that have been introduced into the Goy customs by our councils and by our theories of rights. But how else could we foment the increasing causes for disorder in the midst of their administration? What other means could we use? Among the most important means for corrupting their institutions is the use of such agents as are able, through their own destructive activity, to contaminate others by revealing and developing their own corrupt tendencies, such as abuse of power and bribery.

---

[18] The Kahal (or Qahal, or Kehila) is a Jewish theocratic system for ruling Jewish society. This is the only such reference in the *Protocols*.

Protocol No. 18

On open and secret defense of rulers

When the time comes for us to strengthen the measures of police protection (the most terrible poison for the prestige of authority), we will artificially organize disorder or simulate the expression of discontent using experienced orators. These orators will be joined by sympathizers. This will give us the pretext for searches and special restrictions that will be put in force by our servants among the Goy police.

Since most conspirators work as amateurs for the sake of chattering, we will not disturb them until we see that they are about to take action; but we will introduce secret service agents in their midst. It must be remembered that the prestige of authority diminishes if conspiracies against it are often discovered, for that leads to the presumption of the weakness of the authority—or, even worse, to the admission of its own mistakes.

You are aware that we have destroyed the prestige of the ruling Goyim by frequent attempts made on their lives through our agents, who were but blind sheep of our flock, easily moved to criminal actions, so long as they were of a political nature.

We have forced the rulers to admit their own weakness by adopting open measures of police protection, and thereby we have destroyed the prestige of their authority. Our Sovereign will be protected only by the most invisible guards, because we will never allow anyone to think that a conspiracy might exist against him that he is unable to crush, and from which he must hide himself. If we were to allow this thought to prevail, as it prevails among the Goyim, we would thereby sign the death warrant, if not of the Sovereign himself, then of his dynasty in the near future.

Observing strict decorum, our Sovereign will use his power only for the benefit of the people, but never for his own good or for that of his personal dynasty. By strictly adhering to this decorum, his authority will be respected and protected by his subjects; moreover, he will be worshiped, because it will be known that the well-being of every citizen of the kingdom depends upon his authority. So too will be the stability of the social order itself.

But to repeat: To openly guard the Sovereign is equivalent to an admission of the weakness of his governmental organization. Our Sovereign, when among the people, will always appear to be surrounded by a crowd of curious men and women, who will stand beside him as though by chance; they will thus hold back the mob as if through respect for order. This example will implant an idea of self-restraint in others. If there is a person in the crowd trying to present a petition, and working his way through the ranks, the person nearest to him must take the petition and present it to the Sovereign in sight of the petitioner himself; in this way, all may know that the petition presented has reached its destination and consequently that the Sovereign is in control. The prestige of authority demands that the people should be able to say, "If only the king could know it," or, "The king needs to know about this."

With the establishment of an official police guard, the mystical prestige of authority vanishes. Under such conditions, and with sufficient audacity, anyone may consider himself superior to authority. Even the assassin becomes empowered and only has to watch for his chance to make an attempt against an official. We preached differently for the Goyim, but we can see the results of open protection.

We will arrest criminals upon the first well-founded suspicion. Simply for fear of a possible mistake, political criminals should not be given a chance to escape; indeed, we will show no mercy towards political crime. If, in exceptional cases, we might allow an investigation of motives that have led to ordinary criminal offences, there is no excuse for those who attempt to deal with matters that no one can understand except the ruler. Moreover, not even all rulers are capable of understanding right policy.

Protocol No. 19

On sedition, political crimes

Though we will not allow individuals to become involved in politics, we will, however, encourage the submission of plans and ideas for furthering the public welfare. This will bring to our knowledge both the shortcomings of our government and the idealistic aspirations of our people. We will answer these suggestions either by favorable action or, if necessary, by rejection, thus proving the lack of intelligence and the errors of those who have submitted them.

Sedition is nothing but a dog barking at an elephant. From the viewpoint of a well-organized government, the dog barks because he doesn't realize his lack of strength. It is only necessary for the elephant to show his strength one time and the dog stops barking; then, he begins to wag his tail the moment he sees the elephant.

In order to eliminate the prestige of martyrdom from political crime, we will place the political criminal on the same level as thieves, murderers, and other disgusting criminals. Then public opinion will regard that class as disgraceful as any other, and will brand them with equal contempt.

We have attempted to prevent the Goyim—successfully, I hope—from using such methods of dealing with seditious activities. In order to attain this end, we have made use of the press and public speeches. Through cleverly-compiled historical textbooks, we have indirectly given publicity to martyrdom as though done for the sake of human welfare. Such an advertisement has multiplied the number of liberals and has swollen the ranks of our agents by thousands of Goyim.

Protocol No. 20

On financial matters, taxation, circulation of money, governmental loans

Today we shall deal with the financial program, a discussion that I have postponed until the end of my report because it is the most difficult, most conclusive, and most decisive point in our plan. In approaching it, I will remind you that I have already suggested that the result of our actions is measured in numbers.

When we become rulers, our autocratic government, for the sake of self-defense, will avoid burdening the people with heavy taxes; it will not forget that its main role is that of Father and Protector. But as government organization is costly, it is necessary to raise the means for its maintenance. Consequently, we must carefully work out the plan of a fair distribution of taxation.

In our government, the Sovereign will have the legal fiction of owning everything in his kingdom (which is easily put into practice), and can resort to legal confiscation of all money in order to regulate its circulation throughout the country. Consequently, the best method of taxation is the levying of a progressive tax on property. Taxes will thus be paid without difficulty or ruin in respective proportion to the amount of property owned. The rich must realize that it is their duty to give a part of their surplus wealth for the benefit of the country as a whole, because the government guarantees the inviolability of the remainder of their property and of the right of honest gain. I say 'honest' because the control of property will prevent legal theft. This social reform must come from above, for the time is ripe; it is becoming necessary as a guarantee of peace.

Taxation on the poor is the seed of revolution, and it acts detrimentally to the government, which loses the great in its pursuit of the small. Moreover, the taxation of capital will reduce the increase of wealth in private hands, in which at present we have concentrated it as a counterweight to the governmental power of the Goyim—namely, to the state treasury.

Progressive taxation, assessed according to the amount of capital, will produce much more revenue than the present system of taxing everyone at an equal rate, which is useful to us now only as a means of exciting revolt and discontent among the Goyim. The power of our Sovereign will rest mainly in equilibrium and in guarantees of peace. For these, the capitalists must cede a part of their income so as to protect the action of the government machine. Public needs must be met by those who can best afford to do so, and by those from whom there is something to take. Such a measure will eliminate the hatred of the poor towards the rich, as they will be regarded as the financial supporters of the state and the upholders of peace and prosperity. The poor will also see that the rich are providing the necessary means to insure this end.

To prevent intelligent taxpayers from being too discontented with the new system of taxation, they will be furnished with detailed reports on the disbursement of public funds—excluding those appropriated for the needs of the throne and administrative institutions.

The Sovereign will not own property, since everything in the state will seem to belong to him, and these two conceptions would contradict each other. Private means would eliminate his right to own everything.

The Sovereign's relatives—aside from his descendants, who will also be supported by the state—must join the ranks of government officials, or otherwise work for the right to hold property. The privilege of being of royal blood must not entitle them to rob the state treasury.

Sales, profits, or inheritances will be taxed by a progressive stamp tax. The transfer of property, whether in cash or otherwise, without the required stamp, will place the payment of the tax on the original owner, dating from the time of the transfer, until the time of the reported failure to record the transaction. Transfer vouchers must be shown weekly at the local branch of the state treasury, together with a statement of the names and permanent addresses of both the original and the new owner. The recording of the names of those participating in a transaction will be necessary in all transactions involving more than a certain amount for ordinary expenditure. The sale of prime necessities will be taxed only by a stamp tax, which will represent a certain small percent of the value of the particular article.

Just imagine how many times the amount received from such taxes will exceed the income of the Goy governments!

The state bank must keep a definite reserve fund, and all sums in excess of this must be put back into circulation. The cost of public works will be met out of this surplus fund. The initiative of such works emanating from the government will also tie the working class to the interests of the government and the rulers. Some of this money will be allotted to prizes for inventions and for the purposes of production.

Even small sums in excess of a certain definite and broadly-calculated fund should not be allowed to be kept in the state treasury, because money is intended to circulate. Every impediment to circulation is detrimental to the governmental mechanism, which the money lubricates; the congestion of lubricating substances can impede the proper functioning of the machine. The substitution of bonds for a portion of the currency has created just such an impediment. The result of this has already become sufficiently clear.

We will also establish an auditing office, so as to enable the Sovereign to find a full account of state revenues and expenses at any time, except for the current month not yet made up, and that of the previous month not yet presented.

The only person who will not be interested in pilfering the state treasury will be the Sovereign, its owner. This is the reason why his control will prevent the possibility of loss or misappropriation.

Receptions and ceremonies for the purpose of etiquette, which waste the Sovereign's valuable time, will be abolished so that he may better attend to affairs of the state. His power will not be frittered away on the people surrounding the throne for the sake of appearance and splendor, and who have only their own and not the public interest in mind.

Economic crises were created by us solely for the Goyim by withdrawing money from circulation. Huge amounts of capital were kept idle and thus taken away from the nations, which were thereby compelled to come to us for loans. Payment of interest on these loans burdened the state finances and made the states subservient to capital. The concentration of industry, having taken production out of the hands of the artisan and put it into the hands of capitalists, sucked all the power out of the people and also out of the state.

The present issue of money generally does not coincide with individual need, and consequently it cannot satisfy all the needs of the working classes. The issue of currency must correspond with an increase in population, and children must be reckoned as consumers from the day of their birth. The revision of the issue of currency is an essential problem for the whole world.

You know that gold currency was detrimental to the governments that accepted it; it could not satisfy the requirements for money, since we took as much gold as possible out of circulation.

We must issue a currency based on the value of labor. We will issue money in proportion to the normal demands of every subject, adding a certain amount at every birth and decreasing it with every death.

Every governmental unit, every district, will be in charge of its own accounts. To avoid any delay in paying government expenses, the terms of such payments will be decreed by order of the Sovereign; this will eliminate any favoritism toward the ministry of finance over any other department. The revenue and expenditure accounts will be placed side by side, in order that they may always be compared with each other.

*****

We will present plans for the reform of the Goy financial institutions and of their principles, as planned by us, in such a manner that no one will be alarmed. We will demonstrate the need for reform by the disorderly chaos produced by Goy financial disorganization. We will show that the first reason for this confusion lies in the drafting of rough estimates for the budget, which increases annually. This annual budget is made to last during the first half of the year, but only with great difficulty; then a revised budget is demanded and the funds thus allotted are spent in the next three months, after which a supplementary budget is called for, and all this is concluded by a liquidation budget. As the budget of the following year is based on the total expenditure of the preceding year, the divergence from normal reaches 50% annually, so that the annual budget triples every ten years. Owing to such a procedure, resulting from the carelessness of the Goy governments, their treasuries became empty. The period of loans followed and used up the remainder, and brought all the Goy states to bankruptcy.

You can well understand that we could never adopt the system of management of financial affairs that we imposed on the Goyim.

Every loan proves the impotency of the government and its failure to understand its own rights. Loans, like the sword of Damocles, hang over the heads of the rulers; instead of placing temporary taxes on their subjects, they stretch forth their hands and beg for charity from our bankers. Foreign loans are leeches that can never be removed from the governmental body until they either fall off themselves or the government itself manages to get rid of them. But the Goy governments, instead of throwing them off, *increase their number*, so that these governments must inevitably perish through a self-inflicted blood-letting.

Indeed, what is a loan, especially a foreign loan, if not a leech? A loan is the issuance of government obligations that involve the liability to pay interest in proportion to the sum borrowed. If the loan pays five percent, then in 20 years the government has unnecessarily paid in interest an amount equal to the principal sum borrowed. In 40 years, it has paid twice; in 60 years, it has trebled the sum, while the loan still remains an unpaid debt.

From this calculation, it is evident that the governmental system of universal taxation takes the last penny from the poor taxpayers in the form of taxes in order to pay interest to foreign capitalists, from whom the money was borrowed, instead of collecting these same pennies for its needs, free from all interest.

As long as the loans were domestic, the Goyim only shifted the money from the pockets of the poor into those of the rich; but when we bribed the proper persons to make the loans *foreign*, then national riches poured into our hands and all the Goyim began to pay us this tribute. The carelessness of the reigning Goyim in statesmanship, the corruption of their ministers, and the ignorance of other officials of financial problems, has forced their countries into debt to our banks to such an extent that they can never pay off their debts. It should be realized, however, that we have gone to great pains in order to bring about such a state of affairs.

Impediments to the circulation of money will not be allowed by us. Therefore, there will be no government bonds, except one percent bonds, so that the payment of interest should not hand over state power to the sucking leeches. The right of issuing bonds will be exclusively granted to industrial corporations, which will easily pay the interest out of their profits. The government, however, does not derive profit on borrowed money as these corporations do, since the state borrows money for expenditure and not for production.

Industrial bonds will also be bought by the government—which, instead of being, as at present, the payer of tribute on loans, will become a sound creditor. Such a measure will prevent stagnation in the circulation of money, as well as indolence and laziness, which were useful to us as long as the Goyim remained independent, but are unwanted by us in our government.

The purely bestial brains of the Goyim are so shortsighted! This first appeared when they borrowed money at interest. It did not occur to the Goyim that this money, with the additional interest on it, would have to be taken from the national resources and paid to us. Would it not have been simpler to take the needed money from their own people?

This proves the genius of our distinguished mind; we were able to present the question of loans to them in such a way that they saw loans as advantageous.

Our estimates, which we will produce when the time comes, will be based on the experience of centuries, on all those experiments that were conducted by us at the expense of the Goy governments. Our estimates will prove to be clear and definite, and will obviously demonstrate the advantage of our new system. They will end all those abuses that made it possible for us to master the Goyim, but which cannot be permitted in our reign. We will so organize the accounting system that neither the Sovereign himself nor the humblest clerk will be able to deflect even the smallest sum from its destination or direct it into a different channel than intended.

*****

It is impossible to govern without a definite plan. Even knights and heroes perish when they take a road not knowing where it leads, or start on their journey without being properly provisioned.

We once advised the Goy rulers to neglect governmental duties for grandiose receptions, etiquette, and pleasures; such things only concealed our rule. The accounts of the powerful favorites who replaced the leaders were drawn up by our agents, and they always satisfied shallow minds by promises that, in the future, there would be savings and improvements. Savings from what? From new taxes? This might have been asked but was not asked by those who read our reports and plans.

You yourselves know the state of financial chaos they have come to by their own negligence; they have ended in bankruptcy, despite all the hard work of their subjects.

Protocol No. 21

On domestic loans

I will add one more detail regarding domestic loans, in addition to the report that I made at the last meeting. I will not speak further about foreign loans; they have already filled our coffers with the national money of the Goyim. There will be no foreigners in our government, no outsiders.

We profited by the corruption of the Goy administrators and by the negligence of their rulers, receiving sums that were doubled, trebled, and even more, by loaning money to the Goy governments that they didn't need at all. Who could do the same with us? No one. Therefore, I will only set forth details regarding domestic loans.

In announcing such a loan, governments open a subscription to their bonds. To make them accessible to all, they vary the denomination from 100 to thousands, and the first subscribers are allowed to buy below face value. The following day, the price is artificially raised, on the pretext that everyone hurried to buy the bonds. In a few more days, there is a pretense that the treasury is filled and no one knows what to do with the money that has been oversubscribed. (What was the use of taking it, then?) The subscription is evidently considerably in excess of the amount needed. Therein lies the true effect: by such means, the public demonstrates its confidence in the government obligations.

But after this farce has been played out, the fact of the debt remains, and it is usually a heavy one. In order to pay the interest, new loans have to be issued, which do not liquidate but increase the original debt. Then when the borrowing capacity of the government has been exhausted, it becomes necessary to meet the interest on the loan—not the loan itself—by new taxes. These taxes are nothing but a debt used to cover another debt.

Then comes the period of loan conversions.[19] But these only decrease the payment of interest; they do not annul the debts. Moreover, they cannot be made without the consent of the bondholders. When a conversion is advertised, an offer is made to return the money to those who are not willing to convert their bonds. If everyone were to demand his money, the government would be caught in its own net and unable to

---

[19] What we today would call "refinancing".

return it all. Fortunately, the Goy subjects, ignorant of financial affairs, always preferred to suffer a decline in the value of their securities and a reduction of interest to the risk of new investments; thus, they have given these governments more than one opportunity for ridding a deficit of several millions. At present, with the existence of foreign loans, the Goyim cannot play such tricks because they know that we would demand all the money back. By such action, the government would openly admit its own bankruptcy, which would plainly show the people that their own interests have nothing in common with those of their government

Pay attention to the above circumstances, as also to the following: At present, all domestic loans are consolidated into so-called 'temporary loans'—in other words, loans of short-term repayment. Such debts consist of money placed in savings banks. Being at the disposal of the government for a considerable length of time, these funds vanish in the payment of interest on foreign loans, and they are replaced by an equal amount of government securities. The latter cover all the deficits in the Goy government treasuries.

When we mount the world-throne, such financial expedients, being detrimental to our interests, will vanish. We will also destroy all stock exchanges, for we will not allow the prestige of our authority to be shaken by the shifting prices of our securities. We will legally set the full price of their value, without any possibility of its fluctuation. (A rise leads to a fall, and this was precisely what we did to the Goy stocks and bonds at the beginning.)

We will replace the stock exchanges by great government credit institutions, whose function will be to tax commercial values according to governmental plans. These institutions will be in a position to issue millions of shares of industrial stock per day, or to buy up a similar amount. Therefore, all industrial enterprises will become dependent upon us. You can well imagine what power that will give us.

Protocol No. 22

On restoring social order

In all that I have reported to you so far, I have carefully tried to show a true picture of the mystery of present events, as also of those of the past, which all flow into the stream of great events. We will soon see the results of this process. I have explained our secret plans that govern our relations with the Goyim, as well as our financial policy. There is little left to say.

We hold in our hands the greatest modern power—gold. In just a few days, we can get any quantity desired from our treasuries. Is there any more need for us to prove that our rule is decreed by God? Doesn't such wealth prove that all the evil that we were forced to commit over the centuries has, in the end, served the cause of true happiness—the restoration of order? It may yet require some level of violence to restore order.

We can prove that we are benefactors who have brought true welfare and individual freedom to a tortured world, also ensuring the possibility of enjoying peace, quiet, and dignified relationships—upon the condition, of course, that all are obedient to the laws we will establish.

We will also make it clear that freedom does not mean license to do whatever people please, no more than dignity and power imply the right to promote destructive doctrines like freedom of religion, equality, and similar things. Individual freedom by no means includes the right of disturbing oneself and others, or of disgracing oneself by making ridiculous speeches in disorderly gatherings; it implies that true liberty means individual inviolability through an honest and strict obedience to social laws; that, moreover, human dignity implies the conception of one's rights as well as the idea of inhibitions that discourage fantastic but selfish dreams.

Our power will be glorious because it will be mighty. It will rule and guide, and not helplessly crawl after leaders and orators, shouting insane words that they call 'great principles,' and which in reality are simply idealistic. Our power will lead to order, which, in turn, brings happiness to the people. The prestige of this power will excite mystical adoration, and the people will bow before it. True power does not yield to any right, even that of God. None will dare attempt even a minuscule diminishment of its power.

Protocol No. 23

On the arising of the Sovereign

In order to teach the people obedience, they must be taught modesty. And to accomplish this, the production of luxuries must be limited. We will thus improve public morality, which has been demoralized by competition resulting from luxury.

We will restore handicraft, which will undermine the private capital of manufacturers. This is necessary because big manufacturers often subconsciously sway the people's thoughts against the government. A people who practices handicraft does not know the meaning of unemployment; this makes them cling to existing conditions and consequently to the power of authority. Unemployment is most dangerous for a government; its work will be completed—as instigated by us—when we obtain power.

Drunkenness will also be forbidden by law, and will be punishable as a crime against human decency; man becomes bestial under the influence of alcohol.

*****

I say once again that people blindly obey only the hand that is strong and entirely independent of them—the hand that wields a sword of defense against the blows of social misfortune. Why should the Sovereign have an angel's heart? The people want to see in him the personification of power and might.

A Sovereign must arise who will supersede existing governments—governments whose people have been demoralized by us through the flames of anarchy. Such a ruler must begin by extinguishing these flames, which are incessantly springing up from all sides. Therefore, he must destroy any such society, drowning it, if necessary, in its own blood; he must resurrect it as a well-organized army that consciously struggles against the infection of further anarchy. Our Sovereign will be chosen by God and appointed from above, in order to destroy all ideas influenced by instinct and not by reason, or by brutal principles and not by humanitarianism.

These anarchic forces are now triumphant, and assume the form of theft and violence exercised in the name of liberty and rights. They have destroyed all social organizations, and now help to establish the throne of the King of Israel. But their role will be ended with his coming to power. Then it will be necessary to sweep them from his path, so that not a speck of dust impedes his way.

Then we will say to the peoples: "Pray to God, and bow before he who bears the mark of predestination—to he whose star God has guided, so that none but He Himself will free you from sin."

Protocol No. 24

On the Sovereign, the King of Israel

Finally, I shall refer to the manner in which we will strengthen the dynasty of King David, so that it will endure until the final day. This method will consist chiefly of the same principles that enabled our Wise Men to conserve their power in order to cope with universal problems and to educate humanity at large.

Certain members of the seed of David will train the Sovereigns and their successors, who will be selected not by right of inheritance but according to their personal ability. We will confide in them the deep political mysteries and the plan of our rule, but in such a wise manner that none will know these secrets. The aim of this method is to prove to everyone that power will only be given to those initiated in the mysteries of political art. Only such men will be taught how to apply the above-mentioned plans in practice, by comparing them with the experiences of many centuries; only they will be initiated in the conclusions drawn from all the observations of political, economic, and social movements and sciences; in short, only they will know the true spirit of the laws irrevocably established by nature for the purpose of governing mankind.

Direct descendants of the Sovereign will be prevented from inheriting the throne if, during their period of study, they show signs of frivolity, lenience, or other tendencies detrimental to authority that would make them incapable of governing and thus dangerous to the prestige of the Crown. Only qualified men, even if cruel, will receive the reins of government from our Wise Men.

In case of illness, loss of will-power, or any other form of incapacity, the Sovereigns will be compelled to hand over the reins of government to new and able hands.

The Sovereign's immediate plan of action and its future application will be unknown, even to the so-called closest advisers. Only the Sovereign and the three who initiated him will know the future. In the person of the Sovereign, with his unshakeable will over himself and humanity, the people will see *Fate itself*, with its mysterious ways. No one will know the Sovereign's aims when he issues his orders, and thus no one will dare oppose him.

Naturally, the Sovereign's mental capacity must be equal to the plan of rule outlined here. For this reason, he will not mount the throne before his mind has been tested by our Wise Men.

To make people know and love their Sovereign, it is necessary that he should address the people in public places, thus establishing a harmony between two forces—the people and their ruler—that are now separated from each other by mutual terror. This terror was necessary for us, until the time came to make both forces fall under our influence.

The King of Israel must not be influenced by his passions, especially by sensuality. No particular element of his nature must have the upper hand and rule over his mind. More than anything else, sensuality upsets mental ability and clearness of vision by deflecting thoughts toward the worst and most bestial side of human nature. The Pillar of the Cosmos, in the person of the World Ruler, sprung from the sacred seed of David, must sacrifice all personal desires for the benefit of his people. Our Sovereign must be irreproachable.

PART THREE

NATIONAL SOCIALIST COMMENTARIES

ROSENBERG ON THE *PROTOCOLS*

Editor: The following is drawn from Alfred Rosenberg's Introduction and short Afterword to his book *The Protocols of the Elders of Zion and Jewish World-Politics* (1924)—never before translated into English. The Introduction is of interest because it emphasizes the reality of the Protocols' 'prophecy' of Jewish world domination. Here, the 30-year-old Rosenberg presents detailed evidence for Jewish control over several major nations and over the UN-precursor, the League of Nations. In this way, he demonstrates the truth value of the Protocols, even if their origins remain uncertain. For his detailed study of the Protocols themselves, the reader will have to await translation of the remainder of his book.

When the Protocols appeared in the German language at the end of 1919, they immediately caused a tremendous sensation. Millions suddenly found in them the interpretation of many otherwise inexplicable phenomena of the present day; the most important of these events suddenly seemed not to be coincidences but rather the result of a previously secret, now revealed cooperation of the leaders of apparently opposed classes, parties, and peoples. The publication in 1919 received tremendous weight from the fact that it was demonstrably not a recently-constructed program, but rather reproduced a document that had already played a cautionary role decades ago—but without earning the necessary attention.

Naturally, the most violent attacks by the entire Jewish world press were directed against this, when the appearance of the book—despite all efforts—could no longer be prevented and it could no longer be hushed up. The publishers claimed that the work had been handed over to the British government by the Russians as early as 1906 and was in the British Museum under a certain catalogue number. This is where the Jewish campaign began first. A report out of the "Jewish Press Center in Zürich" made the rounds through all Jewish and Jewish-influenced newspapers of all nations (accounting for 90% of all major papers), claiming that the document was a blatant fabrication. A member of the Zürich Museum

Society, in order to know the truth, inquired in London whether it was true that the Russian work was classified under the number "3296 d 17." A Christian scholar in London replied that this was not true. Consequently, one of the biggest lies of the "reactionary anti-Semites" was exposed as such (see, for example, the *Tribüne juive*, No. 65, 1921.).

Monsignor Jouin in Paris, who should be commended for the disclosure of the Jewish plans, then had investigations carried out in London as well, resulting in the discovery that the work in question really is in the British Museum, under call number "3926 d 17." As can be seen, the Jews gave it a false number by rearranging two of the numbers, and then announced to the world that the malign work, which the anti-Semites had lied about, was not there.

Such attempts at falsification have been made several times. For a while, the German colony of Jewry spread the myth that the Protocols were largely copied from the novel *Biarritz*, an "anti-Semitic pamphlet." The novel in question, from 1869, has now been loaned out from the Munich State Library, and a local group, the *Deutschvölkische Schutz- und Trutzbund* (the German Nationalist Protection and Defense League) in Nuremberg offered a large prize for successfully proving the above assertion. The price is still outstanding today. The second attempt at deception was unsuccessful.

It was no different with the claim coming from the Paris ghetto that Russian anti-Semites had plundered Monsieur Joly's *Dialogues aux enfers entre Machiavelli et Montesquieu* from 1871. It turned out that this Joly himself was a Hebrew (born Moses Joël) and one of the leaders of the commune.

Incidentally, those who know Judaism claim that the thoughts and plans express in the Protocols are not unheard of in Jewish history, but rather, can found in Jewish literature through all the centuries up to the present time.

Similar to the aforementioned attempts at deception, a number of other maneuvers were made to make the Protocols appear to be a forgery. But all the efforts of *Tribune juive*, *Peuple juif*, *L'Univers israélite*, *Archives Israélites* of *Jewish World*, *Jüdischen Rundschau*, *Israeliten*, *Hamburger Israelitisches Familienblatt* and all the other openly and covertly Hebrew newspapers and magazines, ended with new defeats. Through these attempts, however, the probability of authenticity became a certainty even for many doubters. The story that Russian secret police, after the First Zionist Congress in Basel in 1897, had procured a copy of the minutes, lectures, discussions, or whatever one might call the collection, and handed it over for publication to Sergei Nilus, known as a connoisseur of Judaism—and still living in hiding in Russia today—remains the most probable.

It goes without saying that the anti-Jewish camp looked around for the actual author of the Protocols, and the writings of the most important Zionists and participants in the Zionist Congress of 1897 were thoroughly examined. Three men, in particular, were investigated: Theodor Herzl, Max Nordau, and Ahad Ha'am (Asher Ginzberg).[1] Let us consider each of them for a moment.

Theodor Herzl's diaries did not appear until 1922, but their style betrays a different character from the Protocols—although they clearly show that this fervent Jew was well informed about the power of Jewish high finance, that he knew exactly how the private stock market intended cancerous damage for the peoples of Europe, and he proposed defensive measures for the Jewish state. Even his public speech at the Congress in Basel leaves nothing to be desired in terms of clarity and menacing tone, despite all its "submissiveness." Also of great interest is a 1919 confession by the Zionist Littmann Rosenthal (in the *American Jewish News* of September 19), which reports that Nordau gave a speech in Paris in 1903 (!) that prophesied World War [One], the [Versailles] peace conference, and a Jewish state of Palestine under the protectorate of England—in other words, exactly what happened in 1914 and ended in 1919 in San Remo, with the British Mandate. In this speech, Nordau said, among other things: "Herzl knows (!) that we are confronting the whole world with a terrible shock." Herzl knew it. Why? Because he knew of forces that were consciously working towards catastrophe.

And then 22 year later, the Berlin *Jüdische Rundschau* (No. 86, 1918) reported, in a disarmingly naïve way:

> Two things must be made clear: that the English (!) declarations are not a miraculous coincidence, but instead, *the*

---

[1] Herzl (1860-1904), Nordau (1849-1923), and Ha'am/Ginzburg (1856-1927) were leading Zionist intellectuals circa 1900.

> *result of 25 years of systematic (!!) work* carried out by and for the Jewish people; and secondly, that it calls the Jewish people to new responsibilities, conversions (!!), and for a determined effort unprecedented in our history.

That's actually more than one can ask from a Jewish mouth in black-and-white; and whether the Jewish world stock exchange now believes that it has achieved its goals or not, it is openly admitted that there is a plan, a decades-old plan, behind today's Jewish world politics. The things that flow unconsciously from Jewish pens, so to speak, are therefore all the more valuable testimonies.

But to the point, no matter how well-informed Nordau and Herzl may have been, they themselves hardly wrote the proposals laid down in the lectures—even if they certainly participated in their elaboration.

Leslie Fry's suspicion arguably comes much closer to the truth when she tried to prove (in the journal *Vieille France*) that Ahad Ha'am—one of the most important Hebrew writers, who is now living in Jerusalem and is praised by all Zionists as the "great prophet"—is also the actual author of the Protocols. Her booklet (*L'auteur des Protocols : Ahad Ha'am, et le Zionisme*, 1921) devoted to this investigation (translated into Russian and German) is quite interesting in some respects, but, to tell the truth, its argument is unconvincing. The question of authorship therefore, for the time being, remains open.

More important are the comments about Ahad Ha'am by Dr. Shmaryahu Levin, one of the leading American Zionists, at a large mass meeting in Berlin:

> For the time being, the right place for the idea [of a League of Nations], which is only anticipated, can be found neither in Geneva nor in The Hague. A Jewish thinker, who is not only a strict logician, as some believe, but also a great seer of our future, Ahad Ha'am dreamed of a temple on Mount Zion, where the representatives of all nations will dedicate a temple to eternal peace (*Jüdische Rundschau*, No. 82/83, 1921).

These words, which call for the Masonic-Jewish Temple of Solomon in Jerusalem to be the center of world politics, are no longer spoken about in secret sessions but in public meetings. And Ahad Ha'am is the "soothsayer" of these times.

*****

Various weak, paranoid passages, sometimes apparently crazy, were cited in the Protocols as proof against its authenticity. If, it was said, the whole plan for the destruction of Europe was so ingenious and so well thought out, that measures that were declared almost "crazy" had already become a fact today, then it would mean that the Jewish spirit would be overestimated if one wanted to acknowledge the above concerns as valid. It is characteristic of the whole of Jewish history that the Jews, whenever they exercised financial control in any state, finally lost their self-control; then, apparently in inexplicable, short-sighted impudence, they called all forces *against themselves*. Thanks to this lack of restraint, they brought about their own downfall.[2] This narrow-mindedness—which, despite all comprehension, sharply breaks through everywhere—coupled with a blood-red hatred of everything non-Jewish, speaks in the Protocols (and elsewhere) of a Jewish conspiracy; this is true from the Talmud to the *Frankfurter Zeitung* and the *Rote Fahne*.

So, as things stand today, neither legally conclusive proof for its absolute authenticity, nor for its fabrication, can be produced. Some of the leaders of the Zionist Conference of 1897 have died, and others will be very reluctant to admit the truth. And the Russians who procured the original copy 25 years ago are also long dead. But apart from the obviousness of today's world situation, there are still documents from earlier times, as well as from the most recent present, which ooze out from both the deepest Jewish subconscious and from a power-conscious arrogance, and which have exactly the same meaning as the reviled *Protocols of the Elders of Zion*.

A Most Revealing Pamphlet

Before the war, the center of Jewish world politics was in London. It was Herzl who described England—"which spans the world with its gaze"— as the "starting point" of the Zionist idea. Here, the almighty House of Rothschild had its headquarters, and Disraeli-Beaconsfield systematically

---

[2] See Rosenberg's book *The Track of the Jew Through the Ages*.

prepared the foundation.³ With the permission of the British government, a book entitled *The Jews Among the Entente Leaders* was published in 1918 for private use. This work, which has so far only been completely translated into French, contains a short biography of 16 leading Jewish personalities from the Entente states. Here we see judges, bankers, politicians, and labor leaders together as brothers and sisters, openly proclaimed as Jewish representatives. This alone should be enough to point out the fraud—as if these people became "English", "French", or "American."

The book begins with the following words: "The purpose of this little pamphlet is to give a sketch of the careers of some (!!) of the most important leading Jews among the peoples of the Entente, and to indicate their part in this world-struggle for the Allied cause." Furthermore, after repeated reference to the diplomatic achievements, it refers to:

> The Earl of Reading [Rufus Isaacs], on his mission to the United States to establish the spirit of brotherhood between the two great English-speaking races on either side of the Atlantic Ocean; Mr. [Bernard] Baruch and Mr. Samuel Gompers, charged with looking after the economic resources of the United States in order to direct and control this world struggle; and Mr. [Otto] Kahn, who—although of German origin—shook off the yoke of Prussian militarism and proved a devoted and enthusiastic supporter of the Allied cause by his largesse and testimony, which testified to the justice of this cause. They are all representatives of thousands of Jews, each of whom plays a part in the allied nations in the struggle for the triumph of democracy and liberty.⁴

Anyone who is impartial will admit that these words indicate an awareness of the domination of the political and economic life of the Entente peoples. When all the power of control over American industry lies in the hands of two men, openly claiming to be Jews, this signifies a recognition

---

³ Benjamin Disraeli (1804-1881), 1ˢᵗ Earl of Beaconsfield, was the first Jewish prime minister of the UK.
⁴ Isaacs, Baruch, and Gompers were, of course, all Jewish.

of a Jewish financial dictatorship.[5] Bernard Baruch was also in charge of all commercial agreements between the United States and 26 Entente powers. He delivered all profitable purchase orders to the Lewinsohns, the copper king Guggenheim,[6] and the steel trust magnate Charles Schwab.[7] Systematically, the proceeds of labor from entire nations were channeled into the pockets of Abraham's sons.

When Jakob Schiff died—he who financed Japan's war against Russia and later the 1917 Revolution (which the "Jewish Press" reported triumphantly on 15 October 1920)—the courts in New York celebrated for two full days, and the *Israelit* declared in unison with all Jewry: "Among the great Jews of our age, Jakob H. Schiff's name will shine forth in the first place" (No. 40, 1920).

Soon afterward, the head of the house of Guggenheim died, and the Jewish newspapers of the world gleefully announced that he might have been the richest Jew—and after Rockefeller, the richest man—in America, adding unanimously: "The Guggenheims control the world's (entire!) copper market".[8]

In the course of my publications, I often address similar portents to our shameful contemporary situation. In this regard, I recall the words that close the introduction to the pamphlet, and with which the Protocols themselves could conclude, so much do they correspond to their spirit:

> Let us hope that the joint efforts of the Jewish representatives of the Entente Powers are the symbol of a greater unity that will be born after the war, not with a goal of annihilation and destruction, as is presently inevitable, but to create a better and happier world in which Hebrew (!!) ideals of right and justice will prevail.

---

[5] Rosenberg adds a parenthetical note to see Henry Ford's *International Jew*, volume 2.
[6] A reference to either Isaac or Daniel Guggenheim.
[7] Schwab (1862-1939) was an American steel magnate who ran Bethlehem Steel for many years. He is apparently unrelated to Charles R. Schwab (b. 1937), founder of the American financial agency that bears his name.
[8] *Israelitisches Wochenblatt für der Schweiz,* No. 44, 1922; *Hamburger Israelitisches Familienblatt,* No. 40, 1922, etc.

So an even greater consolidation of Jewish financial power is prophesied, and Hebrew "ideals" are to rule the world. If anything speaks for the authenticity of the Protocols, it is this testimony from a Jewish pen, which saw the light of day 21 years after the First Zionist Congress. It represents—in terms of content and tone—the fulfillment of plans from the 19th century, and already points bluntly to further goals.

But in order to forestall the objection that this pamphlet might also be a "forgery," and a delusional product of anti-Semitism, it should be noted that this work, which was only intended for a small number of Hebrews, has been recognized as genuine by the Central Association of German Citizens of Jewish Faith. The photographs, together with precise details of the photographers and other things, made denial impossible from the outset. But at least it's interesting how the ever-vigilant Central Association of so-called German Citizens would like to portray this Jewish triumphant cry as innocuous. A certain Mr. B. S. writes in the *C. B. Zeitung* (No. 14, 1922):

> The little book is not uninteresting; it contains the biographies of some Jewish personalities in the Entente states, who, as politicians and statesmen…, rendered excellent service to their home countries during the war. It is kept in a simple tone, without any (!) boasting and pandering… If this writing had reached the general public through the book trade, it would have come across as boastfulness and importune. Therefore (!), it was only intended for narrow circle (!).

The proclamation of Jewish rule also has a "simple tone" for "German" Jews. And how humble the Hebrews suddenly become when writings meant for their "narrow circle" come to light.

Four "Great Englishmen"

It remains for the time being to emphasize the individual points that the Jewish authors of this above-mentioned highly interesting work identify with full satisfaction, in order to thus obtain an immediate general picture of present-day world politics.

First, there is the former Mayor of London (the fifth Jew since 1900!), and Member of Parliament, Herbert Louis Samuel. Of this "Englishman," it is proudly told that he "enthusiastically surrendered himself to the interests and pursuit of the goals of Zionism." This means that, as an "Englishman," he can openly pursue Jewish nationalist aspirations.

Incidentally, he was appointed Viceroy of Palestine, endowed with the highest decorations by the English King, received an audience with the Pope on the journey to the "Land of the Fathers," and then sailed into Jaffa on an English battleship amid the thunder of the harbor batteries. Today he lives in the appropriated German Protestant hospital in Jerusalem, has almost exclusively Jewish officials around him, and rules the promised land as a Hebrew autocrat with the help of British soldier coolies. For these English mercenaries of the Jewish Stock Exchange of London, the British taxpayers have to pay £500,000 a month.

The acknowledged leader of the World Zionist Federation, Chaim Weizmann, was right when he said of Herbert Samuel: "He is a product of Judaism... It was we who put Samuel in this post" (*L'Univers Israelite*, 16 September 1921, p. 513).

The second leading Jew mentioned is Edwin Samuel Montague, the second son of the Jewish Lord Swaythling, a "Pillar of English Jewry" and a Member of Parliament. In 1906 he became "private secretary" to Mr. Asquith.[9] Montague was later appointed Secretary of Finance, then Minister of Munitions (again a post involving supervision and dictatorial distribution of raw materials). It should be noted that this Montague is closely associated with the Montague Jewish bank in London, which—together with the Sassoons, of whom David Sassoon is governor of Bombay—can claim a monopoly on the exploitation of India.

Just behind Montague is Lord Reading, born Rufus Isaacs, notorious as a fellow speculator with Lloyd George in the Marconi scandal. He was made the first Chief Justice of England, then made Lord, presumably

---

[9] Compare: the Jew Philipp Sassoon as "private secretary" of Lloyd George; the Jew Hugo Oberndoerffer of Loubet; the Jew Mandel as "private secretary" of Clemenceau; before the war it was the Hebrews Cornelius Herz, Goudchaux, and Roth; the Jew Louis Strauss as "private secretary" of the American food dictator [Herbert] Hoover; the Jewish "private secretary" and press officer Tschitscherins, Rosenberg; the Jewish "private secretary" Cahen at the German peace delegation in Versailles, later at Brockdorff-Rantzau in Moscow.

because of his predisposition to "Jewish ideals of justice." During the war, he was "English" Ambassador in New York, and now Viceroy of India—which he helps to plunder with the opium-Jew Sassoon, the Jewish Secretary of Finance Lionel Abrahams, and others.

The fourth great "Englishman" is Alfred Mond, "one of the most important authorities in England on economic questions." He is involved in the "largest industrial ventures in the world," and also owns a number of newspapers.[10]

In summation, it notes about Alfred Mond: "Sir Alfred is one of those English Jews who is proud of his Jewish origins; he is a very energetic representative of the Zionist movement." I add that this English Minister for Public Works is on the board of the United Israel Appeal and has, more than once, made threatening speeches to the very state that tolerates him as a Minister. For example, as an English minister, he once said in a speech at Oxford:

> Firstly, I wish to state in advance that I am not speaking in my capacity as a member of His Majesty's Government, but as a Jew. I would consider myself a coward, quite unworthy of the citizenship I possess, if I chose another path. The Jewish Race must interest those who have the honor of belonging to it. ...
>
> This (Balfour) declaration was, it seems to me, a great act of statesmanlike wisdom and characteristic of the great man who gave it, one of the greatest of living British statesmen. It had the intended and immediate success of uniting on the side of the Allies, in the midst of the World War, a tremendous sum of Jewish sympathy in the countries of all (!!) continents. And although I know many may

---

[10] The extent to which the English press is directed by the Jewish stock exchange is shown in the *Völkischer Beobachter* (No. 103, 1923), where 29 newspapers and magazines are listed, all of which are dependent on Jews or belong to them directly. For example, *The Times*, by Leiter Preuss and Ellermann; *Daily Telegraph* is owned by the Jewish Lord Burnham (Levy); *Westminster Gazette*, owner Alfred Mond; *Daily News*, the organ of Cocoa, Cohen & Co.; *Daily Graphy*, spiritual director Lucien Wolff, etc. See also Winzer, *The Jewish Question in England*.

think superficially (!) that sympathy, for such a mighty empire, is of little importance, and that the effect of the sympathy thus won has not been very significant. But I would remind you that the next largest foreign population in the United States after the Irish is the Jewish population, and that the sympathy and support of a large stratum with a significant influence on public opinion was not without value at the time when the Americans were preparing to join the war with the Allies. ... [*In other words, the Jews drove America into war against Germany.*][11]

The Mandate was given on the basis of a clear (!) commitment that a Jewish national home should be established there, and that no home should be established there unless the Jews were allowed to go there.

The land must be handed over to the people [*i.e. taken from the Arabs and handed over to the Jews*], and any countermeasures could not be justified and upheld (!!) before a body such as the League of Nations…

There were other states that would have been proud (!!) to accept the Mandate and implement it on the basis of the provisions of the Balfour Declaration, but they believed firmly in the word of the British government and the British people, and wished that Great Britain should take over the Mandate... (*Jüdische Rundschau*, No. 20, 1922).

After these ingenious Englishmen followed two "Frenchmen" from the Jewish world ghetto. First, the French-Jewish Minister of Finance during the war, Lucien Klotz, and the present Deputy, who can't get enough of insulting Germany and demanding more and more in extortion; secondly, Joseph Reinach, the notorious journalist and Knight of the Legion of Honor of the Rothschild Republic.

Shortly before Italy was about to enter the war, a significant appointment took place there: Sidney Sonnino, the Alexandrian-born son of a Jewish banker, millionaire, high-degree mason, and friend of England, became Italian Foreign Minister. Everyone who knew anything about

---

[11] For details, see T. Dalton, *The Jewish Hand in the World Wars* (2019).

politics now knew that the hands pointed to war. The Jewish work states dryly: "Italy had not yet entered the war [after Giuliano's death], but under the leadership of Baron Sonnino, after a few months, she took her place at the side of the Allies, and has always been a loyal ally in their successes and in their tragedies." They are followed by Luigi Luzatti, the Italian Minister of Justice, and the Trentino Jew Barzilai (Burzel), Minister without portfolio.

Top American Jews

Then we may examine the American Hebrews. At their head is a leader of American Zionism, Chief Justice Louis Dembitz Brandeis (high brother in the all-Jewish Order of B'nai B'rith). It literally says of him:

> Since his election to the Supreme Court and his move to Washington (!), he has been one of the closest and most favored advisers to the President [Wilson]. Not only has he been consulted on all matters relating to commerce and industry, on which he is a well-known authority in the United States, but his sound (!) judgment was also requested by the President when the international situation was concerned. A committee, consisting of the House of Lords and Mr. Brandeis, was appointed to study world issues and lay down the broad lines of American policy at the Peace Conference.

At this "Peace Conference" the leadership of the American Asian policy was handed over to the Jewish nationalist Zionists: Brandeis, [Julien] Mack, and [Louis] Marshall. As the *Revue antimaconnique* reported at the time, Wilson was accompanied by 156 advisors. Of these, 117 are said to have been Jews.

In addition, it should be added that the all-Jewish financial paper *Frankfurter Zeitung* cynically declared that under Wilson, the party machines—all, not just one—were "almost exclusively" determined by high finance (9 October 1922). In plain language: Jewish finance rushed America into the war to make profits in the war and in the stock market. And all along, the Jew whispering in Wilson's ear was: Louis Brandeis.

And yet another did the same: the trade union leader Samuel Gompers, who is also listed as a great Jew among the "leaders of the Entente." He was followed by Oskar Strauss, who was born in Otterberg (Germany). The "German" Jew was the American Ambassador in Constantinople three times; he was also President of the Chamber of Commerce, the International Law Association, etc. The Jewish pamphlet hailed him as one of "the most influential Jewish leaders of modern times." Oskar Strauss' brother, Nathan Strauss, is said to have been a great "philanthropist". The "German" *Hamburger Israelitisches Sonntagsblatt* (No. 37, 1921) also celebrated him as such. This Strauss was one of the biggest agitators against Germany and declared in a letter to the French ambassador that the enthusiasm for the cause of the Entente among the Jews could be described as unanimous.

After the Strauss brothers comes the aforementioned Bernard Baruch, America's unrestricted economic dictator. The Jewish writing says of the Bureau of Industries, for which the hitherto virtually unknown Baruch was appointed chairman:

> This office is not only an agency for production, but it is also the broker of [that is, *all*] Allied purchases, and it effectively controls the world's supply of essential materials. Indeed, Mr. Baruch has complete authority over everything that industries receive in the United States.

Is there anything more that can be said in black-and-white?!

A particular favorite of pan-Judah seems to be the "American" Otto Hermann Kahn, who was born in Mannheim. He is described as having a good knowledge of Germany and, as I said, the most loyal supporter of the Entente, so he is again one of the thousands of examples that have already been given of "German" Jews becoming Germany's most venomous enemies. This does not prevent German Reich Chancellors, such as Dr. Karl Wirth, from asking us to pray for the help of this Otto Kahn.

On 1 June 1918, the Parisian *Journal* published an interview with Mr. Otto H. Kahn. This man was summoned by a German chancellor and openly declared that he wished for the defeat of the new Germany. "And I can assure you," he continued, "that 70 percent of the 12 million German-Americans share the same hope." So, when asked if he preferred

France to Germany, this scoundrel replied: "Most certainly; isn't France admirable? Be assured that all America is on your side. Hold out for three or four months, and you will hear no more cannon fire here from Paris, and that will be victory." The representative of the *Journal* concludes with the expression: "Ah, if only all Germans could be like this one in the future!" The essay is headed: "A German-American who hates Germany." To complete the disgraceful picture, it should be noted that this German Jewish American warmonger and banker is a Knight in the French Legion of Honor.

Finally, the book names Abraham Elkus, America's ambassador to Constantinople after the Jew Henry Morgenthau. And to complete the honor roll comes Paul Hymans, the former Belgian Minister for Foreign Affairs, the retired President of the League of Nations, and current President of the Council of the League of Nations.

Jewry in England

Thus ends this highly important document, which I have dealt with in some detail because it is completely unknown in Germany—only Count Reventlow mentioned it once in his weekly, *Der Reichswart*. In order to understand its full scope, a general overview is necessary because the 16 personalities mentioned represent only a fraction of those men who today almost autocratically determine the politics of all countries. If we follow the same state divisions as given in the Jewish pamphlet, we can add a number of other names to those of Reading, Herbert Samuel, Montague, and Mond.

Since the reign of Edward VII, when baronetcies and peerages were sold to profiteers of all kinds for massive amounts of money, Jewish high finance has increasingly nested in the English nobility; today we already see a dozen Jewish lords sitting in the English upper house. In addition to the rule of India and Palestine by the representatives of high finance, there are now a number of other colonies ruled by the Hebrews. For example, as Zionist leader Cohen notes with great satisfaction, the President and Vice-President of the Parliament of New South Wales [Australia] are

Jews, and the House once had to suspend its work because these two Jews were...in the synagogue (*Jüdische Rundschau,* Nr. 33/ 34, 1921).[12]

Furthermore, the commander of the Australian Army Corps, John Monash, is a descendant of Abraham, as is Matheus Nathan, Governor of Queensland (*Forward,* No. 277, 1921). And the English representatives at all major world conferences were of course always accompanied by a representative of Jewish high finance (mostly by Anthony Rothschild). It was therefore understandable when old Lord Balfour publicly declared at a mass meeting in London: "We have embarked on a great enterprise—I say expressly we, the Jews and England. We are comrades in this enterprise" (*Jüdische Rundschau,* No. 49, 1920). Jewish financial dictatorship in England found its expression in the well-known Balfour Declaration, the wording of which cannot be emphasized to all Europeans often enough. This note reads, in full:

> His Majesty's Government view with favour the establishment in Palestine of a national home for the Jewish people, and will use their best endeavours (!) to facilitate the achievement of this object, it being clearly understood that nothing shall be done which may prejudice the civil and religious rights of existing non-Jewish communities in Palestine, or the rights and political status enjoyed by Jews in any other country.

As the Jews, beaming with joy, discovered after the war, this note was not written by the British government but by Zionist leaders, and then presented to Lord Balfour for signature, who in turn sent it to Lord Rothschild. As can be seen from the wording, the English state took on the

---

[12] The following exploits of George V of England are also perhaps worth noting. In honor of his birthday, he made the merchant Jew David Stern a baronet; knighted the government expert in the diamond trade, the Jew Arthur Levy; Lord Reading (Rufus Isaacs) received the Grand Cross of the Order of Victoria; the Jew Isaacs, Judge in the Australian High Court, was made a member of the Private Cabinet. In Palestine, the celebration of the royal birthday was postponed because of a Jewish festival (*Jewish Chronicle,* 9 June 1922). On the same day, this Jewish newspaper reported that the King of Italy had received a Jewish delegation in Trieste and had shown great interest in Jewish affairs.

obligation to stand up for the so-called rights of the Jews *in all countries*. In other words, British politics made itself the servant of pan-Judah high finance. In recent years, the English government has carried out these agent services in Poland (where England's representative for a long time was the Jew Müller; see *Journal de Pologne* 5 May 1922), Hungary, and Romania (which was represented in Washington by the Jew Leon Feraru). For all the details, see my work, *Der staatsfeindliche Zionismus* (Subversive Zionism).

Jewry in France

France behaved very much like England before the war, and even more so during and after it. Apart from the world-political facts mentioned, one must not forget that in Clemenceau's time, the Jew Georges Mandel stood by his side as "private secretary," and through his fingers ran all the diplomatic files of the French Prime Minister. Raymond Poincare, who was addressed as a tyrant, also had to repeatedly express his "willingness" to stand up for the so-called rights of the Jews in many interviews forced upon him.

After the war, as a senator and future Prime Minister, Poincare received the director of the Jewish press office in France, Heinrich Braunstein, in an audience in which he promised his support for Judaism. *Le peuple juif* reports (21 July 1921) that, after this conversation, Mr. Braunstein declared in a circle of journalists and politicians that he had been delighted with this reception. And the correspondent of the journal *Die Zeit* featured the interview of a Zionist with Poincare, in which he advocated the immigration of Jews to France, adding that the Jews in France would quickly become French patriots: "There is no danger of anti-Semitic excesses in France," concluded Poincare, "since the smallest attempt carries the heaviest penalties" (*La Tribüne juive*, 9 September 1921).

There can therefore be no doubt about Poincare's position; the consequences of such a kowtowing are evident in the increasing number of new appointments of long-established and newly-immigrated Hebrews. Thus a Monsieur Heugle, Director of Departmental Administration, was appointed Councilor of State. Mr. Dadoune, Algerian Jew, was appointed Sub-Prefect of Florac. Thanks to the protection of powerful financiers, Mr. Levi-Brühl rose to become a lecturer on French law. A Mr. Kahn was appointed procurator in Melun. Mr. Alphandery was appointed vice-president of the Parisian Commercial Court. And the Jew Bernhard Wellhof rose to become the Freemasonic Grand Master of the Grand Orient de France, whereby the *Archives Israelites* (29 September 1921) added with satisfaction that the Scottish rite already knew two other Jewish Grand Masters—namely, Adolf Cremieux and Marco Allegri.

It should also be added that three Jews hold decisive positions on the Budget Commission of the French Republic: Leon Blum, the Socialist; Lucien Klotz, the former Minister of Finance; and Maurice Bokanowski, a Jewish profiteer from Poland. Bokanowski was appointed Chief Officer on the French budget (*L'Univers Israelites*, 8 June 1921, p. 266). Poincare later made him Minister of the Navy.

The Republic of Rothschild was crowned with dignity by Mr. Alexandre Millerand. The grandfather of this ex-president of France was a clerk in the synagogue in the street Notre Dame de Nazareth; the young Alexandre was brought up by his uncle Ephraim Cahen, who was loyal to the Talmud (*Archives Israelites*, 30 September 1920). On the occasion of a church celebration, this Jewish newspaper triumphed: "The services in the cathedral were attended by: M. Millerand and the Marshals of France. A piquant detail: Father Cahen's grandson was greeted here by a whole procession of cardinals and archbishops" (*Archives Israelites*, 10 September 1920).

When Millerand became president, the London *Jewish Chronicle* explicitly celebrated him as a Jew and compared him to Leon Gambetta. In the spring of 1922, Millerand set out on a journey to Tunis. *La voix d'Israel*, the organ of North African Jewry and Zionism, published in large letters an article titled "One Page of History," which contained the triumphant declaration of the Jewish origins of the President of the Republic of France. *La Depêche tunesiénne* of 2 May 1922 describes in detail Millerand's journey, emphasizing his Jewish enthusiasm. Finally, consider the distinctions he granted. No Frenchman was decorated, but Eugène Bessis, the President of the Israelite Community, and Yossef Guez, former director of the Jewish Charity Society, received the Cross of the Legion of Honor (*La Vieille France*, No. 277, 18 May 1922).

When the city of Montrouge wanted to inaugurate a monument in mid-May, this was done under the chairmanship of the Jew Paul Strauss, a minister in Poincare's cabinet. This Jew had previously been sentenced to three years' hard labor for desertion (see the trial report, *Vieille France*, No. 265, 23 February 1922). One could go on for hours with similar taunts. This brief overview may suffice for now. As a sign of the times, it alone speaks the clearest language about the domination of Jewish money, and about the feelings of nationalism and honor among the peoples of Europe.

Therefore, it is not surprising if one explains that the French invasion of the Ruhr came about under pressure from Jewish high finance. Ever since the armistice, the French Jew Aaron has been in Essen, unrecognized, as the French representative and informer for the entire Ruhr area. When the negotiations about German subjugation began after the occupation of the Ruhr, this gentleman, who had been quite unknown up to that point, suddenly introduced himself and took the place of the previous French representative. All of France's press propaganda in the Ruhr area was in the hands of a four-member commission. As the Parisian *Vieille France* (26 April 1923) noted, of the four gentlemen, three are Jews. Thus, all "information" and lying propaganda emanates from a verifiable Jewish center in the Ruhr area. It should be added that two of France's main generals in the occupied territory—Simon and Levy—are also Hebrews, and the *Vieille France* gives Germans the right to behave anti-Semitically, since they regard all the French troops as mercenaries of Jewish high finance.

In May 1924 new elections were held in France that brought a "leftist" majority to the helm. Twelve Jews moved into the French Parliament as deputies, distributed across all parties. The radical Socialist Edouard Herriot became Prime Minister. The inevitably Jewish "Secretary General" was named Israel. Paul Painleve became President of the Chamber; the Jew Heilbronner became its "Secretary General". In place of Millerand, Gaston Doumergue became President of the Republic. The *Jüdische Rundschau* said of him (No. 64, 1924):

> The President of the French Republic, M. Gaston Doumergue, in his youth held a humble post as a judge in the Town of El Arab in Algiers, which is mostly inhabited by Jews. The young judge frequented the circles of the local Jewish intelligentsia and was often a guest with Jewish families. When a vacancy became available for a secretary's

position at the El Arab Jewish community, Mr. Doumergue, who as a judge earned only 120 francs a month, offered to fill the position of secretary at the Jewish community on a part-time basis. The office was gladly given to the popular civil servant. The secretary, Gaston Doumergue, wrote and signed all the parish circulars on religious and social matters, and in time learned to use Hebrew terms where necessary.

These secretarial fees can probably be regarded as indirect bribes. The notion that a real judge, i.e. a just man, could be popular with the Hebrews in Algiers—represented by sex traffickers, brothel owners and liquor smugglers—is probably out of the question.

Jewry in Italy

If we take a look at the situation in Italy, a confession from the *Berliner Tageblatt* about the origins of the World War [One] is of the greatest interest. This paper, managed exclusively by Jews, wrote on 8 March 1923, after general information had been announced concerning anti-papist activities of the Italian government:

> During the whole time that an anti-clerical spirit reigned in Italy, Freemasonry, which belonged to the acme of the nation, and therefore the government as well, became a schematic, ossified anti-clericalism… [T]hese were the elements of life in which, until a few years ago, the politics of Italy moved.

After describing the internal political upheavals that took place later, above all the founding of the Italian People's Party, the *Berliner Tageblatt* makes the following comments:

> The anti-clerical elements, especially Italian Freemasonry, which was formerly omnipotent, but now was severely compromised by its mysterious relations with France in 1914 and 1915, were tacitly eliminated, so that, since the war years, it has hardly played a role.

After a description of the fascists' pro-church policy, it is stated that they outlawed Freemasonry and forbade membership in the Lodge. And then the *Tageblatt* continues, referring to it as:

> A measure that one can address this Italian Freemasonry; for it, which has played such a large part in Italy's decision to go to war, must now be regarded as the main factor of the military intervention from 1914-1915...

These confessions of the Masonic-Jewish *Tageblatt* are highly noteworthy—above all, because at the head of Freemasonry at that time, which the *Tageblatt* itself admits, was the main driving force behind the war, was the former Jewish mayor of Rome, Ernesto Nathan (son of Mazzini and Sara Nathan from Pisa). When Nathan died in 1921, he was characterized by the entire Jewish world press as one of the greatest Hebrews, and the Jew Peter Ryss wrote in the *Tribüne juive* on 14 May 1921: "a Jew as mayor of the Eternal City [is] the symbol of the new times."

Professor Preciosi in Rome has also earned great credit for his clarification of the domination of Italian politics by Jewish high finance. He published extensive statistics in his monthly journal *La vita italiana*, which precisely demonstrated that, behind the scenes of Italian political life, stood the same elements as in the other states. Despite the fact that there were only 50,000 Jews in Italy, international high finance had managed to shove their own, one after another, into important positions in Italian politics. 3,259 Jews were civil servants. There were 64 in parliament, 54 in diplomacy, 317 in the administration of the interior, 470 in the management of the tax office, etc. The Italian people knew just as little of these things as the other peoples of the continent.

Fascism, as a national counter-reaction against the international chaos, was at first thoroughly Masonic, but then came out very sharply against Italian Masonry and pursued a church-friendly policy. But even Mussolini has so far preferred not to take action against Jewish high finance, with which he is certainly unfamiliar. And so it became possible for the Minister of the Interior, Cosi Aldo Finzi, to be claimed as a Jew by various Jewish newspapers, even though he was baptized (see *Berliner Tageblatt,* 8 March 1923). Mussolini's court Jew Finzi was the confidante of the bank Jew Toeplitz, who was director of the Banca

Commerciale di Roma. Mussolini's recognition of Soviet Russia was undoubtedly due to Jewish pressure. Thanks to this contamination of national sources, fascism is certainly faced with other issues than the well-known Matteotti affair.[13]

Jewry in the USA

The center of gravity of today's world-politics is in New York. The six Jewish politicians mentioned form only a [small] selection from the circles of those powerful financial groups, before which today all of Europe is lying on its belly. As mentioned, President Wilson was always surrounded only by Jews: Simon Wolf, who presented him with a gold medal in the name of the Jews after his return from Versailles; Jacob Schiff and his son Mortimer; Otto Kahn; Felix Warburg; and an endless array of other financial figures.

As I said, Samuel Gompers was at the head of a labor organization, but care was taken to ensure that the head of the anti-Gompers union was also a Hebrew: Sidney Hillman.[14] (For more details, see *The International Jew*, Vol. 1.) Ninety percent of the land of the city of New York belongs to Hebrews; theaters and cinemas likewise. Of the city's large department stores, only one is not in Jewish hands. One-third of the population consists of Jews; well over 1 1/2 million Jews live in the largest city in America, and this city in the "freest country on Earth" is also the largest ghetto in the world.

Shortly before Wilson's departure, he made one more significant appointment, elevating an old stock jobber turned wartime admiral to the position of Supreme Commander of all Union Naval Forces in the Pacific. This was Mr. Joseph Strauss, a relative of the aforementioned Nathan and Oscar Strauss. The *Israelit* expressly described this Strauss as a "conscious Jew" (No. 5, 1921).

---

[13] A political conflict between liberals and fascists after the assassination of Giacomo Matteotti in June 1924; the fascists, led by Mussolini, emerged victorious.
[14] This is standard practice in the present day, where Jews attain leading positions in all parties and across the political spectrum, precisely in order to monopolize all sides of all issues.

Things didn't change when Warren Harding became president [in 1921]. Immediately after taking office, he wrote a letter to the Zionist leader Hartmann in which he expressed his admiration for the Jewish people and praised their "loyalty to the laws of the country in which they live" (*Jüdische Rundschau,* No. 83, 1920). Later, on 5 November 1921, on the feast of Rosh Hashanah, he congratulated world Jewry and extolled the usefulness of the Jewish people (*Israelit,* No. 44, 1921). And even later he never hesitated to kowtow again and again to New York's high finance. On 16 February 1923, the "Jewish Press Center" in Zurich was able to print a letter from Harding to the Union of Hebrew Congregations in America, which said, among other things: "One of the wonders of human history has always been the strength and power of the Jewish faith and the uninterrupted influence and power of the Jewish people." Having continued to glorify the Jewish faith, Harding concluded by acknowledging that other religions had a "great debt to pay" to the Jewish faith.

Much more could be said about this tragicomedy called President Harding, but the indications in this one direction must suffice; it should only be added that as soon as he took office, Harding promoted the Zionist Bernhard Rosenblatt to the position of New York's Municipal Justice of the Peace. Furthermore, the Jew Robert Lasker became President of the American Shipping Board; the newly-elected president also appointed Mr. Lewis Einstein American Ambassador to Czechoslovakia, and Rabbi Josef Kornfeld was appointed US Ambassador to Tehran.

When Professor Albert Einstein and Chaim Weizmann came to New York [in April 1921], official buildings hoisted the Jewish national Zionist flag alongside the American one; the two Jews were made honorary citizens of the city of New York.

Of course, things did not change in the slightest when Harding went to his eternal rest in mid-1923. Mr. Calvin Coolidge took his place. When the Jewish-American Congress opened in New York on 15 October 1923, Coolidge wrote to its chairman, Rabbi Stephen Wise, expressing his subservience to the stock exchange Jews as follows:

> American Jews are doing right in striving to secure the rights of their brethren in all countries where those rights are threatened. The President has a special interest in the

efforts of American Jews to build up Palestine under the British Mandate in order to restore a home to the homeless Jewish people there. Contrary to the allegations that the restrictions on immigration to America are being exercised with particular severity against the Jews, and that Jewish emigrants are often treated unfairly by the American consuls, the President declares that his government will never sanction or condone anti-Jewish tendencies on immigration or in the other questions in the future. The President is certain that a thorough investigation (if one were necessary) would provide evidence that these alleged impairments were unreal. (*Jüdische Rundschau*, 23 October 1923).

In No. 258, 1923, the *Jüdische Presszentrale Zürich* published statistics on the Jews in America as compiled by the Jewish Statistical Office in New York. According to this, in January 1922 the "freest country in the world" was home to 3.6 million Hebrews, of which 1 million lived in New York alone, 250,000 in Chicago, 200,000 in Philadelphia, etc. If you consider that the Jews always underestimate their number, then America houses the largest ghetto in world history. And yet President Coolidge has promised his help that it will be further enlarged.

Jewry in the League of Nations

It only remains to point out that Paul Hymans, the chairman of the League of Nations who only resigned at the end of 1923 and soon afterwards became chairman of the Council of the League of Nations, was not the only Hebrew to head a highly political association, but that he has a lot of friends who run kosher sweatshops alongside him.

The general Jewish joy about the splendid "League of Nations" in Geneva is quite naturally justified. For no sooner had the General Director of this institution, Sir Eric Drummond, arrived in Geneva, than he did what is a matter of course, given the monetary power of Jews today: he went to an audience with Grand Rabbin Ginsburger. In his address, Drummond said he and his associates "would unite in defense of the Jews, and he has every confidence that the League of Nations will do its duty (!) for the Jews. He hopes that all Jewry everywhere will soon rejoice in all human and civil rights. Henceforth the Jews would no longer appeal in vain to the justice of mankind". (*Israelit*, 11 November 1920, No. 45.)

This promise is all the more understandable when one knows that Jews represent all countries in the most important sections of the famous League of Nations: Dr. Hamel (representing Holland), a Hebrew native of Germany; the Director of the Political Department is the Jew Mantoux (formerly interpreter in the "Supreme Council" in Paris during the Versailles negotiations); the head of the Traffic Department is the Jew Haas; France is represented by Andre Weiss, Spain by Mr. Steegmann, and San Domingo by Mr. Cuhnhardt. In addition, the Jews have secured themselves the section for "fighting" the white slave trade, which was their business for centuries (*Deutschlands Erneuerung*, Nr. 4, 1921). Finally, "Poland" is represented by the Jews Prof. Askenazy and Strassburger.

In November 1923, the former Jewish-American ambassador in Constantinople, Henry (Hirsch) Morgenthau, went to Geneva to chair the special commission of the "Rehabilitation Work" of the League of Nations for the Greek-Turkish refugees and prisoner exchange (*Jüdische Presszentrale Zürich*, No. 267, 1923). Immediately after his arrival he gave a lecture at the B'nai B'rith Order in Thessaloniki, in which he promised to be of use to the Jews; he concluded with the words: "I will do everything possible for your congregation, as for all the Jewish communities of Greece, which I shall visit" (J.P.Z., No. 269, 1923). From these words, the real purpose of the Morgenthau's mission is clearly evident.

In December 1923, the Jew Dr. Abraham Flexner (of the Rockefeller Foundation) was appointed the League of Nation's Chairman for "Women and Children's Welfare" (J.P.Z., No. 271, 1923). "The International Committee on Intellectual Cooperation," a League of Nation's commission, meets under the chairmanship of the Jew Henri Bergson (J.P.Z., No. 271, 1923). In the same month, the leaders of the League of Nations delegated two Jews to their Hygiene Section: Professor Ottolenghi (Italy) and Professor Lion Bernard (France) (J.P.Z., No. 272). It is therefore more than understandable when the *Jewish Echo* wrote as early as 1920 (No. 53, 1920):

> The Jewish people see in the principles of the League of Nations the realization of the brotherhood of nations, proclaimed in Jewish prophecy, and it hopes that the League of

Nations will succeed more and more in making the conflicts between nations disappear and in freeing the Jewish people from their terrible fate.

For our part, however, we agree with Henry Ford, who, in October 1923 (according to the J.P.Z., No. 262, 1923) told a Canadian journalist that he regarded the League of Nations as a completely inadequate instrument for preventing war. Ford said, "One should get the 50 leading Jewish financiers of the world together and render their manipulations of money impossible—because these financiers are causing the war... Wall Street is the Jewish Mecca".[15]

Jewry in Germany

How things were (and are) in Germany can be found in a literature that has grown enormously; the essentials must already be presupposed here (I refer to W. Meister, *Judas Schuldbuch*; Kernholt, *Schuld und Sühne*; Armin, *Die Juden im Heer,* etc.)

In the context of this overview, it should be emphasized that the parallel structure of Baruch-Montague-Rathenau is downright astonishing. Just as the Jew Baruch, out of obscurity, became dictator over the American world state, just as Montague, as Minister of Munitions, practically ruled over the British army, so the Jew Rathenau appeared before the German Kaiser a few days after the outbreak of war with a completed plan. This, of course, was the same man who wrote a book (*Der Kaiser*) after the fall of this same emperor, in which he coldly recounts that he had already told a good friend at the time that if Wilhelm II and his paladins were to ride victoriously through the Brandenburg Tor, "world history would have lost its meaning". What the "meaning of world history" consisted of, the same man had already declared on 25 December 1909 in the Viennese *Neue Freie Presse*: high finance was called upon to seize the reins of government in place of emperors and kings.

In the *Neue Züricher Zeitung*, Emil Ludwig (Cohn) dedicated an essay in homage to his friend Walter Rathenau on the occasion of his self-appointment as Minister of Reconstruction. He writes:

---

[15] *Indiana Jewish Chronicle*, 5 October 1923, p. 1.

[Rathenau's] heights are called: firstly, (Hugo) Stinnes; secondly, anti-Semitism; thirdly, collegiality—because Rathenau, despite all formal conciliation, has the mindset of a dictator, only learns according to relevance, and would rather go away than change the path he has been following for a decade. His spirit must permeate the cabinet or give way entirely.

This time it is easy for the viewer to get to know this path in advance. Since peace, Rathenau has published proposals for building a new society, a new economy, and a new sociology about every three months, in the form of a brochure. Theoretically, he has long been the "development minister," and by always trying to be pro-Europe (!!), he has something of Hoover about him, who thinks in terms of *states* and *millions*. State socialism, as he created it in Germany during the war, is his plan for peace.

It is unfair to define such a loner in political life in terms of keywords, but for today it should be said that Rathenau is anti-militarist, anti-nationalist, and anti-capitalist. He teaches simplification, dematerialization, planned economy, and international economics. So he is actually a candidate from abroad, namely England, but only very few know that he alone prevented the break in Spaa, August 1920, and thus brought about the only agreement that has occurred between the wartime opponents since 1918. (D.Z. 8 June 1921).

And after the "proletarian", "anti capitalist" revolution of November 9, 1918, this representative of Jewish high finance and "a candidate from abroad"—in other words, of our enemies—rose to become the man who openly dominated Germany. At the Cannes Conference in January 1922, he said words that could have been the motto of the "Protocols of the Elders of Zion": "The path that one wants to take seems right to me: an *international* syndicate and a *private* syndicate at that" (*Berliner Tagesblatt*, No. 27, 1922). The *Tagesblatt* prints the last words in bold, a sign that it knew exactly where to go.

The objective consequence of the Rathenau system was the same as the rule of Bernard Baruch: wartime societies fell almost exclusively into Jewish hands (for more shocking evidence, see Armin: *Die Juden in den Kriegsgesellschaften* ["The Jews in Wartime Societies"]). The whole nation cried out against these exploitative syndicates, but the government was incapable of taking action against them; it was not allowed to. And for that very reason, it fell under the blows of the protective troops of plutocratic usury, under the blows of social democracy. A deserved end—except that the German people must pay for it with tremendous humiliation and slavery.

A sober overview of the political situation in the world shows us everywhere the same picture. Behind what the British, American, French, or German government likes to call themselves, stands the rule of pan-Judah high finance (not ignoring the influence of other forces), organized into national, "philanthropic," and "religious" alliances, which do not recognize state borders.

How did that happen?

Afterword

The foregoing essays and documents no longer leave any doubt as to the similarity of the mode of thinking as it emerges in the Protocols and in other Jewish literature. The politics of the present corresponds exactly to the details of the intentions and plans as they were discussed and laid down more than 25 years ago. I had to limit myself with the evidence, but I always took another country as an example for every important case, so that we can see Jewish activity and its successes in all major states, but also in Switzerland, Austria, Czechoslovakia, Poland, and so on. Everywhere the same picture, the same disgrace.

"How did that happen?", I asked in the Introduction. One of the most profound statements about the Jew comes from Richard Wagner. He called him "the plastic demon of decay of humanity".[16] This means that when a people or many peoples together enter an epoch of spiritual drought, uncreative spirituality, an epoch of rootless, inauthentic, inorganic striving, then, as it were, the Jew appears in a leading position as a

---

[16] In his essay of 1881, "Know thyself."

symbol of this decline. Because we have been unfaithful to ourselves, he grows in power; because we did not preserve our holiest, he was able to seize it. We renounced love and the curse of gold came over our world. The Jew stands in our story as our metaphysical counter-image. However, this has never been clearly grasped by us. We have always draped our robes around his desert figure, presupposed in his beautiful words motives that weren't there, and transferred our soul and spirit into his form without suspecting that the Jew's demon didn't want all that, couldn't receive it, that he lived on deep down on another plane of the soul.

Today, at last, it seems as if the eternally foreign and hostile, having risen to such tremendous power, is felt and hated as such. For the first time in history, instinct and knowledge rise to clear consciousness, and at the highest point of the greedy peak of power, the fall into the abyss awaits the Jew. The final fall. After him the Jew has no more room in Europe and America.

Today, in the midst of the collapse of an entire world, a new epoch is beginning, a fundamental departure in all areas from many ideas of the past. As one of the portents of this coming struggle for a new world formation stands for the knowledge of the nature of the demon of our present decline. Then the way will be free for a new era.[17]

---

[17] Alfred Rosenberg (1893-1946) was considered the leading theorist of National Socialist philosophy. Born in Estonia in 1893, he spent time in Russia, earning a PhD in engineering there in 1917. He migrated to Germany the next year, becoming a journalist and political activist. Rosenberg first met Hitler in late 1919, and soon joined the newly-formed NSDAP party. Eventually he was named Reich Minister for the Occupied Eastern Territories. Rosenberg was captured after the war, tried at Nuremberg, found guilty, and hanged in the early hours of 16 October 1946. For more on his story, see *Streicher, Rosenberg, and the Jews* (T. Dalton, ed.; 2020).

HITLER AND GOEBBELS ON THE *PROTOCOLS*

Editor: Following his failed Beer Hall Putsch in November 1923, Adolf Hitler was arrested and sentenced to 13 months in prison, covering most of the year 1924. During this time, he dictated volume one of *Mein Kampf*. There, in Chapter 11, section 4, he offered some brief comments on the Protocols. These would be his only such remarks in speeches or writings.

11.4 How much the whole existence of this people is based on a permanent lie is proved in a unique way by *The Protocols of the Elders of Zion*, so infinitely hated by the Jews. With groans and moans, the *Frankfurter Zeitung* repeats again and again that these are forgeries: the best proof of their authenticity. Here, what many Jews unconsciously wish to do is clearly set forth, and that's what counts. It doesn't matter from what Jewish brain these revelations sprang; the important thing is that they disclose, with an almost terrifying precision, the nature and activity of the Jewish people, exposing both their inner contexts and final aims.

The best way of judging them, however, is reality. If historical developments of the last few centuries are studied in light of this book, we will immediately understand the constant outcry of the Jewish press. The moment that the general public gets hold of this book, the Jewish danger will be stamped out.

Editor: Joseph Goebbels kept a near-daily diary for over 20 years. Four of these entries mention the Protocols: two in near-succession in April 1924, one briefly in 1939, and then a final longer entry in 1943. Coincidentally, the 1924 entries were almost concurrent with Hitler's dictation of *Mein Kampf*.

8 April 1924
The Jewish Question is the hottest issue at the moment. It has to be solved before one can go on to the re-fortification of Europe. Maybe Russia will make a start. What I already suspected—namely that the current Russian situation is only Jewish soap scum atop a heavy nationalist dishwater—I now find confirmed in all authentic opinions.

I read Henry Ford's *The International Jew* today. The book is very interesting and salutary. But one shouldn't let oneself be too taken in by the author's captivating evidence. He also writes a bit 'to the home crowd.' All the same, a lot is revealed in the book. One can see the implications of the Jewish Question in the non-German lands. Strange: Henry Ford, the richest man in the world, makes Jewish capitalism his target. The world is a big theater.

Lenin, Trotsky, [Georgy] Chicherin are Jews. How stupidly one can sometimes judge political and economic processes, if one doesn't know the most necessary material. A major part of Ford's book discusses the *Protocols of the Elders of Zion*. But the text itself is missing [from Ford's book]. I have to reorient myself about this question another time. I won't rest until I have clarity about the Jewish Question. The solution to these things may change my whole inner nature.

10 April 1924
I believe that the *Protocols of the Elders of Zion* are a forgery; not because the worldview expressed in it or the Jewish aspirations seem too utopian and fantastic to me—one can see today how the claims of one protocol after another are realized, how a systematic plan of decomposition leaves the world in ruins—but because I don't consider the Jews to be so boundlessly stupid that they couldn't keep such important records secret. Hence, I believe in the inner, but not factual, truth of the protocols.

One's hair stands on end when reading these shameful pieces. And yet race and system lie within it. The biggest mistake of anti-Semitism is that it underestimates the Hebrews in their spiritual resources. It may perish due to this.

One thing has now become for me an unbreakable truth: the Jew is, in reality, for the Faustian man, "the plastic demon of decay," "the ferment of national decomposition".[1]

It's up to us to help ourselves. No one helps us. If our national strength is no longer large enough to overcome the Jewish corrosion, then we deserve to go under.

I stand on the folkish side: I hate the Jew out of instinct and out of reason. In my deepest soul, he is hated and repulsive.

3 November 1939
With the Führer. I give him a report on my trip to Poland, which interests him greatly. Above all, my exposition on the Jewish problem earns his full support. Jewry is a waste product. More a clinical than social issue. … We are considering whether or not we should bring out the Zionist *Protocols* for our propaganda in France.

13 May 1943
I once again thoroughly studied the Zionist *Protocols*. Until now I had always been told that they were unsuitable for current propaganda. Reading them today, I find that we can use them very well. The Zionist *Protocols* are as modern today as when they were first published. One is amazed at the extraordinary consequence with which Jewish striving for world domination is characterized. If the Zionist *Protocols* are not genuine, they have been invented by a brilliant critic of the time. I went to the Führer around noon to talk about this topic. He argues that the Zionist *Protocols* could claim to be absolutely genuine. No one can spell out Jewish striving for world-mastery as brilliantly as the Jews themselves. The Führer is of the opinion that the Jews did not need to work according to a fixed plan; they work according to their racial instinct, which will cause them to act again and again in the same way that they have throughout their entire history.

The Jewish Question will, the Führer thinks, be of decisive importance in England. We just have to cleverly adjust our propaganda to this goal, we must not get too sluggish in our approach, and we have to

---

[1] Goebbels is here quoting phrases from Richard Wagner and Theodor Mommsen.

place it more in the news than in speeches. At this stage of the war, propaganda again has an extraordinary task to accomplish. However, one shouldn't forget that the English audience is of course not as open to the Jewish Question as the German people. We must therefore never let our intention be known, in order not to arouse any suspicion. If the Jews act according to their racial instincts, that doesn't mean that there aren't civilized Western European Jews who would also be aware of the secret intentions of this racial instinct. They work not only by race, but also by insight. As a result, there will always be some defectors of the Jewish race who, with a startling sincerity, lay out Jewish goals in front of the public. There can be no talk of a conspiracy of the Jewish race against Western humanity in a flat sense; this conspiracy is more a matter of race than of intellectual intentions. Jews will always act according to their Jewish instincts. ...

Jews are the same all over the world; whether they live in the eastern ghetto, in the bank palaces of the City or Wall Street, they pursue the same aims and, without coordination, use the same means. One could raise the question here, Why are there any Jews in the world order at all? It would be the same as asking, Why are there potato bugs? Nature is governed by the law of struggle. There will always be parasites that will speed up the fight and intensify the selection process between the strong and the weak. The principle of struggle also prevails in human coexistence. You just have to know the laws of this fight to be prepared for it. The intellectual man doesn't have a natural defense against the Jewish danger because he is essentially broken in his instinct. As a result, peoples with a high level of civilization are the most vulnerable. In nature, life always acts in the same way against parasitism; this is not always the case in the existence of nations. This actually results in the Jewish danger.[2]

---

[2] Entries taken from *Goebbels on the Jews* (T. Dalton, ed.), 2019.

NSDAP INTRODUCTION TO *PROTOCOLS OF THE ELDERS OF ZION*

Editor: Leading figures in National Socialist Germany—including Hitler, Goebbels, and Rosenberg—saw great value in the Protocols, viewing them as accurate and reliable guides to Jewish thinking and action. They also saw much educational value in them, given that the general public could be significantly enlightened as to the nature of the Jewish threat. Upon coming to power in 1933, the 'Nazi' party (NSDAP) began to produce popular editions of the Protocols that included a lengthy Introduction—translated here from the 1938 edition. The author here is anonymous, but the text bears all the hallmarks of Rosenberg's careful analysis and citation. In any case, this text was one of the last major NS statements on the Protocols, and in particular, on the evidence from daily life that supports the assertions in the Protocols. If reality aligns with the 'predictions' in the Protocols, then we have good reason to take them seriously.

The *Protocols of the Elders of Zion* have brought together important statements about Jewry's plans for world domination; these have had a huge political impact and are highly revealing about the nature of global Jewry. In this way, millions of people have become informed about the corrupting character of Jewish thought and action. People then strive to learn more and to keep a close eye on their fellow "Jewish citizens"; in doing so, they find that the central points of the Protocols are confirmed. No other book has generated such Jewish hatred and animosity, and consequently, Jews have employed all means in their attempt to defame or destroy the Protocols.

The oldest verifiable evidence of the Protocols is found in the Russian magazine *Snamja*, in 1903. In 1905 or 1906 at the latest, a text by

Georgy Butmi de Katzman titled "The Root Cause of Our Problems" appeared in St. Petersburg. By 1907, a third edition appeared, titled "The Enemies of Humanity." Apart from Butmi, the text was also published in 1905 by the Russian writer Sergei Alexandrovitsch Nilus as an appendix to the second edition of his book *The Great within the Small: The Antichrist as a Coming Political Possibility*. Further editions of this book appeared in 1911, 1912, and 1917. There is a copy of the 1905 edition at the British Museum in London. The third printing of Nilus' 1911 edition was translated into German and published by Müller von Hanson under the pen name Gottfried zur Beck, using his *Auf Vorposten* publishing company. The rights were transferred in 1929 to the *Zentralverlag der NSDAP*, Franz Eher, in Munich.

At the present time, it is unreasonable and impossible to research the origins of the *Protocols of the Elders of Zion* in a Judaized Soviet Russia; therefore, we must limit ourselves in this Introduction to examining the accuracy of the Protocols on the basis of evidence provided by Jews in Germany. We want to choose several of the many individual passages and sections from the Protocols for which there is frightening evidence from Jewish literature—particularly from the post-war [WWI] period—that demonstrates how they have been followed and realized. Recent writings differ from the Protocols statements only in form and in linguistic changes from the turn of the century to the present post-war period.

An unbiased reader will see from these citations that Jewry has worked even harder at corrupting the German portion of European culture than is evidenced in the Protocols. During the post-war period, Jews had unlimited freedom in Germany; it seemed to them to be the beginning of Jewish domination of the German people, and thus they openly and plainly displayed their drive for power. Whenever a Jew speaks or acts as a Jew, his statements or actions will be shown to be consistent with the theses of the Protocols.

Since the betrayal of German soldiers at the Front [in 1918] and the resulting parliamentary domination at the start of the post-war period, we will begin with the section of the Protocols titled "universal suffrage":

> [W]e must force all to vote, without class distinction; that is, to establish *an autocracy of the majority*, which cannot be obtained from the intellectual classes alone. (Protocol 10)

The history of the World War [One] and the post-war period in Germany alone provides an impressive collection of evidence, such that one can speak of strict adherence to and systemic realization of a carefully thought-out plan. We have to limit ourselves here to a few compelling examples. The overwhelming role played by "German" Jews in treason and agitation against Germany during the war can be seen in a book by "a French journalist" titled *Behind the Scenes of French Journalism* (1925). In it, a Jewish puppet-master, the American financial Jew Otto Kahn, reveals this filthy and dishonorable business:

> The *Freie Zeitung* was established in Bern, a newspaper of the worst sort. It employed journalists with rather broad consciences, such as [the Jew] Grelling (the author of *J'accuse* and similar writings; Röselmaier, [the Jew] Fernau, and Edward Stilgebauer (author of the novel *The Ship of Death*, which portrayed the torpedoing and sinking of a huge ship in gruesome detail). They were under the direction of the Maison de las Presse (in Paris) and twisted the facts intentionally, subtly selecting documents and discovering bloodthirsty German atrocities. The Swiss government was powerless. It should not be forgotten that the well-known American banker [and Jew] Otto Kahn contributed $50,000 to establish the *Freie Zeitung*.

This is how Jewry worked against a strong Germany that was determined to resist. In Germany itself, we have the Jews Alfred H. Fried, Alfred Einstein, Eduard Bernstein, privy councilor Witting-Witkowski, Wulfsohn, Siegfried Balder, Magnus Hirschfield, Dr. Oskar Cohn, Hugo Haase, and Kurt Eisner—among whom Maximilian Harden (Wikowski) particularly stands out. Even before the war, they worked hard to bring down the monarchy. Their racial comrade Max Reinhardt said:

> If one could trace the important events of this period to their origin, one would have to admit that all the threads led to a single man in Berlin-Grunewald [i.e. Harden]. Whatever the results of the great upheavals of the present may be, later observers will have to conclude that he was their cause.

After the war, and amidst Germany's greatest poverty, Harden celebrated his triumph in an unsurpassable hate-filled way:

> [Germany] may regain its rights only when it has the courageous dignity...to admit its injustice. (*Zukunft*, 1919, I, p. 328).

No greater infernal monstrosity of Jewish thinking can be found in the Protocols. It corresponds to the practical proposals in the conclusion of the London Plan to impose war debts on Germany through a consortium, and later through the Dawes Plan:

> Germany's first task in the consortium, as debtor to its creditors, as the defeated to the victors, is to provide all necessary means for building up Russia—experts, technicians, skilled labor, tools, and finished products—which will help it to recover, along with industry in Northern France, and English and American commerce. (*Zukunft*, Nr. 23, 4.3.1922).

These facts and evidences give a picture of widespread Jewish efforts against Germany's will to resist, wherever it was found. This was the preliminary work for the Weimar Constitution, created by the Jew Hugo Preuss. It followed the Protocols' call to establish "the absolute power of the majority" down to the smallest detail.

The importance to the Jews of "creating" new constitutions that affirm the absolute power of the majority is proven by the surprising fact that nearly all German "democratic" and "republican" constitutions have Jewish authors. The creators of the first Reich constitution [in 1848] were the Jews Gabriel Riesler and Johann Jacoby. The former was "reorganizer" of the Democratic Party of Prussia and spokesman for international democracy; the latter was one of the most prominent attorneys in the "German Citizens of the Mosaic Faith." They, along with their baptized racial comrade Eduard von Simson, created the first German Reich constitution.

That same revolutionary year of 1848, the Jewish demagogue Adolf Fischhof prepared a "representative constitution" in Vienna. It demanded complete freedom of the press (which means the unrestrained incitement of public opinion), the abolition of the death penalty, and "absolute majority rule." It was followed exactly in the republican federal constitution of German-Austria, which was the work of the Jew Kelsen. And the Weimar Constitution of the German Republic not only agreed with the demands of the *Protocols of the Elders of Zion*, but was prepared by an exclusively Jewish committee.

The Jew Paul Nathan published the following details about the history of this Constitution in the newspaper *Vorwärts*, edited by his racial comrade Stampfer:

> Hugo Preuss, who usually did not pay visits, surprised me by coming to my home and said: "Ebert has asked me to draft the German Reich constitution. Should I do it?" And I instantly replied: "Naturally, if you are guaranteed a free hand." An hour later, we were with Theodor Wolff of the *Berliner Tageblatt*. Soon we were joined by Witting, Maximilian Harden's brother. All of us whom Preuss had brought together were agreed that Preuss—as long as his independence was assured—should agree to Ebert's request, and that he must do it. Thus Preuss moved from Jerusalem-Strasse to Wilhelm-Strasse. (*Vorwärts*, 9. 10. 1925).

From Jerusalem-Strasse to Wilhelm-Strasse! With that began the rule of the Jewish spirit over Germany in the preparation of the Reich Constitution, the law that governed all Germans.

Knowing these facts, one can understand why the Jews were so happy after the successful "German Revolution," as they called the November revolt of 1918. In the "serious" Jewish magazine *Der Jude* we find an article, not from the pen of a popular author but rather from the editors of the magazine itself. It represented a broad circle of the Jews in Germany, and displayed a spirit absolutely identical with the Protocols:

> The German Revolution is the first powerful phase of the beginning of the liquidation of war, and this phase shows the scale and effects that the individual phases of this liquidation will have. For us Jews, the concluding phase of the

war will be of enormous significance, determining the future perhaps even more than the years of the war itself.

The Coming Jewish Age

Then followed a genuinely Jewish interpretation of the November revolt and a prophesy about the post-war period that, as we learned, turned out to be all-too-true:

> We will feel bound to it [the present age] and the ideas guiding it, and with the goals for which it is striving. It will set spirit against force, justice against power, and peace between the peoples against war between the peoples; we will know that Jewish ethos and Jewish pathos are at work. An age of the breakthrough of the Jewish spirit in the world comes once more, an age in which humanity moves forward to save itself. How could we stand aside when other peoples are transforming their lives? We will also experience this age in a positive and affirming way, fully aware that we are the children of the prophets.

Hidden behind these vague phrases is the claim that, after the work before and during the war, the future will be a Jewish age. In the following passage, this is said openly, in a way that leads back to the theses of the Protocols:

> The collapse of these three powers [Germany, Austria-Hungary, and Russia] in their old form means that Jewish policy is much easier to conduct. The fact that the same war that inaugurated a globally-recognized Jewish national policy also led to the collapse of three great powers hostile to the Jews is a unique combination of events that may give one pause to think. (*Der Jude*, v. 3, 1918/1919).

In truth, these facts agree with the points of the Protocols we have mentioned. Yet another point of the Protocols is relevant: the policy of hampering the resistance of non-Jews through war—even a global world war. It says:

> We must be able to overcome all opposition by provoking a war with the neighbors of any country that dares to oppose us. Should, however, those neighbors, in turn, decide to unite against us, we must respond by creating a world war. (Protocol 7)

Those three states whose defeat was celebrated by the Jewish magazine *Der Jude* already had publicly-active anti-Semitic groups before the war. And after the war, these three countries were the first to suffer, and suffer most terribly, as hostages of Jewish communism.

A Statement from Lucien Wolf

Before we explore further points from the Protocols to see whether or not they were realized in post-war Germany, we must consider the accuracy of the statement in *Der Jude* that the coming age, the years after 1918, would be Jewish. The Jew Lucien Wolf, a leader of the English Jews, had unsurpassed insight into the political activities of his racial comrades. With cynical openness, he provided an eloquent, if not exhaustive, insight into the role of the Jews in international politics after the war, particularly those who devised the Treaty of Versailles. In his lengthy essay in the *Jüdische Press-Zentrale Zürich* he wrote:

> The great progress of the second decade of the 20th century and its democratic consequences offers the possibility for a significant increase in diplomatic activity on the part of the Jews. During the war, two Jews who followed the example of those of their faith in the 16th and 17th centuries helped to defend against new attacks on Europe's freedom and on the balance of power. Lord Reading...and Baron Sonnino brought about the Treaty of London in 1915 that dissolved the three-party pact and led to Italy's entrance into the war.
>
> Other than these two men, we Jews had no leading diplomatic representatives during the war. However, numerous

Jews were quickly employed in the newly-established intelligence and propaganda agencies that were part of all the foreign ministries, since they possessed the traditional broad cosmopolitan vision and could speak other languages.

A significant but not widely known fact is that none of the warring nations knew how to properly use the Jews. The foreign ministries in London, Paris, and Berlin organized special Jewish departments that concentrated on the analysis of Jewish matters. The history of the competition between these departments with regards to Palestine, which Zionist leaders used so effectively, must still be written. From the beginning, the Zionist leanings of London's Foreign Office was clear. The head of the new Jewish Department, although not a Jew himself, shared the name of a cousin who was a famous diplomat, journalist, and writer, and who was a pioneer of the Zionist idea. The Jewish Departments in Paris and Berlin were headed by famous Jewish professors who were, however, lukewarm about Zionism. One was Professor Sylvain Levi, the eminent Sanskrit scholar and current president of the Alliance Israélite Universelle, the other Professor M. Sobernheim, also an eminent Orientalist. The British and French departments have been eliminated, but the Jewish Department on Wilhelmstrasse is still functioning and remains under the leadership of Professor Sobernheim. In recognition of Professor Sylvain Levi's services to the Quai d'Orsay, his son Daniel Levi was accepted into the distinguished circle of French diplomacy. He is currently consul in Bombay.

Many Jews in the background at the conference [Versailles, where Oscar Strauss represented Taft], ephemeral representatives of a future state that hoped for recognition from the great powers. Lithuania was represented by the Kovno attorney Rosenbaum who was an assistant to the foreign minister. The Ukraine delegated two Jews, the Kiev attorney Arnold Morgolin and Samuel Sarachi, a physician who had had a practice on London's Whitechapel Road. We find the signatures of a small group of other outstanding Jews on the final act of the peace conference. Baron Sonnino signed the Treaty of Versailles for Italy, Edwin Montagu for India, Louis Klotz on behalf St. Germain for France, Auguste Isaac for Trianon (also for France). Several of these representatives were also signatories to the treaties with Poland, Rumania, and Czechoslovakia. The treaty with Poland was signed by no fewer than three Jews, Sonnino, Klotz, and Montagu, while the other two main treaties were signed by Klotz.

Diplomatic activity by Jews after the treaty can be discussed briefly. Europe [!] had a Jewish foreign minister in the person of the deceased Walter Rathenau... Working closely with him was a Jewish ambassador, the very capable Dr. Lujo Hartmann, a historian who represented Austria in Berlin. In London, Mr. Henry Rabbinowitsch was chancellor of the new and fully recognized Lithuania. Until recently, the outstanding Russian-Jewish historian served in the same capacity in the legation of the Ukraine. Another outstanding historian, Professor Szymon Askenasi, is the chief of the Polish delegation to the League of Nations in Geneva.

Both the Soviet government and the ephemeral military government that fought the Bolshevist usurpation had a number of Jewish diplomats. The most prominent among the Bolshevists was Litvinov, the former ambassador to Great Britain and current assistant to Foreign Minister Kamenoff, as was his successor in London, Radek, who was also the first Soviet ambassador in Berlin. Salkind and Rothstein served as Soviet ambassadors to Teheran. On the other side, the old Russian attorney and senator Vinaver severed as foreign minister in the government of General Denikin, while the well-known international jurist Mandelstamm represented the same government in Paris.

In addition to those named above, others who should be mentioned include, among others: Judge Abram Elkus of New York, former American ambassador to Constantinople; Mark Hyman of New York, general consul of the U.S.

Shipping Board; Max D. Kirjassof, American consul in Manchuria; and the American consuls Samuel Sale and Samuel Sokobin in Kalgan [China]. Furthermore, there was Jacques Georges Nunberg, first secretary of the Polish embassy in Bern, and Milan Schwarz, Southern Slavish consul in Zürich. There were also several prominent Jews among the delegates to the League of Nations.

After this overview of the Jewification [*Verjudung*] of diplomacy from a professional Jewish pen, there can be no doubt that during this period, "Jewish ethos and Jewish pathos" were at work, and that the leadership of world affairs was almost entirely in the hands of the "children of the prophets."

Jewish Political Agitation

During the post-war period, Germany experienced the realization of another point of the program: "The constitution as a school of party discord":

> Constitutional governments were born of liberalism, which replaced the autocracy (monarchy) that was the salvation of the Goyim. The constitution, as you well know, is nothing more than a school for dispute, discussion, disagreement, fruitless party agitation, dissension, and party tendencies—in other words, a school for everything that weakens governmental efficiency. (Protocol 10)

This development could already be seen at the turn of the century. The Jews had a leading role in founding all political parties. Of the parties that they founded (or helped to found) and controlled in every way, we will name only the National Liberal Party, one of whose founders was the Jew Eduard Lasker; the Freethinker's Party, one of whose founders was the Jew Ludwig Bamberger; the "Right Center" at the National Assembly in Frankfurt, founded and led by the baptized Jew Eduard von Simson; and finally the Democratic Party in Prussia, which was "reorganized" by the Königsberg Jew Johann Jacoby. At the same time in Vienna, we find Adolf Fischhoff, spiritual leader of the Democratic Party, who for a time during the Revolution of 1848, held the fate of Vienna in his hands as president of the security service. The Conservative Party of the pre-war period was founded by the Jew Friedrich Julius Stahl, who let himself be baptized. He built the intellectual foundation of Christian (!) conservative political thought. He was also the leader of the conservative faction in the upper house and had a central role as member of the Evangelical Church Council (!).

But the strongest centers of Jewry's corrupting power are the two Marxist parties. The General German Workers' Union was led by the Jew Ferdinand Lassalle's (Lassal). And one can note that the Social Democrats and the Communist Party have the same father, Karl Marx-Mordechai, whose Jewish nature in both his works and person was accurately characterized by a Jew in this way:

> His [Marx's] spirit found a direction that forever overcame all supernatural forces because he showed how they were bound to the physical world; without realizing it himself, he became in his deepest self a Jew in tradition of the prophets.[1] (*Neue Jüdische Monatshefte*, 25.4.1918).

Not only was the theoretician and founder of Marxism a Jew, but Jews are also the best-known Marxist practitioners, whose deeds will forever be among the most terrible atrocities in history. We do not need to search for the names, but only refer to an essay by the Jew Georg Hermann in which he celebrates the atrocities as a revelation of Jewish nature, as a Jewish contribution to the history of humanity. He says:

> I hear Jews say nervously: "They hurt us, that is not good, it leads to bad blood." To the contrary: Let us be proud that a Marx, a Lassalle, a Singer, a Rosa Luxemburg, a [Kurt] Eisner, even a [Hugo] Haase, etc., are Jews. They represent the ancient human soul of our tribe better than any religious renewal is able to do. Let us cheerfully admit that also in Russia, and in Hungary, many of those—whether they are

---

[1] This is a revealing quotation: that Jews sometimes (often? always?) manifest longstanding Jewish propensities subconsciously, "without realizing it."

> correct or not, I dare not say—many of those who seeking to bring the oppressed, miserable masses to new, better, humane forms of life—a Trotsky, a Bela Kuhn—are Jews. They only prove that human thought is best advanced by the Jews. (*Neue Jüdische Monatshefte*, v. 3. Nr. 19/20).

Georg Hermann, the author of the well-known novel *Jettchen Gebert*, was fully aware of the significance of his words that he directed to his racial comrades in a Jewish magazine. In another book from the same time directed to the broader German public, his *Randbemerkungen* (1919), he presented himself as an "opponent of nationality"; and in a statement directed to the Germans, he wrote: "We must finally learn to put humanity above nationality."

At the same time that he glorifies Jewish-Communist murderers like Trotsky and Bela Kuhn in a Jewish magazine as real leaders of modern Jewry, Hermann tries elsewhere to take the German readership's faith away from its great men:

> Humanity would be better off had it never known its great statesmen, generals, and rulers—without great men and without great ages, it would have been much better off. Socially and culturally, it would be 5,000 years ahead. (*Randbemerkungen*, p. 90).

That is only one brief example of many that provides a look at the "school of discord" that the Protocols proposes as means to an end. Marxist Jews promoted class struggle within the people, and subverted national powers of resistance and public morality, while intellectual Jews who pretended to be nonpartisan saw to it that Jewish unity was preserved. This wicked double game—that praises Jewish-Marxist atrocities on one hand while subverting and weakening non-Aryan peoples by inciting them against themselves through carefully prepared slogans—is well-grounded in the plan of the Protocols. One can easily take the following passages and translate them from the language of the turn of the century into that of the post-war period:

They have not yet discovered and will not discover that this dream [of equality] is a clear infringement on the principal law of nature, which, from the beginning of the world, created each being unlike all others, precisely for the sake of expressing one's individuality. If we were able to lead them to such insane and blind beliefs, does it not obviously prove the low level of development of the Goy mind as compared to our own? It is precisely the thing that guarantees our success. (Protocol 15)

And:

The word 'liberty' brings all society into conflict with all authority, whether it be natural or divine. This is why, at the moment of our enthronement, we shall strike this word from the dictionary as being the symbol of a brute power that turns the masses into bloodthirsty beasts. It is true, however, that these beasts will sleep as soon as they have tasted blood, and then it is easy to shackle them; but if they don't get their blood, they will not sleep but rather struggle and fight. (Protocol 3)

Or: "From us emanates an all-embracing terror" (Protocol 9).

Could one hope to find a better expression of the theory and practice of the Jewish rulers of Russia and the Comintern during the post-war period,[2] and which they are doing today in Spain, than they were at the turn of the century?

Protocols on the Press and Culture

It would go beyond the bounds of this Introduction to spend any more time on the Jewish policies of the Marxist parties or list the Jewish actions and statements that prove and justify the historical accuracy of the

---

[2] The Comintern, also known as the Third International, was a Soviet organization founded in 1919 to promote global communism and global revolution. It was disbanded in mid-1943.

Protocols. Rather, let us compare another thesis from the Protocols with historical facts. Regarding Jewish domination of the press, it says:

> Not one bit of information will be made public without our control. This is already being done by us, since the news from all parts of the world is received through a few agencies, in which it is centralized. These agencies will then be completely in our power and they will publish only such news as we permit. (Protocol 12)

The extent to which the source of the international press system was Jewified even during the pre-war period is proven by looking at the three leading global press agencies. All three were founded by Jews; and the two that survive today are still fully Jewified. The French *Agence Havas* was founded by the Jew Charles Lois Havas; the English Reuters by Josaphat Beer, the son of a rabbi who later added the name "Reuter"; and the now defunct [as of 1934] Wolff Telegraphic Bureau in Germany was the work of the Jew Bernhard Wolff.

The extent to which Jewry used the power of the press to serve Jewish interests is clear from an editorial in the magazine *Der Jude*, which was published before (!) the end of the war. It threatened the German government with Jewish world power:

> We have a leading role in the international press, in international finance, and in economic life; we influence public opinion, we are an important factor in establishing international attitudes, and—something very important—we are represented everywhere. We are truly a unique international people, spread over every land, active in every aspect of politics, and of immeasurable value to anyone who wishes to be our ally. (v. 3, 1918/19, p. 194).

Closely bound to the press was Jewish influence on Germany's intellectual and cultural life. Jewry had no limits here during the post-war [Weimar] period, able to fully realize the thesis in the Protocols about subversive activity in this field: "We have misled, corrupted, deceived, and demoralized the Goy youth by education along principles and theories known by us to be false, but which we ourselves have inspired" (Protocol 9).

The reader cannot be spared the results of this process, evidenced in the defense of immoral and obscene literature by Jewish writers considered great and important members of their race. They fought laws against immoral and obscene literature, claiming that it was necessary to the intellectual life of the nation and particularly for the education of the youth. They praised it accordingly.[3] The *Berliner Tageblatt*, at the time a purely Jewish newspaper, and one proclaimed by the Jews to be Germany's leading international newspaper, wrote the following about the battle over the law—which ultimately passed, despite Jewish influence:

> Obscenity is absolutely necessary for the youth. Old maids argue the fantasy that young boys and girls are corrupted by obscene literature. In reality, however, the fantasies of young people going through puberty are rather obscene, and these fantasies need obscene literature to redirect their arousal in harmless ways. If one takes obscene literature away from the youth, the number of youthful sex crimes would increase tremendously. An outlet would be closed, and thus an inner pressure would have destructive effects. Obscene literature means as much, even more, to the youth than dirty jokes to adults. What would become of all the fine gentlemen and workers who exchange dirty jokes at pubs, bowling clubs, or evening events if one closed off that outlet—what filthiness would they do, if they could no longer talk about filthiness! (*Berliner Tageblatt*, 1 December 1926).

The Jews have used every means to oppose this [anti-obscenity] law. The Jew Willi Haas's *Literarische Welt*, which otherwise had no interest in Germandom outside our borders, saw Germans abroad as a way around the law. The Jew Heinrich Eduard Jakob proposed the following plan:

---

[3] This has strong echoes in the present day, where, for decades, Jews have played central roles in the publication and distribution of pornographic magazines, films, and websites.

> The Index *liborum prohibitorum* established by this law is valid only for the territory of the Reich. What is the sense of establishing censorship for 60 million German readers when there are 90 million of them in the world? The law does not encompass the purely German population of Austria, Switzerland, or northern Bohemia. It does not encompass the Baltic Germans, those in Alsace or Luxemburg, Danzig or Upper Silesia. The law is so weak that, to give only a few examples, energetic action by three foreign German [Jewish] newspapers—the *Neue Freie Presse* in Vienna, the *Neue Züricher Zeitung*, and the *Prager Tageblatt*—could render it impotent. Will these newspapers do anything? Be assured, they will. They will do it because of their German past, because of their liberal tradition, and for other reasons. (*Die literarische Welt*, Nr. 51 of 17.12.1926).

Today we must grant that these German-language Jewish newspapers abroad did their duty under Jakob's plan in an exemplary way. So too did the Jewish "writer" Franz Wersel, who wrote in the *Literarische Welt* (26.11.1926) that he became a member of the Academy of Literature only so that he could use its "official authority" to "fight this dreadful law against obscenity and immorality" with more force than he otherwise would have.

    Clear evidence of the satanic battle opposing the protection of German youth from obscenity and trashy literature, from moral corruption and moral destruction, comes from the behavior of the Jews in Bern [Switzerland] and all of their racial comrades in the battle against *The Protocols of the Elders of Zion*. They misused the "Law on Movie Theaters and Measures against Immoral Literature" against a publication that in no way injured moral sensibilities, even if it said something "painful" for the Jews. This makes clear to any reasonable person the duplicity and dishonesty of Jewry. They have used every means to morally corrupt non-Jewish youth during the post-war period by fighting the law against trashy and obscene literature. After Jewish world power was shaken by the National Socialist revolution [in 1933], however, a similar law in the canton of Bern was good enough to prevent the unmasking of Jewish world power.

Here, we need not discuss in detail the Jewification of theatrical life, particularly the Jewification of the Berlin stage; a few passing remarks will suffice. A report from one of the few newspapers from that time that dared to oppose the evil spirit of the almost entirely Jewish theater directors had this to say about the theater calendar. It gives us a picture of the Jewish stamp on the holidays of the period—a mockery of everything German and Christian, something that had been impossible up to that time:

> The Lessing Theater is producing Shaw. The asses at the Künstler-Theater dug up Sardou, and the "German" Theater for Christmas is giving us Beer-Hoffman's Zionist play *Jakobs Traum*. The Kammerspiele is doing Wedekind's *Fühlingswachen* in the afternoon, and in the evening, "more Strindberg." Das Kleine Theater is doing *Das unberührte Weib* by the kitschy Pole Zapolka. To improve attendance, the actresses are half naked. Das Kleine Schauspielhaus is doing "Strindberg." Das Theater an der Königgrätzstrasse is performing, of all things, Wedekind's *Schloss Wetterstein*. The Residenz-Theater was at least honestly unashamed: it celebrated Christmas with the bordello drama *Evchen Humrecht*. Long live the theater director who earns money following the principles of the whorehouse! The Tribüne is not only presenting Wedekind's *Franziska*, but more importantly has the theatrical whore [Olga] 'Wojan' stark naked on stage behind a thin veil. Is it hateful for us to say, in combating this Witch's Sabbath during the Christmas season, that Jewish theater directors are responsible for these monstrosities? (*Deutsches Volkstum*, 1920, Nr. 3).

In the revues produced exclusively by Jews during the post-war period, the destruction of family life, and above all marriage, reached its epitome. We must content ourselves here with an overview of the titles of some of these Jewish products: "Undress," "On and Off," "Beautiful and Chic," "Damn—A Thousand Women," "A Thousand Naked Women,"

"Strictly Forbidden," "The Sins of the World," and "Sinful and Sweet." And we add the text of a poster for the James Klein Revue "Undress":

-- COMIC OPERA --
James Klein's
Powerful New Revue Show "Undress"!

An Evening without Morality
in 30 Scenes
With 60 Prize-Winning Nude Models

The Hunt for Beautiful Women
Experience with a 15-Year-Old
The Huge Heavenly Bed
The Woman with a Whip
Sunshine and Naked Magic

Living Bells and Living Flowers and 20 more Scenes
Original Paris Revue Costumes

Furthermore, the extent to which Jewry not only tried to subvert the law against immoral literature and obscenity, but was also actively involved in pornographic films of the worse sort, is shown by the titles of a selection of films of Jewish origin:

How Pure and Beautiful Women Fall;
The Right of Free Love;
Lu, the Flirt;
Sinful Blood;
In the Clutches of Sin;
The Daughter of the Prostitute;
The Courage to Sin;
Those Who Sell Themselves (Those Who Live from Love);
Paragraph 175-Different than the Others;
Paragraph 218-Abortion;
Paragraph 182-Under the Age of Consent;
Lilli's Path to Prostitution

Racial Miscegenation

Closely bound up with the Jewish propaganda for pimps and prostitution that was pressed on Germans with a persistence that makes it clear that it was no accident…closely bound to that is Jewish propaganda for race-mixing, promoted to our people through fashion and the press. An essay by the Jew Claire Goll illustrates the ways the Jews sought to realize their slogan of the "equality" of all who have a human face. It concerns the Niggerfication [*Vernegerung*] of Europe, which in a way revealed the general staff plan of the Jews, showing how they used fashion to advance their instinctual goal of corrupting their host people:

> In New York, the Negroes have their hair straightened; the Whites want curls, Negro hair. That goes well with dark colored skin, the new fashion of brown skin. When one gets to the point where the skin of Negroes can be whitened, racial differences will happily disappear. This will benefit and bless old-fashioned looking White humanity. (*Berliner Tageblatt*, Nr. 489 of 16.10.1928).

Furthermore, and also an explanation as to why the debasement of the host people is a prerequisite for Jewish rule, consider the opinion of the Jew Kurt Münzer, taken from his 1910 book *Der Weg nach Zion*:

> We Jews are not the only ones debased and at the end of a worn-out culture that has been sucked dry. All European races have corrupted their blood as we have—perhaps *we* have infected *their* blood. Everything today is Jewified. Our essence is in everything living, our spirit rules the world. We are the masters; what has power today is our intellectual child. We can no longer be driven out, we have overcome the races, corrupted them, broken their strength; everything is worn out, rotten, and decayed because of our culture. Our spirit can no longer be exterminated.[4]

Jewish subversive activity like this, especially that which is directed specifically toward non-Jewish youth, proves clearly that the Jews have acted consistently with the cited passage from the Protocols.

---

[4] A remarkable statement from over 100 years ago. One can only wonder how much worse things are today.

Jewish 'Pacifism'

Along these lines, we must not forget the propaganda for pacifism that Jews such as Kurt Tucholsky (under several aliases) used to try to break the people's will to defend themselves. The following citations from Tucholsky's pamphlets reveal the aggressive and combative tone that he used to attempt to win over the always active and battle-ready German youth to his pacifism. Although he never was at the Front, he had these clear words to say about his conduct during the World War:

> I shirked the war for three-and-a-half years however I could—and I regret that I did not have the courage to say no and refuse military service, like the great Karl Liebknecht. I am ashamed of that. I did what many others did, using every way I could find to avoid being shot at and having to shoot. (*Mit 5 PS*, p. 85).

He built his own treasonous ideology:

> What judges call 'treason' does not bother us [Jews], and what they call 'high treason' is for us not dishonorable. We are left cold by what they call 'perjury,' 'destruction of documents,' and 'breach of peace.' (*Deutschland, Deutschland über Alles*, p. 167).

If that were not enough, he calls for direct acts of treason:

> For us pacifists...if required to preserve the peace of Europe, if demanded by our consciences—and I am fully aware of what I am saying—there is no German military secret that I would not give to a foreign power if it seemed necessary to preserve peace... We are traitors. But we betray a state that we renounce in favor of a land that we love, for peace and for our real fatherland: Europe. (*Weltbühne*, 27.3.1928, p. 473).

Tucholsky was not the only Jew who thought this way, as is proven by an essay by the Viennese Jew Alfred Polgar in the *Berliner Tageblatt* of 1922. He wrote this about the Germans of 1914:

> Cattle are cattle... Animals about to be slaughtered have no idea what is coming. The proof of that was brought *en masse* when the war began. They [Germans] cheered in the streets, heads high, those that would fall to the axe. (*Deutsches Volkstum*, 122, Nr. 3, p. 130).

For 15 years, Jews in Germany followed *The Protocols of the Elders of Zion* in a striking way, working to stifle the will of German youth to fight. They did this not only in magazines and pamphlets, but also in university lecture halls. On 1 April 1933 there was a total of 1,066 Jewish professors at German universities. They spread the poison of pacifism and a contempt for German heroism through Jews like Emil Gumbel, Theodor Lessing, and their comrades.

The reader must realize that such treasonous statements in word and image were not prohibited because the governmental press office in Prussia was in the hands of Jews. In Prussia in 1930, the press was under the patronage of Jewish State Secretary Dr. Weissman, with his subordinates: Superior Councilor Gosslar as press secretary for the Prussian government, and Senior Councilor Dr. Pfeifer as his deputy; Councilor Dr. Weichmann as press secretary in the Prussian Department of State; and Dr. Hirschfeld as press secretary in the Prussian Interior Ministry. The same was true for the Reich Federation of the Press, headed by the Jew Georg Bernhard. The same was true in the Protective Federation for German Writers, which had the following leaders in 1928:

Chairman: Walter von Molo (non-Jew)
Vice Chair: Arnold Zweig (Jew)
First Secretary: Paul Guttmann (Jew)
Assistant Secy: Frau Adele Schreiber-Krieger (Jew)
Treasurer: Dr. Léon Zeitlin (Jew)
Assistant Treasurer: Dr. Theodor Bohner (non-Jew).

Board Members: Erich Baron (Jew),
Johannes R. Becher (non-Jew),
Robert Breuer (Jew),
Dr. Max Deri (Jew),
Dr. Annie Jacker (Jew),
Sami Gronemann (Jew),
Egon Erwin Kisch (Jew),
Dr. Alfred Kuhn (non-Jew),
Bruno Shoenlang (Jew),
Paul Westheim (Jew).

Jews on Homosexuality and Abortion

Another active account of Jewish deeds is the propaganda for the abolition of Paragraph 175 of the legal code, which penalized homosexuality. This, too, was demanded by the Protocols as a way of corrupting non-Jewish youth. The Jew Magnus Hirschfeld had worked in this area long before the war. He created the "Scientific Humanitarian Committee," an organization of homosexuals that spread throughout Germany, as his papers clearly prove. Even before the turn of the century, it had offices in Berlin, Hamburg, Munich, and the Rhineland. These cells recruited doctors, attorneys, and even clergymen who supported the Jew Hirschfeld and gathered lists of names for petitions to relevant government offices.

During the post-war period, this organization—founded and led by Jews—had absolute freedom. There was a "press for homosexuals," and in one of their periodicals, *Friendship*, the following sentences could appear unhindered, without in any way being restricted by the Constitution:

> Homosexuals. These people hope that, over the years, the government and people will finally realize that the legal paragraph should be eliminated and that all Germans should enjoy the same rights. (*Das Freundschaftsblatt*, 1928, Nr. 52).[5]

Besides this public mockery of the German people, the Jew Willi Haas's *Literarische Welt* printed the following propaganda for lesbianism on the occasion of the Max Reinhardt-Goldmann's premiere of *Gefangenen* by Bourdet (which treated homosexuality):

> Two men speak in one scene about a lesbian drama that presumably takes place behind the scenes. When will we finally see a play in which this love itself—its uniqueness, its psychology, its different language, the dialog of an eroticism foreign to men—receives serious literary treatment? Above all, the hopeless alienation against this unapproach-

---

[5] Again, we see an early manifestation of present-day Jewish-led activity in favor of LGBTQ- and Trans- "rights."

able, incomprehensible relationship? That would certainly be new material for our theater, which needs it. (*Literarische Welt*, 1926, Nr. 24/25).

Closely connected to the battle against Paragraph 175 is the subversive Jewish effort against Paragraph 218, which forbids abortion. Here, too, the Jew Magnus Hirschfeld was a leader in a crime against the German people. From among countless articles by Jewish authors—not to mention the actual crimes of Jewish doctors against budding life—we mention only the following:

- "Abortion or Birth Control?" by Dr. Martha Ruben-Wolf;
- "Struggle against Paragraph 218," by Dr. Friedrich Wolf;
- "Blessing of Children, Fertility Control, Abortion," by Dr. Fritz Bruchbacher;
- "Contraception," by Magnus Hirschfeld.

This overview of the culturally and morally subversive influence of the Jews is only a brief summary of the available material on several important points. It is enough to show that each point of the *Protocols of the Elders of Zion* about the corruption of non-Jewish youth has been more than fulfilled.

The best way to measure the practical effects of this attack on the existence of a healthy German nation is to consider the Jewification of the medical and legal professions, the latter of which is always ready to defend its racial comrades of other professions in court. In Berlin, the percentage of non-Aryan physicians on 1 October 1933 was 52.2%—at a time when many Jews had already left Germany. The percentage for attorneys as of April 1933 was 50.9%. In January 1933, 28.4% of Berlin's judges and 15.1% of its States' Attorneys General were of Jewish descent.

Each point of the Protocols could be handled in the same way. In Germany alone, there is enough material from the post-war period to prove the accuracy of the statements collected in the *Protocols of the Elders of Zion*. We will not cover further points simply because it would take far more space than is available in this Introduction. Some statements in the Protocols would require lengthy historical research; others would require specialized scientific methods.

Words from an American Jew: Samuel Roth

In closing, we want to give just one more example of the Jewish hope for absolute world domination that always surfaces in Jewish literature and essays. The old Jewish hatred of the Goyim, familiar from the Talmud and *Schulchan Aruch* and in Jewish history from ancient times,[6] is brought up to the modern era in the *Protocols of the Elders of Zion* where it receives a political discussion of opportunities and prospects. This Jewish hatred is manifested anew each day in the private lives of individual Jews.

This form of Jewish hatred was especially expressed in novels during the post-war period, such as *Der Weg nach Zion* by Kurt Münzer and Arthur Landsberger's novel *Asiaten*. The American Jew Samuel Roth gives a classic example of the private expression of Jahwe's revenge on non-Jews in his book *Now and Forever*. It takes the form of a dialogue between himself and Israel Zangwill. *Reichsleiter* Alfred Rosenberg discussed it in his major speech at the Reich Party Rally in 1937. The following is a long quotation from this significant Jewish writing:

> *Roth*: "They envy our intellectual leadership of Europe, whose thought is Jew-born and Jew-bred. Europe not only thinks in Jewish terms, but all her enterprises are motivated by the personalities of Jews. Only once, for one trembling moment, did the mind of Europe raise itself above the turmoil of its mental slavery, in the rhythmic, sentimental meditations of Descartes. But not till the rise of Spinoza did Europe achieve a philosophy. Spinoza is at the heart of European thought: he prevented Descartes, who came before him, from becoming a prophet, as he prevented Immanuel Kant, who came after him, from becoming a lawgiver. As it was in the beginning, so it still is now. There is not a program, a sentiment, or a conviction a European can choose to follow but he must follow a Jew—whether it be Bergson, Marx, or Freud.

---

[6] For an elaboration of these very points, see *Eternal Strangers* (T. Dalton, 2019) and *The Book of the Shulchan Aruch* (E. Bischoff, 2023).

Why should not the intelligentsia of Europe hate us? Time and again we have humiliated them. We began by giving them Christianity, and for two thousand years they have been trying to live up to it. A continent-full of savages loving plunder and thieving, exulting in rape and incest, were saddled with a religion enjoining them to love their neighbors as themselves. Those mountain chieftains with hidden daggers kept in readiness to strike, those bands of idlers accustomed to hiring out their soldierly services at so much per day, were advised to turn the other cheek. If they had only had the presence of mind, how they would have answered their Christian teachers! But the poor European has from time immemorial suffered certain periodic lapses of shyness in which it is difficult for him to deny any one anything. In such a moment, it is easy to make him believe that he is good and noble and nothing else. In such a moment, Christianity was imposed on Europe. And even though Europeans have not permitted themselves to be swung entirely out of their natural preference for pillage and brigandry, this religion we foisted on them has confused their speech and freighted their treaties with vows they do not mean and cannot understand.[7]

But Christianity was only the first of a long series of Jewish enterprises of which Socialism is the culminating imposition. Instinctively Europe is as much against Socialism as she has always been against Christianity. Why are they gradually accepting Socialism? Europe is simply living though another one of her periods of shyness. But don't worry. Europe will soon recover. Only see what has just happened here in England. Why did the railway workers and the longshoremen allow the Government to starve the coal miners into submission? 'You held better and steadier jobs than we did during the war, so you can afford to strike.' Was that not the substance of the reply of the rail-

---

[7] For an elaboration on this important point, see the two essays by the Jew Marcus Savage in *Classic Essays on the Jewish Question* (T. Dalton, ed.; 2023).

road workers and the longshoremen to the appeal of the coal miners? I tell you that just as Christianity has failed to make Christians of them, Socialism will fail to make men of them.

In the meantime, Socialism and Christianity are abiding, irritating symbols of Europe's mental enslavement to Israel. When the Chestertons and the Bellocs talk of race purity and patriotism, they lie in their throats. They know that we are racially purer than they are. They know that we are better patriots than they are. It is their intellectual slavery which rankles in them, and once this is understood, we can afford to ignore them completely."

Zangwill: "Suppose I grant you our intellectual leadership—I do not think it is possible to deny it—have not the Europeans leadership in everything else, in the conduct of great cities, in the arts, in military science? That is having so much more than we have that I still do not see why they should be angry or envious." […]

Roth: "There will be Jews in Russia, in Germany, in Austria and in Italy. But the greater number of the Jews will be massed in India, Persia, China and all the neighboring countries. Jews will be spread plentifully throughout the entire East, which will float strange colored banners fresh with triumph. The whole East will be alive with planning and with building. But in the midst of all this, a strange, a terrible man will arise, the like of whom has never before been seen on earth, and he will go through the marketplaces of the East, and he will speak only a loathing of Europe.

He will wander from man to man and from city to city, and his speech will be very scant and quiet, but something in his eyes will open up in their beholders great sluices of wrath, so that slowly, silently, desperately, his following will increase, and all with little clamor, all with little wagging of the boneless tongue.

In time, this man will become leader of an enterprise of vengeance which will start out modestly from Calcutta, but by the time it reaches Constantinople will number several millions of men, carrying secreted in their clothes little yellow phials. Sweeping up the Steppes, their numbers will increase as by a miracle, and their great hordes will seem to darken the face of the earth.

For six days and six nights, the world will remain in the grip of these dark forces, for it took six days for God to create the world. The yellow cloud will slowly descend in their midst and breathing will become as painful as pulling nails from living fingers. A strange confusion will spread throughout the world during those dreadful six days. Having gone out for a stroll, a man will find, on having reached the front door of his dwelling, that he is legless. Sitting opposite a beautiful woman, he will find himself gone blind. The water in his cup will taste like foul blood. His bones will snap like dry twigs.

The lives of the peoples of Europe will flow out of them through the mouth, through the eyes, and through the dense, undented skin, in streams of foul blood wherever the strange man and his silent army will have passed through.

In Russia, only sucklings and illiterates will be spared—the rest will make huge graveyards of Moscow and Petrograd. Of Poland and the Ukraine, he will make a howling wilderness, all the women in those countries will be put to shame before being killed as a reminder of what once happened to a defenseless people in their midst. The docks will spout foul blood where Danzig receives the sea.

Of Belgium and Germany, he will make such a slaughter-house that it will be necessary to build new and taller dykes around Holland, that the smell of the carnage might not befoul a country for which his outraged memory will have no terrors. Through France, he will sweep as a conflagration sweeps through a cornfield…"[8]

---

[8] *Now and Forever*, from chapters 5 and 17 (1925; R. McBride and Co.)

This bloodthirsty desire for murder and revenge against undying peoples is constantly repeated in Jewish literature and novels, and in the most varied ways. It is frightening and revolting, but nonetheless a genuine and accurate picture of the eternal enmity Jews have against non-Jews. The statements and demands in the Protocols are consistent with this well-nourished racial instinct, which, as we have seen from the effects of the Jews in Germany, unscrupulously and steadily works to oppose and destroy all existing values of community, culture, justice, and morality.

If we review once again these comments on the *Protocols of the Elders of Zion*, we must conclude that the theses and facts proclaimed in the Protocols, and evidenced by the activities of the Jews in Germany, have been fully proved. The Jews in post-war Germany have behaved consistently with what is written in the Protocols.

This conclusion has a large and pressing significance for all the cultured peoples of the world. They, too, must thoroughly study the Jewish Question in their countries. At the moment, Germany is Enemy #1 of the Jews. It has freed itself from this poison in its racial body through the Nuremberg Laws. Each people and each country, however, must sooner or later defend itself against subversive Jewish activity.

For we Germans, the memory of this time of subversion is only a warning. We have freed ourselves from the nightmare of Jewish dominance. In all other states and peoples, however, one can find daily evidence of similar or identical Jewish subversion. As long as they do not recognize and solve the Jewish Question and the Jews continue to determine the fate of peoples—just recently, Leon Blum's French cabinet was 37.5% Jewified—so long will it be impossible to speak of peace between peoples. For the future, therefore, and for every country, there is but one warning call to reason, which also includes a call to knowledge and defense: *Peoples of the world, defend your holiest possessions!*

INTRODUCTION TO THE *PROTOCOLS*
JULIUS EVOLA

Editor: Julius Evola (1898-1974) was an Italian philosopher, political theorist, and alleged 'neo-fascist' thinker whose work was influential in both Mussolini's Italy and in the German National Socialist movement. He was criticized as both an anti-Semite and a racist, although he believed that race was a 'spiritual' rather than biological construction, and thus had fundamental conflicts with NS policy. When the Protocols were published in Italian in 1938, Evola wrote the following Introduction, which contributed greatly to the spread and influence of the document in Italy. Several years later, after the war, Evola wrote a book entitled *Men Among the Ruins* (1953). There, he argued that the Jews alone could not have the power portrayed in the Protocols because there were other, higher, 'occult' powers at work in the world—referring, vaguely, to worldviews, myths, and perhaps even spiritual entities. His short update on the Protocols in that book is included below, following the original Introduction.

The importance of this document [the Protocols], which *Vita Italiana* has just reprinted, cannot be sufficiently emphasized. It presents a spiritual 'motivation' like few others, it reveals unsuspected horizons, and it draws attention to fundamental problems related to action and to knowledge, which must not be neglected or postponed, especially in these decisive hours of Western history, on pain of seriously prejudicing the offensive of those who fight in the name of spirit, of tradition, and of true civilization.

Two aspects particularly demand attention in the Protocols. The first concerns the Jewish question directly. The second has a more general importance, and leads us to tackle the problem of the true forces at work in history. For the reader to understand perfectly what we mean here, we think that it is suitable to bring forward certain considerations essential to a good orientation on this matter.

For this purpose, it is first necessary to examine the famous problem of the 'authenticity' of the document, on which certain parties have attempted tendentiously to focus all of the public's attention, by means of which alone they endeavored to determine the importance and the validity of the text. This is really a very childish approach. Obviously, one can simply deny the existence of any secret directive force behind historic events. But one cannot admit, even as a mere hypothesis, that there may be something of that sort, without acknowledging that it must then become necessary to do a kind of research very different from that which is based on 'documentary evidence' in the common sense. Here, as rightly pointed out by Guénon, lies the decisive point, which puts the question of 'authenticity' into perspective: the fact is that no truly and seriously secret organization, whatever its nature, leaves behind written 'documents'. It is only by inductive processes that the importance of texts such as the Protocols can be determined. This means that the problem of their 'authenticity' is secondary to the far more serious and essential problem of their 'veracity', as was already emphasized by Giovani Preziosi when he published them for the first time seventeen years ago. The serious and positive conclusion of the whole controversy which has developed since is that, even if we assume that the Protocols are not 'authentic' in the narrow sense, it comes to the same thing as if they were, for two capital and decisive reasons:

1) Because the facts show that they describe the real state of affairs truthfully;
2) Because their correspondence with the governing ideas of both traditional and modern Judaism is indisputable.

As the Bern trial provoked by the Protocols was widely talked about, we shall describe it here, so that the reader knows where he stands and does not let himself be influenced by tendentious reportage. The Bern trial was really just a maneuver on the part of international Judaism, which attempted to use Swiss justice, or, to put it better, Swiss Marxist 'justice', to obtain a sort of official legal determination of the non-authenticity of the document which so troubles Israel. That it was really just a maneuver becomes clear from the very impossibility of raising the question of the authenticity of the Protocols there. Basically, the Bern court admitted the complaint made by certain Israelite communities against a certain Silvio Schnell, who had distributed some copies of the German edition of the Protocols in a nationalist meeting, on the basis of Article 14 of the law of the Canton of Bern regarding subversive and immoral literature. Starting from this basis, from a strictly legal point of view, the Berne court should not have taken any interest in the problem of the authenticity or otherwise of the Protocols, but should simply have decided whether the Protocols, irrespective of their truth or falsity, were or were not reprehensible according to the aforementioned law, as being likely to incite one part of the Swiss population against another. Judaism however distorted this requirement by focusing attention on the problem of authenticity, in order to reach the desired conclusion. In this respect, here is a significant declaration by the great Rabbi of Stockholm: "This is not a process against Schnell and his friends, but one of all the Israelites of the world against all their detractors. Seventy million Jews have their eyes fixed on Bern."

After a year of proceedings, the court of first instance ended up convicting Schnell, from which the Jews happily inferred that they had got rid of the Protocols. This was a short-lived triumph. In November 1937, the Bern court of appeal quashed the previous judgement, acquitted Schnell, ordered the plaintiff Jewish communities to pay costs, and declared itself incompetent to rule on the question of the authenticity of the Protocols. But the question of authenticity had already been raised in the first hearing. For what results? Once again, negative ones. The Jewish front had tried to reach its objectives essentially by two means: by false testimonies and by the thesis of 'plagiarism'. As we cannot go into detail here, we shall limit ourselves to the following remarks: a certain Madam Kolb, already sentenced for fraud and forgery as 'Princess Radziwill', declared, in a deposition skillfully devised in conjunction with one of her woman friends and a certain Comte du Chayla—a more than suspicious character, a paranoiac, adventurer and traitor, once sentenced to the death penalty, then pardoned—that the Protocols were written in Paris about 1905 by three agents of the Russian secret police, with the intention of stirring up an anti-Semitic publicity campaign. However, the Protocols were shown to have been in the possession of a certain Stepanoff in 1895, and of Nilus in 1902, and to have been published fully in the Russian newspaper *Znamja* in 1903, i.e., two years before their purported compilation in Paris! Furthermore, it was proved that none of the three Russians named, to wit, Ratchkovsky, Manuellov, and Golovinsky, were in Paris at the time when, according to Madam Kolb, they supposedly "invented" the Protocols.

The other means of attack was the charge of 'plagiarism'. A serious misunderstanding arose here. Basically, the problem of the value of the Protocols is quite different from that which might arise regarding a literary work, which could be settled by the examination of its originality and the right of someone to consider themselves its author. Here, the issue is totally dissimilar. The *Times* had already raised the question of plagiarism in 1921, by pointing out that the text copies ideas and sentences from a pamphlet published in 1864 by a certain Joly (himself a half-Jew, a revolutionary, and a Freemason) about the methods to be used in a Machiavellian policy of domination. This correspondence, or this 'plagiarism', is real, and not limited to the work of Joly, but applies to various other then-existent works. However, what does this tell us? In deciding whether or not the Protocols correspond to the program of world domination of an occult organization, it makes no difference whether the author has composed and written them from start to finish, or whether, in the course of his composition, he has also used ideas and elements from other works, thus creating, from the literary standpoint, a 'plagiarism'. The anti-Semitic controversy has already brought to light a whole series of 'sources' or antecedents to the Protocols, which generally draw their inspiration from a single current of ideas, and reflect, often in a 'fictionalized' form, the confused awareness of a truth. This truth is that the whole orientation of the modern world conforms to an established plan, as implemented by some mysterious organization.

Thus, the problem of 'authenticity' brings us back again to that of 'veracity'. As far as 'authenticity' is concerned, the outcome of the trial of Bern is, as we have explained, negative: the prosecution did not succeed in proving that the Protocols were false. But legally, the defense is not required to prove the authenticity of an impugned document; it is up to the prosecution to prove its falsity. But since, despite all the efforts of Judaism—the concerted testimonies, the thesis of 'plagiarism', the tendentious documents provided by the Soviets, the maneuvers which succeeded in rendering all the documents of the defense inadmissible (at least, in the court of first instance), an extremely one-sided assessor's report by Loosli, a notorious philo-Semite, and so on—they did not succeed in proving this falsity, the field is clear, and the question of 'authenticity' is liquidated, that is to say, it is once again subordinate to a double test of superior character, which is, let us repeat again: 1) the proof by the facts; 2) the proof by the nature of the Jewish spirit.

*****

Having given these clarifications, it is now possible to move on to the content of the Protocols.

They contain the plan for an occult war, whose objective is the utter destruction, in the non-Jewish peoples, of all tradition, class, aristocracy, and hierarchy, and of all moral, religious, or supra-material values. With this aim in view, an occult international organization, directed by real leaders clearly conscious of their goals and of the methods to be followed to achieve them, would appear for a long time to have been exercising, and continuing to exercise, a unitary invisible action, which constitutes the source of the main forms of corruption of Western civilization and society: liberalism, individualism, egalitarianism, free thought, anti-religious Enlightenment, and various additions which, following on from these, bring about the revolt of the masses and communism itself.

It is important to note that the absolute falsity of all these ideologies is expressly recognized: they are stated to have been created and propagated only as instruments of destruction and, in relation to Communism, the Protocols go so far as to declare:

> If we were able to lead them to such insane and blind beliefs, does it not obviously prove the low level of development of the Goy mind as compared to our own? It is precisely the thing that guarantees our success. (Protocol 15)

Not only they talk about political ideologies which will have to be instilled without anyone being allowed to grasp their true meaning and their goal, but they talk also of a "science" created with the purpose of general demoralization, and significant references are made to the scientistic superstition of 'Progress', to Darwinism, to Marxist and historicist sociology, and so on. "The Goyim are no longer able to think without our scientific advice" (P3), while, once again, the falseness of all those theories is acknowledged (P1, P2, P3, P13).

In the third place, we find discussion of a specifically cultural action: to dominate the principal centers of official teaching; to control, through the monopoly of the popular press, public opinion; to spread in the so-called leading countries an unhinged and equivocal literature (P14); to provoke, therefore, as a counterpart of social defeatism, a moral defeatism, to be increased by an attack upon religious values and their representatives, to be carried out, not head-on and openly, but by stirring up criticism, mistrust, and discreditable rumors regarding the clergy (P4, P16).

The 'mercantilization' of life is indicated as being one of the principal means of destruction; hence, also, the necessity of having a crowd of 'economists' as conscious or unconscious instruments of the secret chiefs. Once the spiritual values which were at the root of the former authority have been destroyed and replaced by mathematical calculations and material needs, all the peoples of the world must be brought to a universal war, in which it is assumed each will follow its own interests, and all will remain unaware of the common enemy (P4). Finally, it is proposed to encourage the ideas of the various competing groups, and, instead of attacking them, to use them to realize the overall plan, so that a capacity for providing support for the most diverse conceptions, from the aristocratic and the totalitarian to the anarchist or socialist ones, is recognized, provided that the effects contribute to the common goal (P5, P12). The necessity of destroying family life and its influence on spiritual education is also recognized (P10), as is that of rendering the masses stupid by means of sport and distractions of all kinds, and stirring up their passionate and irrational tendencies to the point at which they lose any faculty of discrimination (P13). This is the first phase of the occult war: its goal is to create an enormous proletariat, to reduce the peoples to a mush of beings without tradition or inner strength.

Then there is proposed a further action, on the basis of the power of gold. The secret chiefs will control gold globally, and, by means of it, all the peoples already deracinated, along with their apparent, more or less demagogic, leaders. While, on one hand, the destruction will proceed through ideological poisons, revolts, revolutions and conflicts of all sorts, the masters of gold will stir up crises of domestic economy everywhere, with the purpose of driving humanity to such a state of prostration, despair, and utter mistrust towards any ideal or system that it becomes a passive object in the hands of the invisible dominators, who will then manifest themselves, and impose themselves as absolute world-wide rulers. The King of Israel will be at their head, and the ancient promise of the *Regnum* of the 'Chosen People' will be achieved.

This is the essence of the Protocols. The more general problem which is connected to it has various aspects.

The Jew Benjamin Disraeli once wrote these significant words: "The world is governed by very different personages from what is imagined by persons who are not behind the scenes." The importance of the Protocols consists, first and foremost, in arousing the suspicion, the presentiment, that history has a 'third dimension', that an 'intelligence' can be hidden behind apparent leaders and events, and that many presumed causes are only the effects of a subterranean influence. What the Protocols say about a pseudo-scientific mentality, created solely with a pre-established plan in view, is particularly important; the so-called 'scientific' or 'historical' way of looking at history falls exactly within this description, and aims to divert attention systematically from the plane where true causes come into play. Nothing is more significant than this passage from Protocol 15:

> The Goy's purely animal mind is incapable of analysis and observation, and even less so of foreseeing the results to which a given principle may lead. It is through this difference in the process of reasoning between us and the Goyim that it becomes possible to clearly see the stamp of God's elect, as compared to the instinctive and bestial mentality of the Goyim. They see, but they cannot foresee; they cannot invent anything except material things. It is clear, therefore, that nature herself intended us to rule and guide the world.
> ... Regarding the secrets of our political plans, both the masses and their administration are like little children.

It is not by chance that recent history shows us the phases of a systematic and progressive work of spiritual, political, and cultural destruction, and, in this respect, the Protocols offer us, to say the least, what a scientist would call a "working hypothesis", that is, a basic idea whose truth is confirmed by its capacity to organize, via inductive research, a body of facts otherwise apparently unrelated and spontaneous, by bringing out their logic and their unique direction. This is the second aspect which must be borne in mind.

The fact is that the content of the Protocols, in its first part, which concerns the stages and the means of the destruction, corresponds in an impressive way to what has already unfolded, and continues to unfold, in recent history, as if the chiefs of the various governments, the apparent leaders of the various movements, and all those who made 'history' in the previous century, had only been the unconscious executors of a pre-established plan, announced a long time in advance, whether by that text or by others, as we have already mentioned. This is why Hugo Wast (*Oro*, Buenos Aires, 1935, p. 20) wrote: "The Protocols may be false, but they are carried out wonderfully"; and Henry Ford, in the newspaper *New York World* (17 February 1921), wrote: "The only statement I care to make about the Protocols is that they fit in with what is going on. They are 16 years old and they have fitted the world situation up to this time. They fit it now." Henry Ford refers here to the first edition, that of Nilus, but the anti-Semitic controversy has established that they date back to about 20 years earlier, and that the original document was known to Bismarck. History itself thus proves the veracity of the Protocols in a manner that the accusations of their opponents cannot refute, and all the difficulties which 'positive spirits' claim to find, and which they assert change the terms of the problem, result not merely from superficiality but from outright irresponsibility—not from 'objectivity', but from prejudice.

Via capitalism, the mentality of the Ghetto spreads to the Aryan civilizations, which at the same time lays the foundation for the revolt of the working masses. In accordance with this, the Jews Marx, Lassalle, Kautsky, and Trotsky give the masses the most powerful ideological weapons, in the form of materialistic falsifications of the messianic myth, always subordinating the movement to a precise goal: the destruction of every last remnant of true order and of differentiated civilization. Parallel occult tactics, to the same end, engender the most profound international conflicts, and Jewish financiers arm each militaristic front extensively, while, on the other hand, the Judeo-Masonic ideology of liberalism and democracy prepares opportune coalitions. The world-wide conflict of

1914-18 breaks out, whose true signification, according to the official declarations of an international Masonic Congress which was held in Paris during the summer of 1917, was the holy war of democracy, "the crowning of the work of the French Revolution", which had in view not this or that territorial claim, but the destruction of the great European empires and the formation of the League of Nations as an omnipotent demo-masonic super-state. Judeo-American capitalism finances the Russian Revolution (with which the English aristocracy was also involved) and, as, with the collapse of Russia, a first goal is reached, America intervenes directly, without any manifest reason, and the Central Empires meet the same fate as Russia.

After the war, revolutionary flames flare up everywhere, both in the vanquished nations and in the victorious ones, and the power of Judaism takes a phenomenal leap forward, through worldwide debt, through a secret tyranny in the Soviet state, and through the control of public opinion worldwide and general cultural influence. However, since the objectives of the revolt in Europe are not reached, they pass to a new phase.

The Third International abruptly changes tactics and allies itself, via the Popular Fronts, with the Second International and the great capitalist democracies, unveiling thus the framework of the secret war. After the failure of sanctions, all these things happen at once: the Soviets provoke the revolution in Spain, they ally themselves resolutely with Judeo-Masonic France, and they assume, in co-operation with the secret anti-fascist politics of England, a guiding role in the League of Nations. Decisive alliances are prepared in this way. The reader will find an excellent reconstruction of the 'occult war' in a book by Malinski and de Poncins which is called, precisely, '*La guerre occulte*', and in *Vita Italiana*'s article: 'Is Israel provoking a war?' This is indeed the prelude to the final stages of the plan of the Protocols. In reality, to adopt as working hypotheses the essential ideas of this 'apocryphal' manuscript is to find a reliable guide to the deeper unitary meaning of all the most important disruptions of recent times. This is why Adolf Hitler considered it to be undoubtedly the most powerful means of awakening the German people.[1]

---

[1] In *Mein Kampf*, vol. 1, sec. 11.14 (see "Hitler and Goebbels on the Protocols", present volume).

*****

We can now move on to further considerations which demonstrate the veracity of the Protocols, not only as *sigillum veri* ['simplicity is the mark of truth'], but also as testimony to a specifically Jewish influence. Basically, even assuming that the subversion of the West has as its background some superior causality, we still have to prove strictly that the Jews are truly responsible for it. In other words, even assuming that the 'Elders' exist, we must ascertain whether they are really 'Elders of Zion', if we wish not to be suspected of making a tendentious interpretation, derived merely from a determination to hold the Jew responsible for any and all subversion and thus justify an extremist anti-Semitic campaign.

This is certainly a legitimate question, but only to the extent that we can ask it regarding an organization which is *ex hypothesi* occult. In Freemasonry, even the highest dignitaries are unaware of exactly who their so-called 'Unknown Superiors', to whom they owe their obedience, actually are, and they could even stand right next to them without being able to identify them. We cannot therefore be expected to produce the duly authenticated identity cards of the 'Elders' in order to place the problems following on from the Protocols into the context of the Jewish question. This however does not prevent us from arriving at a fairly precise 'evidentiary process'.

Let us start by saying that we cannot support the sort of fanatical anti-Semitism which sees the Jew everywhere, as a *deus ex machina*, and finally falls into a sort of trap. In fact, as Guénon pointed out, one of the means of defense of the real concealed forces consists in drawing the whole of the attention of their adversaries tendentiously upon persons who are only partially responsible for certain upheavals, thus making them into scapegoats of a sort, on which all the reactions are discharged, and leaving themselves free to pursue their game. This is true, to some extent, in respect of the Jewish question. Merely noting the pernicious role that the Jew has played in the history of civilization must not prejudice a deeper investigation, which can make us become aware of forces for which Judaism itself may have been, to some extent, only the instrument.

Besides, the Protocols often speak imprecisely about Judaism and Freemasonry, so that one reads "Judeo-Masonic conspiracy", "our divided Free-Masonry", and at the bottom of the first edition: "signed by the representatives of Sion of the 33rd degree". Since the theory that Freemasonry is exclusively a creation and instrument of Judaism is, for various reasons, untenable—see our 'The relations between Freemasonry and Judaism', in *Vita Italiana*, June 1937, where we show that the Judaization of Freemasonry occurred essentially in the eighteenth century—it follows that it is necessary to refer to a much larger network of corrupting occult forces, which we are even inclined to believe is not purely human. Besides, the principal ideologies indicated by the Protocols as being instruments of destruction, which have indeed have this historical effect, viz., liberalism, individualism, scientism, and rationalism, are only the last links in a chain of causes which are unthinkable without antecedents such as, for instance, humanism, the Reformation, and Cartesianism, all of which are phenomena which no one would seriously think of ascribing to a Jewish conspiracy—except Nilus, insofar as, in an appendix to his edition of the Protocols, he makes the Jewish conspiracy date back to 929 BC.

Perhaps, though, Nilus perceived a certain truth, in a confused fashion. The various stages in the progress of the destructive Symbolic Snake, of which he informs us, are mostly perfectly real, but it is advisable to examine them in a far wider and more objective framework: the fall of ancient, sacral, Dorian Greece, and the coming of the 'humanist' Greece; the degeneration of the Roman empire; the degeneration into absolutism of the Sacred Empire of the German people with Charles V, and the Reformation; the preparation of the French Revolution (Enlightenment, rationalism, absolutism); the anti-traditional maneuvers of mercantile England; the attacks upon Austria and the plots within Germany; and the anticipation of Bolshevism, the point of arrival of the "serpent". However, by contrast, we should remember that the positively destructive action of the international Jewish organization developed in a more recent period, and that the Jews found a ground already undermined by processes of decomposition and involution, whose origins date back to very distant times, which are linked to a chain of very complex causes (cf. *The Crisis of the Modern World*, René Guénon; *Revolt against the Modern World*, Julius Evola). They have used that ground, and, so to speak, grafted their own action onto it, accelerating the rhythm of these processes. Thus they cannot be solely responsible for the entire worldwide subversion. The 'Elders of Zion' are really a much more profound mystery than most of the anti-Semites, or those who, contrarily and for different reasons, reduce everything to Masonic internationalism or something of that sort, can imagine.

We feel that this caveat is eminently justified. However, having established this, the 'presumption' which we have indicated, and which constitutes the second basis of the veracity of the Protocols, is completely justified, and leads to very precise results.

Here, we must distinguish two aspects, the one practical, the other ideological. In practical terms, are we to imagine that so many events which ended as victories for Judaism, along with the infallible presence of Jews, half-Jews, or agents of Judaism in connivance with Judaized Freemasonry, in all the principal seats of modern social, political, and cultural subversion, are fortuitous? Are we to ignore the fact that Israel not only remained united, despite the dispersion, but that agents of Judaism, quoting almost literally the words of the Protocols, have recognized that such a dispersion has a providential character, since it facilitates the universal domination promised to Israel? And, let us not be mistaken, in this respect, there is also a unity which is quite different from the abstract and ideal unity. Israel, the unassimilable cell in every nation, the people within every people, and, in some cases, such as Czechoslovakia, even the state in the state, has its own supra-national parliament, with legitimate delegates elected by the Jews of each country, which regularly meets and takes decisions, without, obviously, being obliged to provide a complete and public report of these to any Goy who wishes for it. On the other hand, there is a domain within which suppositions and inductions give way to overwhelming statistics: the fact is that, wherever the Jews obtained emancipation and equality, they did not use it to establish normal relations with the Goyim, but to rise immediately to all the principal positions of responsibility and social privilege, and thus to develop, more or less visibly, real hegemony. Whether the principles of democracy and liberalism were created by the 'Elders', or not, the fact is that, in all countries and epochs in which those principles have prevailed, the Jew has pervaded, parasitically or tyrannically, the highest rungs of culture and society, where he has undeniably exercised a destructive and corrosive influence and has woven a cord of international racial solidarity which, leaving aside the plane of a true secret war, does have the character of a conspiracy. Is all this mere 'chance'?

*****

But this practical aspect of the Jewish influence is linked at its root to the theoretical problem. To present the Jewish problem properly, so as to understand the true danger of Judaism, it is necessary to work on the premise that what is fundamental to Judaism is not so much race (in the strictly biological sense) as the Law. 'The Law' means the Old Testament, the Torah, but also, and especially, its further developments, the Mishnah, and, finally, the Talmud. It was rightly said that, as Adam, the Jew was shaped by the Law, and the Law, by its age-old influence throughout the generations, has awakened special instincts, a special way of feeling, of reacting, of behaving, has passed into the blood, and has continued to act on the Jew without his even being directly conscious of it or wanting it. It is an essence, an incoercible way of being, which has allowed Israel to preserve its unity, and its principle, Jewish Law, the Talmudic spirit, persists and acts today, fatally, whether in an atavistic and unconscious manner, or in an occult manner, or in some other more or less tortuous manner.

Here another decisive proof of the veracity of the Protocols as Jewish document becomes apparent, namely, that to draw from that Law all its logical consequences on the plane of action means, precisely, to arrive more or less at what is essential in the Protocols: International Judaism has striven to prove that the Protocols are 'false', while always taking great care to avoid the question of whether that document, true or false, corresponds to the Jewish spirit. And it is precisely that question which we would like to examine now. Jewish Law is based on the radical distinction between the Jew and the non-Jew, which is presented more or less in the same terms as that between human and animal, or that between élite and slaves; from this is derived the promise that the universal Reign of Israel will come sooner or later, and that all peoples will have to submit to the scepter of Judah; it is the duty of the Jew to see only violence and injustice in any law which is not his Law, to manifest a torment, and a baseness, wherever his power is less than absolute; from this is derived a double morality which limits solidarity to the Jewish race, while approving every form of lying, trickery, and treachery, in the relations between Jews and non-Jews, thus making the latter into outlaws; finally we find the sanctification of gold and interest as instruments of the power of the Jew, to whom, by divine promise, all the wealth of the earth must peculiarly belong, and who must 'devour' any people that the Lord will give to him. The Talmud goes so far as to say: "Kill the best of the heathens [goyim]".[2] In the Shemoneh Esreh, a Jewish daily prayer, one reads: "May the apostates lose all hope, the Nazoreans and the Minim [Christians] perish on the field, be erased from the book of life and have no contact with the righteous."

In Protocol 9 it says: "We possess boundless ambition, burning greed for merciless revenge, and bitter hatred," and it is difficult to find a more fitting expression for what is revealed to the one who penetrates the Jewish essence. The hope of the Reign has never departed from the Jew, and within this hope lies the secret of the unheard-of force which has allowed Israel to persist and to remain true to its own nature throughout the centuries, tenacious, obstinate, proud, and vile all at once. Even today, yearly, all the Jewish communities evoke the following promise during the celebration of Rosh Hashanah: "Raise your hands towards the sky and acclaim God while rejoicing, for Jehovah, the Most High, the terrible one, will bring all the nations to submission, and will prostrate them at your feet".[3]

Thus, the theoretical convergence between the essence of the Protocols and that of Judaism is indisputable, and we can infer that, even if the Protocols are invented, the author has written what Jews faithful to their tradition and to the deep will of Israel would have thought and written.

*****

One should not imagine, then, that this discussion is a matter of retrospective disinterment, and that the Law is merely a religious myth from a remote and 'outdated' past. Jews faithful to their tradition are far more

---

[2] Soferim 15,10. Repeated in Midrash Tanchuma Beshalach 8:1.
[3] For these textual quotations, and for the declarations of the official representatives of Judaism, even today, we refer the reader to the May and June issues of *Vita Italiana*, and to *Fatti e Commenti*, as well as to the following works: E. Vries de Heekelingen: '*Israël, son passé, son avenir*' (Paris, 1937); U. Fleischhauer: '*Die Echten Protrokolle der Weisen von Zion*' (Erfurt, 1935); E. Jouin: '*La judéo-maçonnerie et l'église catholique*' (Paris, 1921

numerous than is commonly believed, or than one is led to believe. But it is necessary to recognize that the influence of Judaism is not limited to these faithful: the influence of a law followed continuously for centuries does not vanish from one day to the next, but perpetually manifests itself, in one form or another, in any Jewish substance. According to what has been said above about the essence of the Law, which regards as unfair and violent any order which is not led by the 'chosen people', it follows necessarily that the Jew is prone, consciously or unconsciously, to all agitation or subversion, to a continuous project of corrosion. It is so today and so will it be forever. In the classical era, Jewry was already significantly assimilated to the 'Typhonian' stock—that is to say, to obscure disintegrative forces, enemies of the solar god, generators of the 'sons of the powerless revolt'. Theodor Herzl, founder of Zionism, recognized that the Jews, on one hand, always formed the body of non-commissioned officers, as it were, of revolutionary parties, and, on the other hand, always used the terrible power of gold in multifarious ways.[4] The opposition between the two Internationals, the revolutionary one and the financial one, is only apparent, and merely expresses the nature of the two strategic objectives; the Jewish millionaire, Jacob Schiff, who bragged publicly of having financed and brought about the Bolshevik revolution, is only one revealing case among many others, hidden behind the scenes of Western history.

Attention should also be drawn to the destructive work which Judaism has accomplished, quite in accordance with the stipulations of the Protocols, in the specifically cultural field, where the destruction has become protected by the taboos of Science, Art, and Thought. Freud, whose theory aims to reduce internal life to instincts and unconscious forces, or to conventions and repressions, is a Jew; Einstein, whose 'relativism' has become fashionable, is a Jew; Cesare Lombroso, who has perversely equated genius, crime, and madness, is a Jew, as are Max Stirner, the father of absolute anarchism, and Claude Debussy (a half-Jew), Arnold Schönberg, and Gustav Mahler, the main representatives of musical decadence. Tristan Tzara, creator of Dadaism, extreme limit of the disintegration of the so-called avant-garde, is a Jew, and so are Salo-

---

[4] "Where we sink, we become a revolutionary proletariat, the subordinate officers of the revolutionary party; when we rise, there rises also our terrible power of the purse" (*The Jewish State*, 1896/1967, p. 26).

mon Reinach and many representatives of the sociological school, which is characterized by a degrading interpretation of ancient religions. Nordau, who wants to reduce the essence of civilization to conventions and lies, is also a Jew. The 'primitive mentality' is to a large extent a discovery of the Jew Lucien Levy-Brühl, and it is to the Jew Henri Bergson that we owe one of the most striking forms of irrationalism, the exaltation of 'life' and 'becoming' at the expense of any higher intellectual principle. Ludwig, whose biography contains so many tendentious distortions, is a Jew. Wassermann and Alfred Döblin are Jews, as well as a whole series of novelists within whose works corrosive and mordant criticism of essential social values can always be found. And so on. Are we so naïve as to consider all this, once again, a matter of 'chance'?

The same influence emanates from all those personalities, whose destructive effect propagates itself in their respective domains, and one can hear cries of 'barbarism' and 'fanatical racism' as soon as they are impugned. To debase, to make all fixed points variable, to make all certainties problematic, to sensualize, to tendentiously exalt what is inferior in man, to spread a sort of terror, calculated to favor self-abandonment to obscure forces and to pave the way for occult influences of the sort described in the Protocols; this is the true meaning of cultural Judaism. We do not think that there is a genuine plan here, or even a precise intention on the part of every individual; what comes into play is 'race', i.e., an instinct; in the same way, it is in the nature of fire to burn. The fact remains that the whole, disorganized, unconscious influence is in perfect accord with the occult, integral, unitary influence of the hidden forces of world-wide subversion. In order to recognize the existence of international Judaism, it is not therefore necessary to assert that all Jews are led by a genuine organization, and that their whole action consciously follows a plan. The link is established to a large extent automatically, by nature. Once this becomes clear, another aspect of the veracity of the Protocols is confirmed immediately.

*****

What is debatable, however, is the true nature of the main goals of that indisputable influence. The problematic part of the Protocols is that which deals with reconstruction, not with destruction. When Nilus compares, in an apocalyptic tone, the principal ideal of the Protocols to the coming of the anti-Christ (the obsession of the Slavic soul), he simply raves. The truth is that this ideal, basically, is the imperial ideal, no more and no less—and even in a higher form: an absolute and inviolable authority of divine right, a system of classes, a government of men who possess a transcendent knowledge and make light of all the rationalist, liberal and humanitarian myths; defense of craft industry, and struggle against luxuriousness. Gold, once its mission is carried out, will be overcome, as will be demagoguery, all the 'immortal principles', and all the illusions and suggestions used and spread as means. There remains a promise of peace and liberty, respect of property and person, for whomsoever recognizes the Law of the Elders of Zion. The sovereign, chosen by God, will dedicate himself to the destruction of all ideas dictated by instinct and animality; a personification, in a way, of destiny, he will be inaccessible to passion, and master of himself and of the world around him; his power will be so unshakeable that he will not need an armed guard about him (P3, P22, P23, P24).

The Protocols lose much of their significance if one does not separate that part from the rest, for, if that was their true goal, they could basically receive a justification. But, to us, all that is fantasy. We have tried, instead, to analyze the process which has led to the paradoxical association between these revivals of traditional ideas, linked to the ideal of the '*Regnum*', and the motifs of anti-traditional subversion: here, we see rather a deviation, culminating in a true 'inversion', of certain elements from which the original spirit has withdrawn; elements which, left to themselves, have come under the influence of forces of a quite different kind. We have tried elsewhere to determine the successive phases of this inversion and perversion. The positive part, which we have traced in the Protocols, is that from which we have shown how, in all the destructive processes of the modern world, there is something which did not happen 'by chance', something which shows a 'plan' and the presence of hidden forces. We have already talked about the role which the Jew has played therein, and we think that it is wrong to conclude that everything he has done, he has done with the ideal of the spiritual empire, as described in the Protocols, in view. And even if this were not the case, for us who are not Jewish, the result would be the same, for we dispute Israel's right to consider itself as the 'chosen people' and to claim an Empire which would imply the submission of all the other races. We are in no way willing to grant absolution for this crime. We know all the greatness of our former imperial, aristocratic and spiritual Europe, and we know that that greatness was destroyed. We fought against the forces which caused that destruction, and we know what role the Jews played then, and play now, within it, and we know that they can be found necessarily, today, in all the most virulent centers of international revolution. Our knowledge regarding this does not in itself require us to pose for ourselves any additional questions.

We do however acknowledge that most anti-Semitic positions are not up to the true task, since, by the idea of race, of nation, of anti-revolution, of anti-Bolshevism, of anti-capitalism, this or that sector of the Jewish front and of the vaster front of subversion to which it is linked, can certainly be affected, but we will not reach its center. The political myths of the majority do not count for much, their breath is short, their validity is often affected by the evils which they hope to cure. What is necessary is the full return to the spiritual idea of the empire, the precise, hard, absolute, will of a truly traditional reconstruction in every domain, and, therefore, first, in that of the spirit, on which all the rest depends. Protocol 5 contains a really significant remark, recognizing that only a Sovereign drawing his authority from a 'divine right' can really aspire to universal empire, and the Protocols add that only someone similar appearing in the opposite front would be in a position to fight the 'Elders of Zion'; and then the conflict between him and them "would be of such a merciless nature as the world has never seen before."

The Protocols conclude: "But it is too late for them"—i.e., for us. Our view is the opposite of this. At the present time, forces are leaping everywhere to the reconquest, because the destiny to which Europe seemed condemned may be averted. These forces must be completely conscious of the tasks and principles which inflexibly determine their action, and must have the courage to be radical, firstly on the spiritual plane, and to reject all compromise, to prepare the conditions of the formation of an international traditional front, and continue in this direction until the conflict "of such a merciless nature as the world has never seen before" finds them united in a single robust, unshakeable, irresistible block.

From *Men Among the Ruins* (1953)

In this order of ideas, there is an interesting document known as The Protocols of the Learned Elders of Zion. I have discussed the nature and scope of this document in the introduction to its last Italian edition [above]. Here I will only mention some fundamental points.

This document was purported to be a protocol stolen from a secret Judeo-Masonic organization and allegedly reveals a plan that was devised and implemented with the subversion and the destruction of traditional Europe in mind. Regarding the authenticity of the Protocols, a rabid and complex debate has erupted, which can be dismissed, however, by Guénon's correct observation that a truly occult organization, no matter what its nature, never leaves behind written documents or "protocols." Thus, in the most favorable hypothesis, the Protocols could have been the work of someone who had contacts with some representatives of this alleged organization. However, we cannot agree either with those who wish to dismiss this document as a vulgar mystification, forgery, and work of plagiarism.

The main argument adduced by the latter is that the Protocols reproduce and paraphrase in many parts the ideas found in a short book written by a certain Maurice Joly during the period of Napoleon's Second Empire. Allegedly, mysterious provocateurs of the Czar's secret police were responsible for writing the Protocols. This argument is truly irrelevant: those who decry plagiarism should keep in mind that this is not a matter of a literary work or of copyright. For example, when a general writes a plan, he could employ previous materials and writings as long as they contain ideas for his purpose. This would be a case of plagiarism, but it would not affect at all the question of whether or not this plan has really been conceived and carried out.

Cutting short all this—that is, leaving aside the issue of the "authenticity" of the document in terms of real protocols stolen from an international secret organization—the only important and essential point is the following: This writing is part of a group of texts that, in various ways (more or less fantastical and at times even fictional), have expressed the feeling that the disorder of recent times is not accidental, since it corresponds to a plan, the phases and fundamental instruments of which are accurately described in the Protocols. Hugo Wast wrote: "The Protocols may well be a fake, but their predictions have been fulfilled in an amazing way." Henry Ford added: "The only comment that I can make about the Protocols is that they perfectly correspond to what is happening today. They were published sixteen years ago, and ever since then they have corresponded to the world situation and today they still dictate its rhythm." In a sense, we can speak of a prophetic premonition.

In any event, the value of the document as a working hypothesis is undeniable: it presents the various aspects of global subversion (among them, some aspects that were destined to be outlined and accomplished only many years after the publication of the Protocols) in terms of a whole, in which they find their sufficient reason and logical combination. As I have said, this is not the place to engage in a detailed analysis of the text; it will suffice to recall the main points. First of all, the primary ideologies that are responsible for the modern disorder did not arise spontaneously, but have been evoked and supported by forces that knew they knew were false and had in mind only the latter's destructive and demoralizing effects. This would apply to democratic and liberal ideas; the Third Estate had purposely been mobilized to destroy the previous feudal and aristocratic society, while in a second phase the workers were mobilized to undermine the bourgeois. Another basic idea of the Protocols is that, despite all, the capitalist and the proletarian Internationals are in agreement, being almost two columns with distinct ideas but which act in unison at a tactical level in order to achieve the same strategy. Likewise, the economization of life, especially in the context of an industry that develops at the expense of agriculture, and a wealth that is concentrated on liquid capital and finance, proceeds from a secret design. The phalanx of the modern "economists" followed this design, just as those who spread a demoralizing literature attack spiritual and ethical values and scorn every principle of authority.

Among other things, mention is made of the success that the secret front achieved not only for Marxism, but for Darwinism and Nietzsche's nihilism as well. The Protocols at times even encourage the spread of anti-Semitism, while in other cases mention is made of the secret monopoly of the press and of the media in democratic countries as well as the power to paralyze or destroy the most prestigious banks. This power concentrates the rootless, financial wealth in a few hands, and through it controls peoples, parties, and governments. One of the most important objectives is to remove the support of spiritual and traditional values from the human personality, knowing that when this is accomplished, it is not difficult to turn man into a passive instrument of the secret front's direct forces and influences. The counterpart of the action of cultural demoralization, materialization, and disorganization causes unavoidable social crises to grow increasingly worse and collective situations to grow increasingly desperate and unbearable; in this way, a final conflict will eventually be considered as the means to finally sweep away the last residual resistance.

It is difficult to deny that such a "fiction" exposed at the beginning of this century has indeed reflected and anticipated much of what has taken place in the modern world, not to mention the predictions of what is in store for us. It is therefore no surprise that the Protocols received so much attention from those movements of the past that intended to react against and stem the currents of national, social, and moral dissolution in their own day and age. However, these movements often upheld dangerously unilateral positions, due to the lack of adequate discernment; this was a weakness that, again, has played into the enemy's hands.

In relation to this, we must deal with the issue raised by this document concerning the leaders of the occult war. According to the Protocols, the leaders of the global plot are Jews who planned and undertook the destruction of the traditional and Christian European civilization in order to achieve the universal rule of Israel, or God's "chosen people." This is obviously an exaggeration. At this point we may even wonder whether a fanatical anti-Semitism, which always sees the Jew as a *deus ex machina*, is not unwittingly playing into the hands of the enemy. One of the means employed by the occult forces to protect themselves consists of directing their opponents' attention toward those who are only partially responsible for certain upheavals, thus concealing the rest of the story, namely a wider sequence of causes. It could be shown that even if the Protocols were a forgery perpetrated by provocateurs, nonetheless they reflect ideas very congenial to the Law and spirit of Israel.

Second, it is true that many Jews have been and still are among the promoters of modern disorder in its more radical cultural expressions, whether political or social. This, however, should not prevent a deeper analysis, capable of exposing forces that may have employed modern Judaism merely as an instrument. After all, despite the fact that many

Jews are among the apostles of the main ideologies regarded by the Protocols as instruments of global subversion (i.e., liberalism, socialism, scientism, and rationalism), it is also evident that these ideas would have never arisen and triumphed without historical antecedents, such as the Reformation, Humanism, the naturalism and individualism of the Renaissance, and the philosophy of Descartes. Such phenomena cannot be attributed to Judaism, but rather point to a wider web of influences.

In the Protocols, the concepts of Judaism and Masonry are interwoven; therefore, in the literature that this text spawned, mention is often made in careless terms of a Jewish-Masonic plot. Here caution must be exercised. While recognizing the Jewish predominance in many sectors of modern Masonry, as well as the Jewish origin of several elements in the Masonic symbolism and rituals, the anti-Semitic thesis, according to which Masonry has been the creation and the tool of Israel, must be rejected. Modern Masonry (with this designation I allude essentially to the Freemasonry that developed since the creation of London's Grand Lodge in 1717) has undoubtedly been one of the societies that promoted the modern political subversions, and especially their ideological background. However, here too the danger is to be distracted by explaining everything with the action of ordinary Masonry.

Among those who regard the Protocols as a forgery, there are some who have noticed that various ideas in this text are similar to those that have been implemented by centralizing and dictatorial regimes, so much so that the Protocols can be an excellent manual for those who wish to install a new Bonapartism or totalitarianism. This view is partially correct. This amounts to saying that the "occult war" should be conceived, from a positive point of view, within a wide and elastic context, and we should expose the part played in it by phenomena that are apparently contradictory and hardly reducible to the simplistic formula of a Jewish-Masonic global plot.

Regardless of the role played by Jews and Masonry in the modern subversion, it is necessary to recognize clearly the real historical context of their influence, as well as the limit beyond which the occult war is destined to develop by employing forces that not only are no longer those of Judaism and of Masonry, but that could even totally turn against them. To realize this, consider *the law of the regression of the castes*, which I have employed as a hermeneutic tool in my *Revolt Against the Modern*

World in order to assess the effective meaning of history. From a civilization led by spiritual leaders and by a sacred regality, a shift occurred to civilizations led by mere warrior aristocracies; the latter were eventually replaced by the civilization of the Third Estate [i.e. the masses]. The last stage is the collectivist civilization of the Fourth Estate [i.e the media].

When we reflect carefully on things, modern Judaism as a *power* (quite apart from the concomitant, widespread, and instinctive action of individual Jewish thinkers and writers) is inseparable from capitalism and finance, which fall within the civilization of the Third Estate. The same applies to modern Masonry, which prepared ideologically for and supported the advent of the Third Estate. Masonry still presents itself today as the custodian of the principles of the Enlightenment and the French Revolution, its doctrines acting as a kind of secular religion of modern democracy; its militant action has revealed and continues to reveal itself along this line, openly or in semisecret ways. All this falls within the penultimate phase; this phase, the overall cycle of democratic and capitalist civilization of the Third Estate, will eventually usher in the last collectivist phase, to which it has inadvertently opened the way.

It is therefore logical that the role of a central guiding force of global subversion in this last period will no longer be played by Judaism or Masonry and that the main current may turn against both of these groups, as if they were residues to be liquidated once and for all; after all, this can be seen in countries in which regimes controlled by the Fourth Estate (i.e., Marxist regimes) are beginning to be consolidated, even though Jews and Masons contributed to their advent.

But then again, as far as the general radical Jewish-Masonic conspiracy thesis upheld in some milieus is concerned, the actual situation shows its inconsistency. It would be a real abandonment to fantasy to suppose that the leaders of the great conflicting powers—the United States, the USSR, and Red China—receive orders from an international center of Jews and Masons (almost nonexistent in China), and act accordingly in view of the same goal. Again, it is necessary to refer to a wider horizon of influences and to look elsewhere.

PART FOUR

CONTEMPORARY REFLECTIONS

THE FAKE "FAKE PROTOCOLS":
THE PURPOSE AND SIGNIFICANCE OF
THE *PROTOCOLS OF THE ELDERS OF ZION*

CARLO MATTOGNO[1]

Since the *Times of London* revealed in August 1921 that the *Protocols of the Elders of Zion* are drawn in good measure from Maurice Joly's political satire *Dialogue aux enfers entre Machiavel et Montesquieu ou la politique de Machiavel au XIXe siècle*,[2] they were transformed from "proof" of a world Jewish "conspiracy," as it was interpreted in anti-Semitic—or better, anti-Jewish—circles, to "proof" of a "fake anti-Semitism".[3] This interpretation is still in vogue in philosemitic circles.

However, a careful reading of the text, outside of ideological conditioning and cultural bias, and one aimed at identifying what is really in the Protocols, does not confirm either interpretation. But before presenting evidence for this conclusion, I will begin with some philosemitic perspectives on the Protocols.

1. Some (Partly) Revealing Philosemitic Interpretive Cues

The interpretation of the purpose and meaning of the Protocols proposed by the various scholars on this subject is flatly superficial and insulting, being crushed on the preconception of "fake anti-Semitism." Norman Cohn, in a glimmer of lucidity, observed that the Russian anti-Semites whom he believed to be the authors of the Protocols "often paradoxically attributed their own values and aspirations to the imaginary Jewish gov-

---

[1] This is an edited version of an essay originally published in 2010.
[2] Imprimerie de A. Mertens et Fils, 1865. See "A literary forgery" by Philip Graves (reproduced in the present volume).
[3] By "fake anti-Semitism," Mattogno refers to the orthodox notion that anti-Semitism (or 'anti-Jewism') has no real or legitimate basis. According to the dominant view, all anti-Semitism is "illegitimate" or "fake" in the sense that, they say, there is no justification for it. Mattogno disagrees; he finds much justification, both in history and in contemporary events. (ed.)

ernment".[4] But he immediately dropped this fundamental cue, blinded by his philosemitic biases.

Sergio Romano also glimpsed this basic contradiction:

> The most Russian pages of the Protocols, those that most denounce the book's intentions and destination, concern the "King of Israel," the powerful ruler who will rule the world as soon as the Elders have completed—with the help of Freemasonry and revolutionary ideals—the destruction and subversion of the existing order. In fact, their reflections and maxims can be divided into two parts: on the one hand, those in which the strategists of the Jewish conspiracy minutely describe the means they employ for the conquest of power; on the other hand, those in which they describe, directly or indirectly, the political and social regime whose advent they prepare.
>
> As much as the means are diabolical, much of the final regime is positive, even desirable. The Protocols are thus presented as a composite catechism in which, on the lips of the same protagonists, *cunning* alternates with *wisdom*, *revolution* with *restoration*, today's *evil* with tomorrow's *good*. When they slyly use the Trinitarian principles of the French Revolution, when they alternate between capitalism and socialism to corrode the organic and hierarchical societies of the great monarchies, the Elders are treacherous and malevolent characters; but when they announce the Jewish kingdom or describe the ideal regime against which their own weapons would be ineffective, they are paternal and wise rulers, worthy of imitation.

But then he too was dazzled by the "fake anti-Semitic" argument:

> The message addressed to Nicholas II is thus twofold: to crush the Jewish conspiracy and to realize as of now what the Jews intend to do after the conquest of power. Paradoxical as it may seem, there are passages in which the book is objectively 'philosemitic'; and these are those, precisely, in which the paternal and autocratic regime of the 'kingdom of Israel' is described.

---

[4] *Warrant for Genocide* (1967), Harper and Row.

Romano has touched on the true meaning of the Protocols, rightly asserting that "in other passages, the portrait of the king of Israel is actually the positive portrait of the czar, such as was desired by those sectors of Russian opinion in which the Protocols found most attentive readers," so that "between the feared Jewish kingdom and the dreamed-of czarist empire, there runs an extraordinary similarity." He also notes that "the king of Israel is none other than the autocrat of all Russia"[5]—but then he ends up getting entangled again in the "Jewish conspiracy" thesis.

Romano's judgment contains a glaring inconsistency. The message addressed (also) to Nicholas II could not have been to "crush the Jewish conspiracy," if this was an invention of the "Judeophobic" authors of the Protocols; they wished instead to *crush liberalism* and *restore absolute autocracy.*

In a brilliant study devoted to the Protocols, which surpasses in critical methodology those that have previously appeared on this subject, Cesare G. De Michelis approaches this issue from a basic but surprisingly new point of view, because it had been neglected by scholars: the philological point of view.[6] He rightly points out that

> the question of the origin of the Protocols cannot be studied separately from the definition of the text and its correct reading. Otherwise, as has happened, when faced with the impossibility of proceeding further into the unsolved problems, one idea imposes itself: that, all things considered, the history of the *use* of the text is more important than the text itself. This has resulted in the passive acceptance, at least in part, of the traps of mystification.[7]

De Michelis rejects the "hypothesis—in itself plausible, but never proven—of the compilation [of the Protocols] in Paris, around 1897, by P. I. Račkovsky and, with him, the foreign section of the Okhrana".[8] He as-

---

[5] S. Romano, *The False Protocols. The "Jewish conspiracy" from the Russia of Nicholas II to the present.* (*I falsi protocolli. Il "complotto ebraico" dalla Russia di Nicola II ai nostri giorni*). TEA Storica, Milan, 1995, pp. 42-43.
[6] That is, evaluating the structure of the language of the text (ed.).
[7] C.G. De Michelis, *The nonexistent manuscript. The "Protocols of the Elders of Zion": An apocrypha of the 20th century.* (*Il manoscritto inesistente. I "Protocolli dei savi di Sion"*). Marsilio, Venice, 1998, p. 12.
[8] Ibid. See pp. 63-65 and 110-113. The Okhrana was the Russian (czarist) secret police force, established in 1880.

sumes that their origin lies in narrow circles of the Russian "Judeophobic" far right; he accepts the hypothesis of the Polish historian Janusz Tazbir, who attributes the authorship of the Protocols to two Russians: Pavel Kruševan and Georgy Butmi. He writes: "It is still a hypothesis in a 'circumstantial process,' but far more consistent with the available data than the thesis of a forgery fabricated in Paris by the Okhrana".[9]

Regarding the exegesis of the text, De Michelis applauds the interpretive "views" proposed by French philosopher Pierre-André Taguieff, but considers them "not fully satisfactory," pointing out:

> Taguieff does indeed point out the essential nodes of the Protocols (conspiracy, anti-Semitism, forgery, anti-theology) but, working more from an ideological than philological perspective, he offers, in my opinion, an inadequate sifting to their exegesis. However, he takes a step forward from [Norman] Cohn's 'interpretive model' [...] which, by taking as foundational the category of 'collective psychopathology,' ended up transferring an intricate critical-textual and historical-cultural issue to a psychoanalytic terrain.

Then he sets out his own exegetical criterion:

> We will proceed in a similar manner, but reformulating the issues in such a way as to focus on the text more than on ideology, and on scriptural convictions and 'literary' peculiarities more than on psychology—whether individual (of the sender) or collective (of the recipient). This, of course, is in relation to the reconstructed text, leaving in the background both the history of the myth's constitution and the history of its fruition through the various editions or translations, which have already had their scholars.[10]

2. The Talmud and the Protocols

But even De Michelis, by focusing on a single tree, lost sight of the forest. He fell back on the trite thesis that, at the heart of this writing, is the

---

[9] Ibid., p. 75.
[10] Ibid, pp. 79-80.

"Judeophobia" of its authors[11]—and thus it again becomes a "fake anti-Semitism."

In another study, he confirmed:

> In the following decade, it was the Talmud itself (often misread and worse understood) that was placed at the center of anti-Jewish polemic, according to a pattern that was becoming increasingly clear: after all, the Mosaic religion would still be acceptable, although severely invalidated by the failure to recognize the Messiah in Jesus (something that left the Jews deaf to Grace). But today it was in fact no longer the religion of the Torah [first five books of the Old Testament], but that of the Talmud, which would not "explain" but "replace" the Old Testament.
>
> This gave rise to works of a Judeophobic and anti-Semitic bent, such as *The Talmud and the Jews* (1879) by I. Ljutostanskij, or *The Secrets of the Talmud and the Jews* (1880) by V. Mordvinov, which echoed the theses set forth by A. Rohling (*Talmud-Jew*, 1871). In 1892, a Lithuanian priest teaching in Petersburg, Justinas Pranaitis, published a "scholarly" essay on the anti-Christian content of the Talmud, which found echoes in contemporaneous German anti-Semitism. The Protocols provided a stabilization of the standard formula (quotations from the Talmud recur in the self-styled "Translator's Postscript," supporting the thesis that Jews would see in the goyim only "working cattle"). And since then, the anti-Semitic subculture considers the Talmud to be the foundation of the 'secret doctrine of the Jews'.[12]

However, this interpretation is in open contrast to the crass superficiality with which the Protocols paint the essence of Judaism. De Michelis himself acknowledges that

> of the 'Jewish point of view' represented in the [Protocols] by the words of the 'elders,' one is struck not so much by the repeated and distorted value attributed to the concept of the 'chosen people' (who would consider themselves des-

---

[11] Ibid, p. 71.
[12] C. G. De Michelis, *Judeophobia in Russia*. Bollati Boringhieri, Turin 2001, p. 22.

tined to reign over all the peoples of the earth, and not just in the 'promised land' alone), as by the absence of any reference to the Messiah.[13]

The absence of references to the fundamental texts of Judaism, beginning with the Talmud and the *Schulchan aruch*, should be even more striking[14]—although, as De Michelis points out, there was no shortage of reference texts, beginning with those of Rohling, Ljutostanskij, and Mordvinov. A few years before the drafting of the Protocols, in 1892, the book by Pranaitis appeared in St. Petersburg, which could not have been unknown to the Russian 'Judeophobes'[15] and from which they could draw heavily to make the Jewish character of the 'plot' more credible.

Something similar, as De Michelis notes, appears only in the "Translator's Postscript":

> And behold, it has been prophetically declared to them that they have been elected by God Himself from the ranks of men to possess the earth in an indivisible kingdom. Moreover, it was inculcated [upon them] that only the Jews are the sons of God and they alone are worthy of the title of "man," while the others were created as working cattle and slaves of the Jews, and they were given human features so that their services, which boil down to the creation of the throne of Zion over the whole world, would not be too repugnant to the Jews.
>
> Once it has been inculcated in them that they are superior beings, or superhumans, that explains why they cannot unite in marriage with a beastly lineage, with other peoples who, compared to the Jews, are beasts. Considering all non-Jews to be their working cattle[16] created for the

---

[13] De Michelis, *The nonexistent manuscript*, op. cit., p. 118.

[14] The *Schulchan aruch* is a condensation of the Talmud, written by Joseph Karo in the mid-1500s. For a good summary and critique of this influential writing, see Eric Bischoff, *The Book of the Schulchan Aruch* (2023).

[15] A nonsensical and ridiculous term, on par with "homophobia" and "homophobe." Who coins such imbecilities?

[16] An asterisk appears here referring to the following "Author's Note": "See Aram-Chajm, p. A, p. 1; Eben-Gajzer, p. 44, pp. 8, 24; Jebamot, 98, 25; Katebot, 3, 34; Sanhedrin, 74 and 30; Qiddushin, 68." Further notes to the notes (p. 289) "correct" (!) the spelling and explain that "Orech-Chaim" is "a book of the Talmud" and that "Eben-ha-Ezer" is another "Talmudic book."

exaltation of Zion, the Jews treat them accordingly; they consider the property and even the lives of the non-Jews to be theirs, and dispose of them at their discretion when it can be done with impunity.[17]

But these commentaries of rabbinic teachings are mostly drawn from Pranaitis' book and that of Rohling.

In passing, such comments are punctually reflected in rabbinic literature, except for the fact that non-Jews are considered "working cattle." This is a concept that, moreover, results from the fusion of two sets of texts: those that affirm that non-Jews are beasts *tout court*, such as the Talmudic treatise Bava Metzia, 114b2 ("the peoples of the world *['ûmôth hâ'ôlâm]* are not called men *['âdhâm]*, but beasts *[behêmâh]*"), and those that consider them to be beasts in human form to serve the Jews, such as the Sepher midhrâš talpjiôth, (the 'Talpiot' or 'Talpiyyot'), written by Eliyahu ben Solomon Abraham ha-Kohen:

> (God) created them in human form in honor of Israel; for the Akum[18] were created for no other purpose than to serve them (the Jews) day and night; nor can they ever cease from this their service. For it does not befit the son of the king (the Israelite) that beasts in the form of beasts serve him, but beasts in the form of men.[19]

Actually "Orach chajîm" (Path of Life) and "Ebhen ha'êzer" (Stone of Relief) are two of the four parts of the *Schulchan aruch*, not the Talmud. These references, and others not mentioned by De Michelis, are found in the "Necessary Explanations" from Nilus' 1920 edition of the Protocols.

[17] C.G. De Michelis, *The nonexistent manuscript*. op. cit., pp. 287-288.

[18] The term 'Akum' is formed from the initials of the words *abhôdhath kôkhâbhîm ûmazzâlôth*, or *abhdhê kôkhâbhîm ûmazzâlôth*, "worship or worshippers of the stars and constellations" (= idolatry, idolaters). These expressions were created by ecclesiastical censorship, which thus replaced the original words *nokhrî* (foreigner), *gôj* (or 'goy,' non-Jew), *abhôdhâh zârâh* (foreign worship, idolatry), etc., in the text of the *Schulchan aruch*. The Akum are thus the non-Jews.

[19] *Sepher midhrâš talpjiôth*, Smyrna, 1736, p. 194 verso, sub: *'ôth jôd, 'ânâph Jisrâ'êl*. On this subject, see the excellent studies: *The Jewish Question*, 1 August 1998; and *Johann Andreas Eisenmenger and Judaism Unveiled*, 2008. This learned anthology (pp. 84-121) covers the following topics: 1. Why Jews are superior to all the peoples of the world; 2. Why non-Jews are to be considered beasts; 3. Why it is permissible to kill a non-Jew.

Therefore, if the author of the Protocols had truly and primarily had "anti-Semitic" intentions, he would have included these comments, or related quotations, in the text. But he did not.

3. "Operation Protocols": Erasing the real causes of anti-Semitism

The main purpose pursued by [Jewish writer] Norman Cohn in his low-grade propaganda book *Warrant for Genocide*, incredibly passed off as a serious and scientific work, was to eliminate the real causes of anti-Semitism—Jewish behavior and action—using fallacious and flimsy hypotheses.

When discussing the "real causes" of anti-Semitism, one cannot disregard the interpretation of the late 19th-century Jewish writer Bernard Lazare, which must be considered the fundamental hermeneutical criterion of any serious study of the subject:

> If one wants to trace a complete history of anti-Semitism—without leaving out any manifestation of this sentiment, following its various phases and modifications—one must examine the history of Israel from its dispersion; or rather, from the time of its expansion outside the territory of Palestine. Wherever the Jews have settled, ceasing to be a nation ready to defend its freedom and independence, everywhere, anti-Semitism—or rather anti-Judaism—has arisen. [...]
>
> If this hostility, even repugnance, had been exercised toward the Jews only in a particular epoch or in a single country, it would be easy to clarify the specific causes of these outbursts of anger; but this race was, on the contrary, exposed to the hatred of all the peoples in whose midst it was established. It was therefore necessary—since the enemies of the Jews belonged to the most diverse races, lived in countries far removed from each other, were governed by different laws, governed by opposite principles, had neither the same customs nor the same morals, were animated by dissimilar intentions that did not allow them to judge all things in the same way—it was therefore necessary that the general causes of anti-Semitism had always been inherent in Israel itself, not in those who fought it.
>
> This is not to assert that the persecutors of the Israelites always had the right on their side, nor that they did not indulge in all the excesses that the most violent hatreds entail;

but to establish in principle that the Jews caused—at least in part—their own evils.[20]

What we may call "Operation Protocols" completely reverses Lazare's judgment: wherever the Jews settled, they were always persecuted unjustly, through no fault of their own, being victims of irrational "prejudices," so that the cause of anti-Semitism would reside solely and exclusively in those who fought them, never in the Jews themselves.

As the subject matter is rather complex, I will simply indicate schematically the two basic directions of the operation. The starting point concerns an interpretive misrepresentation: anti-Semitism in antiquity was not anti-Semitism. Hence, writes Cohn:

> Anyone familiar with the works of the Reverend James Parker, Dr. Léon Poliakov, Jules Isaac, and Joshua Trachtenberg could not for a single moment attribute to anti-Semitism the tensions that arose from time to time in antiquity between various Egyptian, Greek, or Roman rulers and their Jewish subjects, or the occasional persecutions of Jews that occurred in Muslim countries (those suffered by Christians were much more severe).[21]

But this is an historically unfounded thesis. In his well-documented *Anti-Judaism in Classical Antiquity*, Gian Pio Mattogno notes in this regard:

> The main charges brought against the Jews by Greco-Roman authors—which correspond to as many themes of classical anti-Judaism—can be summarized as follows:
> - Ethnic-religious particularism and exclusivism;
> - *amixìa* (lit. non-mixing, lack of relationships, asociality): designates the desire to "live exclusively in a Jewish environment and outside any relationship with idolaters, the burning desire to make such relationships increasingly difficult, if not impossible."

---

[20] B. Lazare, *L'antisémitisme. Son histoire et ses causes.* Léon Chailley, Éditeur, Paris, 1894, pp. 1-3. (English: *Antisemitism: Its History and Causes*, 1995).
[21] *Warrant*, p. ix.

- impiety/atheism, terms used to denote "the Judaic rejection of all foreign cults, and refusal to participate in them." Ungodly and atheist were therefore synonymous with evil;
- circumcision, as a distinctive sign of election and separation from all other peoples;
- proselytizing, as a means of Judaizing Roman customs;
- *misoxenìa* (= hatred of foreigners);
- misanthropy/ *odium generis humani*, which "seems to be the ultimate accusation";
- aspiration for world domination.[22]

The next step is that (in the words of Cohn),

> the original form of anti-Semitism was *demonological* anti-Semitism, i.e., the idea that Judaism is an organization of conspirators united in the service of evil, busy thwarting God's plans for the world, and plotting relentlessly for the ruin of mankind.

Of course, "demonological anti-Semitism is Christian in origin".[23]

At this point, the question arises: Why were the Jews represented by a "demonological" character? Was it not perchance, as Lazare would say, that *they themselves* were responsible for it, at least in part? Perhaps because of the Talmud? Cohn's response, by which he would like to rule out even the vaguest suspicion of it, is painfully ridiculous:

> In my opinion, this occurs because, in Christian countries, Jews have ideally been placed in a situation to receive the unconscious negative projections associated with the 'bad' parent, and particularly with the 'bad' father.[24]

Here I would note that if Christianity "demonized" Judaism, Judaism "demonized" itself even more; after all, it was Christianity that constituted a dangerous heresy and apostasy of Judaism, and not vice versa; it was Christianity that configured itself as "idolatry" for Judaism, which,

---

[22] Edizioni di Ar, 2002, pp. 16-17. For a similar but more comprehensive study, see T. Dalton, *Eternal Strangers: Critical Views of Jews and Judaism through the Ages* (2020).
[23] Cohn, *Warrant*, p. ix.
[24] *Warrant*, p. x.

already in Deuteronomy 13:7-11, had the tool to remedy it: the extermination, ordered by Yahweh, of the apostates and the instigators of apostasy.[25]

Cohn's psychoanalytic ramblings aim to create an anti-Semitism with no real causes: by now its "cause" will be only a "prejudice" that is thoroughly and absolutely unfounded. In this way, and as a unique case in world history, the Jews become the only *a priori* just and innocent people, the only ones who never committed even the most insignificant fault, the predestined victim of the "prejudices" of brutal anti-Semites, who inevitably become demagogues, tricksters, shadowy characters, semi-crazy, and semi-criminals, semi-paranoids, and so on.[26]

With this, anti-Semitism is equated with paranoia; and criticism of the Jewish worldview and relations with non-Jews—in a word, the centuries-old debate over the Talmud and later rabbinic writings—is trivially dismissed as irrational anti-Semitic "prejudice" or, even worse, as intentional "defamation."

The second main line specifically concerns the way in which philosemitism has used the Protocols and the aims it pursues. It is, in short, a strategy aimed at reinforcing the idea that anti-Semitism has no legitimate causes. Having identified the essence of anti-Semitism with the Protocols, and since they are a "fake," it follows that "fake" is also the cause of anti-Semitism—i.e. that there is no real, legitimate basis for anti-Semitism.

From another point of view, the "warrant for genocide" argument is meant to dissuade one from investigating the real causes of National Socialist anti-Semitism. As noted, Cohn declares that "the myth of a world Jewish conspiracy" developed out of traditional "demonology." This, then, "inspired a whole series of forgeries, culminating in the Protocols," which, in turn, "were used to justify the massacres of Jews during the Russian Civil War." It eventually "took hold of Hitler's mind and became the ideology of his most fanatical followers at home and abroad (thus helping to pave the way for the partial extermination of European Jews)".[27]

---

[25] "If anyone secretly entices you…saying, 'Let us go and worship other gods', whom neither you nor your ancestors have known…you must not yield to or heed any such persons. Show them no pity or compassion and do not shield them. But you shall surely kill them; your own hand shall be first against them to execute them, and afterwards the hand of all the people. Stone them to death for trying to turn you away from the Lord your God, who brought you out of the land of Egypt, out of the house of slavery."
[26] Ibid., p. 28, 34, 95, 200.
[27] Ibid., p. xiii.

Here too, then, nothing but "prejudice." Moreover, this thesis is refuted by Cohn himself already in his bibliography: the number of editions of the Protocols that appeared during nationalist Germany are fewer than those published in democratic France, and the last edition dates back to 1940.[28] Apparently, at the very time when the alleged Jewish extermination was planned and implemented, the Nazis gave no prominence to the Protocols. Needless to say, of his overstated and openly partisan thesis, Cohn offers no evidence in his book.

Another effect of Operation Protocols is the fictitious link created between this writing and the more serious anti-Talmudic polemic. As De Michelis claims, it fixed the Talmudic *topos*, "and since then, the anti-Semitic subculture considers the Talmud the foundation of the 'secret doctrine of the Jews'." Therefore, the apocryphal character of the Protocols is projected back onto the Talmudic question, which in turn becomes an anti-Semitic "prejudice."

Yet another effect is that it aims to banish from all thinking people the concept, not only of "conspiracy" but also of an "aspiration" for world domination by the Jews. Yet this idea is explicitly expressed as early as Deutero-Isaiah.[29] Rabbi Isidore Loeb comments on it as follows:

> What is certain is that, with or without King Messiah, the Jews will be like the center of mankind, around which the Gentiles will gather, after their conversion to God. The unity of humankind will be done through religious unity. Nations will gather to go and pay their respects to God's people (Isa. 60). All the fortunes of the [Gentile] nations will pass to the Jewish people [...]. The riches of the sea and the fortunes of the nations shall come to be themselves to the Jews [...]. The people and the kingdom that will not serve you will be destroyed.[30]

In this messianic event, the Jews will play an active role:

> It must be said at once, for the understanding of what follows, that God's people, in Deutero-Isaiah, are undoubtedly charged with a messianic role. It is true that there will come

---

[28] Ibid., p. 242.
[29] That is, Isaiah 40-55 (the "second part")—written circa 500 BC. Similar sentiments occur in the even older books of the Torah.
[30] Ibid., p. 197.

a personal Messiah who will subdue the nations and kings, make [Jewish] justice triumph on this earth and peace [*pax judaica*] reign, but the Jewish people are also charged with this role and must concur in it. Precisely it, without any doubt, is the new scourge with which God, at the end of time, will shake the mountains, crush the hills and scatter them like bran (Isa. 41:14-16); precisely Israel, God's Servant, appointed and chosen by God when he was still in his mother's bowels, is the sharp arrow that God hides in his quiver to overcome and subdue the peoples (49:1-3,7). His enemies and adversaries will be covered with confusion, destroyed, annihilated (41:8-13); peoples will march in his light and kings in the rays of his splendor (60:3).[31]

And the fact that these are not archaic fixations but constitute the very essence of Jewish messianism is documented, *ad abundantiam*, in Gian Pio Mattogno's study *Jewish Imperialism in the Sources of Rabbinic Tradition*.[32] Thus, even the real and well-documented Jewish imperialism according to rabbinic sources, thanks to Operation Protocols, dissolves into the "myth" of the "world Jewish conspiracy."

But it is also clear that the very first Jewish conception that an anti-Semitic forger would have invoked to make a Jewish world "conspiracy" credible would have been messianism itself. What could have made such a "conspiracy" truer than an imperialistic aspiration and a prophecy of world domination? And what would have embarrassed the philosemites more seriously? The absence of such a perspective in the Protocols is one of the most convincing proofs that they do not constitute *in primis et ante omnia* ['first and above all'] an anti-Semitic writing.

4. A Critique of Liberalism

We turn now to the specific textual evidence for my alternate thesis. The Protocols constitute essentially a political philosophy and a philosophy of history. They are, on the one hand, an indictment against liberalism and an *apologia* for autocracy, and, on the other hand, an explanation of the cause that (for the Protocols' author) produced the ruin of the autocratic form of government and the birth of the republican one.

---

[31] I. Loeb, *La littérature des pauvres dans la Bible*. Librairie Léopold Cerf, Parigi, 1892, pp. 218-219.
[32] *L'imperialismo ebraico nelle fonti della tradizione rabbinica* (2009).

Before analyzing these aspects of the Protocols, it is appropriate to schematically formulate the keys to interpretating this essay. From the standpoint of political action, "we," that is, the "Elders of Zion," represent liberals and all enemies of absolute monarchy (capitalists, socialists, Freemasons, etc.).[33] "Gentiles," "Christians," symbolize absolute monarchies of divine right and their peoples as the object of liberal disruptive action. In such a perspective, "we have done" means "*liberals* have done"; "we will do" means "*liberals* will do, or plan to do." Doctrinally, "we" expresses the principles of liberalism, and "we have done" and "we will do" refer to the present and future consequences of those principles.

From time to time, however, this perspective is reversed. Where the "Elders of Zion" express their vehement disapproval of the people led astray by liberalism and oppose them with their own virtues, they represent the aristocratic advocates of absolute monarchy. This, of course, is especially true of the series of passages in which the "Elders of Zion" expound a cloying *apologia* for Russian czarism.

Putting some order into the great confusion of themes therein, one can identify in the Protocols, as far as anti-liberal and anti-modernist doctrine is concerned, three main lines of refutation:

> 1) a general and specific critique of the principles and institutions of liberalism;
> 2) an exposition of the deleterious effects—in the political, economic, cultural, social, and moral spheres—of liberal principles; and
> 3) A critique of the republican form of government in its concrete actualization.

Let's examine the first point.[34] First of all, liberal principles and theories have an "absolute falsity" (P9), they are "brutal principles" (P23); liberal-

---

[33] Since at least the early 19th century, Jews have been equated with liberalism. This is because they, lacking power, sought to use disruptive and heterological methods to overturn traditional sources of power, stability, and social strength. In the past century, however, as they have gained increasing power themselves, some Jews have shifted to more conservative, power-consolidating strategies. And yet other, socially-oriented Jews continue with extreme leftist forms of liberalism, which they see as a way to weaken and undermine any potential backlash to their predatory and destructive forms of power. (ed.)

[34] The following quoted passages are cited by Protocol number ("P#"). The wording is, in some cases, slightly different than that given in Part II of this book, because Mattogno is working from an Italian translation of the Proto-

ism is a "poison" and a "deadly disease" (P10) that does not lead to "a rational paradise" (P3). In fact, "the concept of freedom is not realizable, because no one knows how to use it with discretion" (P1). It implies "contradictions" and is "the symbol of the bestial force that turns populations into bloodthirsty beasts" (P3).

Equality "does not exist in nature," because "nature herself has established inequality of mind, character, and ability" (P1), so "true equality cannot exist, given the different nature of the various qualities of labor" (P3). The watchwords of "liberty, equality, fraternity" are "abstract"; not only do they not agree, they even contradict each other (P1). The idea of progress conceals "a deviation from the truth" (P13). Freedom of religion and equality are "pernicious principles" (P22). Moreover, "there is nothing more harmful than individual initiative" (P5), and universal suffrage achieves "an absolute majority," which "could not be obtained from the educated classes or from a society divided into castes" (P10).

Let's move on to the second point. "Liberalism gave birth to constitutional governments" (P10), undermining the foundation of the sovereignty of absolute monarchies (P1). Indeed, liberal rights induced the people who advocated them "to regard Kings as mere mortals" (P5). Politically, liberalism weakens parties, states, and monarchs (P1), and it is easier to seize the state in which such "infection" spreads: then "the new government merely replaces the old one, weakened by its liberalism". The "liberal tendencies toward independence" are nothing more than the "misuse" that power-lovers make of their rights (P3).

In the political-constitutional field, "the laws and the personality of the ruler are rendered ineffective by the continuous intrusive liberalism" (P1), and "liberal ideas" undermine the prestige of the laws (P15). In the social field, liberalism has "destroyed the functioning of natural existence" (P1); the ideas of law and freedom "have destroyed all social organizations," performing "a nefarious action" (P23).

As for the people, liberal principles have created bad subjects (P16). The constitutions of liberal states contain "many rights that for the masses are purely fictitious. All so-called "people's rights" can exist only in theories which are not practically implementable." A "worker of the proletariat, bent by his hard labors and oppressed by fate," receives no advantage "from the fact that a waffler gets the right to speak, or a journalist that to print any nonsense." The constitution does nothing to benefit the proletariat (P3).

---

cols; his quotations were then translated back into English for the present essay. (ed.)

Furthermore, liberalism gave the people fictitious rights. Freedom leads to all-out war against all order: "The word 'freedom' leads society to fight against all powers, even the powers of God's Nature" (P3). It also tolerates the unlimited consumption of alcoholic beverages (P1). The "watchwords" of "liberty, equality, brotherhood," then, "robbed the world of prosperity and the individual of true personal freedom". They corroded "the welfare of Christians [= absolute monarchies]" and destroyed "their peace, their constancy, their union, thus ruining the foundations of states" (P1). Finally, progress "leads directly to utopia, from which anarchy and hatred of authority were born" (P12).

We now come to the third point. The "brutal principles" of liberalism constitute a legalization of theft and violence: "At the present time these concepts prevail with great success, and the consequences are theft and violence carried out under the banner of law and freedom" (P23). And in fact, liberals are actually anarchists (P12). The constitutional regime "is nothing but a school of dissensions, disagreements, contentions and useless party agitations: in short, it is the school of everything that weakens the efficiency of government" (P10).

The republican state is born of violence and is nourished by it (P4). In addition to a secret organization, liberal regimes are also slaves to gold: "Today, the power of gold has overwhelmed liberal regimes" (P1).

Presidents of parliamentary republics are "a caricature" of the autocratic ruler (P10), while "Presidents of Councils of Ministers" are "dictators" who commit with impunity "abuses for the smallest of which" liberal peoples "would have killed a hundred kings" (P3). Liberal governments are "arenas where party wars are fought." Parliamentary institutions are in the grip of anarchy. Republican officials are mere interchangeable puppets, while "the tribune, as well as the press, contributed to making governments weak and inactive, thus rendering them useless and superfluous; and that is why they were dismissed in many countries" (P10).

Universities churn out "inexperienced young people, imbued with ideas about new constitutional forms, as if these were comedies or tragedies; or devoted to dealing with political issues that even their fathers did not understand" (P15). Judges "are indulgent toward all delinquents." Lawyers are cruel and immoral (P17). The people in liberal regimes are enslaved as never before in autocratic regimes (P3). The "Christian peoples," i.e., peoples infected with liberalism, "in their immense baseness" lend themselves to force, are merciless to the weak, cruel to faults and indulgent to crimes, and finally "are patient to the point of martyrdom in enduring the violence of a bold tyranny". The masses are illogical because the "despots" (= liberals) "persuade the people, through their agents, that the abuse of power with obvious detriment to the state is done for a high purpose, namely, to obtain the prosperity of the people and for the sake of international brotherhood, union and equality." The people, under republican rule, condemn the innocent and acquit the guilty (P3). The mass has a destructive and anarchic character. In conclusion, liberal societies are in shambles (P5).

5. Defense of Autocracy

The *apologia* for autocracy is carried out through a timely contrasting of the principles and effects of absolute monarchy with those of the liberal regime. Liberal rights led peoples to regard kings as mere mortals, but "when peoples regarded their rulers as the expression of God's will, they quietly submitted to the despotism of their monarchs" (P5). Autocracy is the foundation of civilization: "Without absolute despotism, civilization cannot exist, because civilization can only be promoted under the protection of the ruler, whoever he may be, and not by the masses" (P1). It is therefore "the only healthy form of government" (P10). Only the autocrat is a true politician (P1).

The parliamentary regime is contrasted with the dynastic regime: The aristocracy was "the only defense that nations and countries" (monarchical) possessed against liberal principles (P1). It defended the people, so that "today the people, having destroyed the privileges of the aristocracy, have fallen under the yoke of cunning exploiters and people from nowhere" (P3). It also defended the working classes and safeguarded personal freedom: "The aristocracy, which—by right—shared the earnings of the working classes, took an interest in ensuring that these classes were well fed, healthy and robust". But the liberal advocates of the principles of the French Revolution "took from the world prosperity and from the individual true personal liberty, which before had been so well safeguarded" (P1).

There is no shortage of *apologia* for castes. True social science would "convince the world that work and employments should be assigned to distinct castes, in order to avoid human suffering resulting from education unresponsive to the work which individuals are called upon to perform." Knowledge of this science would induce the people to submit "voluntarily to the governmental powers and the castes of government as classified by them" (P3).

True liberty is that which is realized in autocratic regimes (P4). Notably, contrary to the liberal conception, "freedom does not consist in debauchery, nor in the right to do as one pleases"; true freedom "consists solely in the inviolability of person, domicile and property for anyone who honestly adheres to all the laws of social life" (P22). Like civilization, neither can the people exist without an absolute monarch, in the absence of whom it is a blind and destructive force: "[F]or the blind force of the people cannot exist for a single day without a leader to guide it" (P1). The people have a "blind power" (P3); the mass "is a blind power," incapable of self-government, because "those who, emerging from it, are called to government, are equally blind in matters of politics," the only true politician being the autocrat (P1).

Other passages insist on the inability of the people to govern themselves, much praised when they submit to "the order established by God on earth," equally denigrated, even in appellations (mass, plebs, crowd) when they accept liberalism (P1). Only the autocrat can do this. The plebs are also ignorant and gullible (P3), stupid (P5), petty, inconstant, lacking moral equilibrium, and incapable of understanding and respecting the very conditions of their well-being and existence (P1). The plebs are anarchists and enemies of all established order: "The plebs, given this state of mind, destroy everything stable and create havoc everywhere" (P3).

This explicitly didactic aspect of the Protocols, hitherto unexplored, is surprising in itself, but even more so is the political conception advocated by the "Elders of Zion," which is just as explicitly an idealized autocracy, called precisely "our autocracy" ruled by "our autocrat" (P10) within the framework of a monarchy of divine right.

6. "Jewish Kingdom" or Czarist Autocracy?

The political philosophy of the "Elders of Zion" is set forth in a series of statements scattered throughout various Protocols and treated systematically in the last one. This does not detract from the fact that it constitutes a very small part of this writing and, above all, a part totally inadequate to what should be the ultimate goal of their "conspiracy." It consists in fact of an idealized czarist autocracy clumsily disguised as a Jewish Kingdom.

In fact, expressions such as "King of Israel" (Ps15, 17, 23, 24), "dynasty of King David" (P24), or "sprung from the sacred seed of David" (P24), are a cover—one that, moreover, betrays itself in pseudo-Jewish epithets such as "a despotic sovereign of Zionist blood" (P3) or "despot of Zionist blood" (P5). At the same time, others, such as "World Patriarch" (P15), "Patriarch of the International Church" (P17) or "true Pope of the World" (P17), are drawn directly from the hierarchies of the Church of the East and West. Others are openly czarist.

The "King of Israel" is in effect a "Universal Sovereign" (P12), a "World Ruler" (P3)—that is, an absolute monarch of divine right "chosen by God and anointed from above" (P23), at the same time father and god of his subjects. This political conception, which traces the apologetic themes previously examined, is in fact essentially an ardent *apologia* for czarist autocracy, which takes on some of the tones of Russian Messianism. This is even clearer from the ultimate purpose of this reign: "Our Sovereign will be chosen by God and consecrated from above for the purpose of destroying all ideas influenced by instinct and not by reason, by brutal principles and not by humanity" (P23). In other words, the task entrusted by God to the Sovereign is to destroy liberal ideas in all fields—political, social, moral, economic, and financial—and to restore an ideal autocracy based on nonhereditary dynastic succession (P24) and castes (P16).

With this, the author of the Protocols shows his cards: He is nostalgic for the *Ancien Régime*, someone who sees the principle of absolute monarchies of divine right collapsing at the hands of liberalism and parliamentarianism and who tries to counter them by describing the nefarious and, in his view, real face of liberalism. He does so by contrasting it with the idealized greatness of autocracy. The "Elders of Zion" is thus a literary fiction that expresses its judgment of liberalism where they harshly criticize this doctrine, and at the same time its conception of autocracy where they fervently praise this political form and set it as the foundation of their coming Kingdom.

7. The "Elders": Aristocrats *and* Liberals

If the part of the world "conspiracy" yet to be realized—the establishment of the Universal Kingdom—betrays the political philosophy and politico-social aspirations of the author of the Protocols, the part already realized—the occult domination through liberal "infection"—appears in its true meaning precisely because of this key reading. This also clarifies the real meaning of the "conspiracy" and its true functionality as far as its properly Jewish aspect is concerned.

The "conspiracy," in its aspect to be implemented, does not end in the monarchy of divine right with marked paternalistic features already examined, but presents another in stark contradiction to the first: that of *a brutal and terrorist despotism*, one that appears either already implemented or soon to be implemented. In relation to this twofold aspect of the "conspiracy," the "Elders of Zion" are the literary embodiment of the plebeian despotism that the author of the paper saw implemented in liberal regimes, and at the same time of the extreme consequences, or aims, or threats that he believed he could identify in them.

8. The World "Conspiracy": Liberalism and its Consequences

We come now to an examination of the actual meaning of the world "conspiracy," which is that of a disguised critique of liberalism that takes up and develops the critique already analyzed.

True sovereignty comes from God; liberalism, by advocating the principle of popular sovereignty, bases the state on brute force: "Our [liberals'] right lies in force" (P1). In order to destroy the very foundation of true sovereignty, atheistic liberalism has attacked Christianity (Catholic and Orthodox), whether by asserting freedom of religion, favoring the principle of free examination of Protestantism, or discrediting the clergy—especially the Jesuits, the liberals' most fearsome enemies. It aims finally at absolute atheism (Ps 4, 14, 15, 17).

The mock attack against the Jesuits takes on overtly apologetic tones (P5). By suppressing the foundation of true sovereignty, liberalism has stifled all legitimate forms of government; constitutional monarchies have a purely virtual, i.e., non-actual, legitimacy (P9). Propounding the "immortal principles" of the French Revolution, liberalism also abolished the privileges of the aristocracy, promoting the development of plutocracy and capitalism (P1).

Thus the enemies of absolute monarchy took over the government by substituting liberal institutions for monarchical ones (P9). By establishing the parliamentary regime, liberals have thrown the state into anarchy: "We have turned governments into arenas where party wars are fought. Before long disorder and failure will appear everywhere" (P3). Liberalism, being founded on false principles, is only apparently the realm of freedom. In reality, it is a terroristic dictatorship, one that is exercised "covertly" (P9).

The parliamentary regime, at once dictatorial and anarchic, cannot bring well-being and prosperity to the people, who are incapable of governing themselves on principle, and who drown in incompetence and corruption. The presidents of parliamentary republics themselves are "wormy individuals," and all state officials are men of malfeasance, who inevitably aim at their individual gain. Parties, finally, are a disruptive force in the state structure (P10).

Throughout the fabric of the republican state and in all fields of public and private life, corruption and hypocrisy reign. The parliamentary regime confuses the people, incites them to luxury and debauchery, corrupts them with filthy literature, misleads them with false science, and deceives them with the press (Ps1, 5, 6).

In his indictment against liberalism, the author of the Protocols also throws into the cauldron those he considers its precursors: Darwin, Marx, and Nietzsche (P2). Even science is felt to be a danger because it undermines the monopoly of Christian culture previously held by the aristocracy (P3). On the other hand, the new science is also blamed for being liberal, that is, anti-Christian and anti-traditional (Ps2, 7, 14).

Confronted with the supineness with which the people "blindly believe in the printed words and erroneous illusions conveniently inspired" by liberals, the author of the Protocols cannot restrain his indignation, which shines through in the crude expressions with which he brands the bestial obtuseness of the masses (P15). But the people are at the same time also victims, a pack of sheep before the liberal wolves (P11). Not even in the face of the liberals corrupting the people can the author of the Protocols mask his disdain, which he depicts thus: "[We liberals] have boundless ambition, a devouring greed, a ruthless desire for revenge, and an intense hatred" for kings and aristocrats.

Let's turn to the economic and financial aspect of the "conspiracy"—that is, what the author of the Protocols believes liberalism has already done and plans to do in this area to unhinge traditional societies. First of all, liberalism, by destroying the privileges of the aristocracy, has generated capitalism and plutocracy, which exercises dictatorship through international finance. Liberal regimes are slaves to gold, which the plutocrats have seized (Ps1, 22). The liberal plutocrats obtained this gold by foreign loans, making slaves of their banks to the monarchies of Europe (P20). With the riches thus obtained, the liberal plutocrats provoked the economic crises by forcing the states into further debt.

The critique of "capitalist despotism" is based on Marxist arguments: exploitation of workers, surplus value (the "abusive profit"), accumulation of capital, proletarianization of the middle classes, starvation of the proletariat, and final revolution (Ps3, 4). For the author of the Protocols, liberalism therefore brings capitalism, which strangles states and workers (Ps1, 3). Conversely, the critique of Marxism is based on "bourgeois" arguments: it pretends to desire the liberation of the proletariat from the yoke of capitalism, but in fact aims to enslave and oppress it (Ps2, 3, 6).

9. Why are the "Elders" "Jews"?

Finally, it remains to explain the anti-Semitic functionality of the worldwide "conspiracy," that is, its attribution to Jewish "Elders." In the autocratic, anti-liberal, and anti-modernist political philosophy expressed in the Protocols, anti-Semitism has a secondary and derivative, almost fallback value compared to the central theme of the liberal, anti-monarchical, and anti-Christian "world conspiracy" that forms the core of their philosophy of history. Indeed, "conspiracy" is introduced there to explain the reason for the decline of divine right monarchy and the triumph of liberalism. How could the "poison" and "deadly disease" of liberalism affect the perfect organism of autocracy? By virtue, precisely, of a "conspiracy."

This idea was, after all, already suggested in Maurice Joly's *Dialogue*, from which the author of the Protocols famously drew so heavily:

> It is thus that the various peoples of Europe have passed, through successive transformations, from the feudal system to the monarchical system, and from the pure monarchical system to the constitutional regime. This progressive development, the unity of which is so impressive, has nothing fortuitous about it; it occurred as a necessary consequence of the movement that took place in ideas before it was translated into deeds.[35]

This explanation, unacceptable to a proponent of the monarchy of divine right, nevertheless contains the cue for the solution of the problem; the destruction of the *Ancien Régime* "has nothing fortuitous about it," it is thus the "necessary consequence" of a "conspiracy."

But who to put in the role of "conspirators"? To arrive at a solution to this other problem, the author of the Protocols simply proceeded by exclusion. It becomes clear that his political philosophy did not allow him to attribute this conspiracy to his natural enemies, the liberals, because then he would not have been able to realize the critical-apologetic purpose that constitutes the essence of the Protocols. Indeed, liberal "conspirators," in literary fiction, could not have failed to harshly criticize absolute monarchy by divine right and enthusiastically exalt liberalism, whereas the author's intent was exactly the opposite.

For the same reason, the cause of the conspiracy could not be a universal democracy, vehemently abhorred by the author of the Protocols. Hence the need for it to tend toward the establishment of an idealized absolute monarchy of divine right, which he regarded as the only legitimate and natural form of government, and which moreover results in an

---

[35] Joly, *Dialogue*, p. 67.

additional *apologia* for autocracy. I speak of "necessity" because a simple terrorist dictatorship, undoubtedly far more consonant with the feral characteristics ascribed to the liberal adversary, would have been in too flagrant a contradiction with the critical-apologetic purpose of the Protocols. Those who firmly believe—like the "conspirators" of the Protocols—in the divine origin of the Sovereign, cannot admit a governing force based on brute force. Indeed, this is the conception they ascribe to the liberal enemy.

With that, in the panorama of forces acting in Europe at the end of the 19th century, the field of likely conspirators narrowed to: Freemasonry and Judaism.

Freemasonry, a proponent of the "immortal principles" of 1789 and therefore itself an embodiment of liberal principles, could not play a conspiratorial role for the same reason that liberals could not. But this is also true of the secret societies of the 19th century, which tended moreover toward democratic and revolutionary radicalism.

Therefore, the choice could only fall on Judaism. This had the added benefit of drawing hatred on the Jews, who are already presented in Joly's *Dialogue* as the models of those who have no other worship of gold and whose customs are mercantile.[36] The Jews, because of their outwardly revolutionary attitude aimed at the acquisition of civil rights, and their inwardly conservative attitude aimed at preserving national and religious unity, were the ideal conspirators. The choice was thus the necessary effect of the critical-apologetic premises of the Protocols; the "conspiracy" served to explain the decline of absolute monarchy, and the "Elders of Zion" served to explain the "conspiracy."

The choice of Jewish conspirators was so obligatory that the author of the Protocols did not even bother to make it credible with references to the Talmud and later rabbinic literature, much less to link the conspiracy to Jewish messianism and to identify the "King of Israel" as the Messiah—as explained above. This also clarifies why the description of the results of a conspiracy hatched "nearly 20 centuries" ago begins with the French Revolution, that is, with the destruction of the *Ancien Régime* and the triumph of liberal ideology.

Having found the required "conspirators," an equally obligatory scheme of conspiracy was found; to destroy the *Ancien Régime*, the "Elders of Zion" provoked the French Revolution and spread its principles throughout Europe by means of Freemasonry, a blunt instrument

---

[36] *Dialogue*, p. 59. This is an interesting situation in light of Joly's Jewishness (ed.).

in the hands of the "Elders" created specifically to exert occult action (Ps3, 4, 9, 12).

From the above, it is clear that the Protocols were not designed to serve as a "warrant for genocide"—the Norman Cohn thesis—that is, to catalyze hatred of the Jews and arouse pogroms against them. From the point of view of practical and factual reaction, they instead explicitly call on the peoples of Europe to reject liberalism and restore autocratic sovereignty. If liberalism is the "poison," the "deadly disease" that has affected them, the only antidote, the only medicine, is absolute monarchy by divine right.

THE *PROTOCOLS* IN THE 21ST CENTURY
THOMAS DALTON

In the present day, some 120 years after they were written and over a century since they were exposed as a "forgery," the Protocols continue to display an enduring fascination and an enduring mystery. They offer a compelling and troubling vision of the future, one that, sadly, seems increasingly realized, if not quite in the way that was anticipated. And surprisingly, even after so many years, no one has yet discovered the true story behind their origins; in many ways, we have no better understanding than did the early commenters of the 1920s and 1930s. Likely much of the truth has been locked away in Russia, which, for most of this period, has been in a cold or (now) hot war with the West, making any Western investigations difficult or impossible. Be that as it may, the Protocols have had a long and illustrious past, and they will surely continue to engage peoples' interest for many years to come.

As a whole, and at the highest level, the Protocols offers a vision and a plan for Jewish domination and control of the major nations of the world, all at the expense of the detested non-Jews or Goyim. Power is to be vested in a single man, the Sovereign, the "King of Israel," the "Patriarch of the World"—a man "chosen by God" but evidently overseen by a nameless committee of Jewish "wise men," rather like a Board of Directors selects, and replaces, a corporate CEO. Under this new king, Jews will presumably flourish with unlimited wealth and power, and the Goyim —the vast majority of the population—will serve as obedient and compliant underlings, performing all the hard work of social existence without any say in governance. There will be a nominal 'order' and 'happiness' among the populace, predicated upon their willing submission to the King of Israel. With the Jews in charge, all will be well—just as prophesied in the (Jewish) Old Testament.

Such a social vision is remarkable both for its audacity and its absurdity. To believe that a small, non-Western minority like the Jews could attain control over Europe, America, the West, and thus indirectly much of the world, is preposterous in the extreme. Today, Jews comprise not more than 2% of the United States population, around 1% of Canada, and about 0.5% in France and the UK. In the other European nations, they are well under 0.2%. There are between 1.3 million and 2 million Jews in Europe today (including Russia), making them a 0.15% minority overall. At no time in history has such a small minority ruled over such a vastly-larger majority. And yet, thanks to the overwhelming economic and military power of one nation—the United States—Jews indeed dominate large portions of Western society, and indirectly, much of the world. "Today, the Jews rule the world by proxy," said Mahathir Mohamad in 2003. It was no exaggeration.[1]

Even back in the early 1800s, there was some evidence that Jews had taken control of much of Europe. The famed Rothschild financial entity arose at that time; the founding member, Amschel Mayer, was widely known as "the Jew of Kings" (a play on the biblical phrase "King of Jews"). From then on, Jewish money became the dominant power in the political sphere. British poet Lord Byron wrote in 1823 that "all states, all things, all sovereigns [the Jews] control." In 1843, Bruno Bauer observed that "the Jew…determines the fate of the [Austrian] Empire by his financial power. The Jew…decides the destiny of Europe." By 1850, Richard Wagner was reiterating these very ideas; he wrote:

> According to the present constitution of the world, the Jew in truth is already more than emancipated; *he rules*, and will rule, so long as money remains the power before which all our doings and our dealings lose their force. (1850/2023: 10).

The result, for Wagner, was a kind of societal curse: "Jewry itself is the evil conscience of our modern civilization," he said (ibid.: 24). Later, in 1869, he wrote of "a press entirely directed by Jews" (ibid.: 32) and of the pernicious consequences that followed from that, not only for music and art but for all of European society. Similar sentiments occurred to

---

[1] Recently there are signs that this may be changing, due in large part to the disastrous Ukraine war, which is destroying American credibility throughout the world and exacting a substantial economic toll. If the non-Zionist nations of the world, and especially Russia, China, and India, can unite against the Zionist American empire, the situation will radically change.

Russian anarchist Mikhail Bakunin, who wrote the following in the same year of 1869:

> The Jewish sect today represents a much more ominous power in Europe than do the Catholic and Protestant Jesuits. They reign despotically in business and finance alike. They control three-quarters of German journalism and a most substantial share of journalism in other countries.[2]

This situation was clear even to observers across the Atlantic; American poet Ralph Emerson wrote with resignation in 1860 that "the Jew" has become "the ruler of the rulers of the earth".[3]

By 1873, a relatively unknown figure, Frederick Millingen (writing as 'Osman Bey') could pen an extensive tract entitled "The Conquest of the World by the Jews." There, he carefully documents the financial, political, and media power of Jews in Europe and America. He traces their history in Europe, demonstrating how, step by step, they entrenched themselves in the higher classes of society, always leveraging a bit of influence to gain yet more influence—power for power's sake. Millingen is blunt in his assessment:

> [T]he Jews have brought things to pass in such a short time that they are now the wealthiest and most influential class of men; and have attained a position of vast power, the likes of which we do not meet in all history. From the height of their immense capital, the weight whereof threatens to crush all other nations, they command the whole world of finance and industry. The most profitable and colossal enterprises of modern times, within and out of Europe, are simply Jewish monopolies...
>
> I have shown that it is no exaggeration to say that the Jews today trample underfoot the power of all the crowned heads and nations of the world.

---

[2] Cited in Ball (1919/1993), p. 145.
[3] All above cited in *Classic Essays on the Jewish Question* (T. Dalton, ed.; 2023). See also *Eternal Strangers* (T. Dalton, 2020).

> In fact, the Conquest of the World by the Jews is henceforth a fixed fact, not to be disputed. What has materially assisted the Jews in this Conquest of the World is the pernicious habit, so prevalent of late, of issuing bonds on the part, not alone of nations, but also of municipalities, etc., thereby mortgaging the wealth of communities, as well as nations, all over the world. ... It is this secret power of compound interest that has enslaved mankind and that has been used as such an effectual weapon by the Jews for their Conquest of the World.[4]

One can only wonder how much more extreme the situation is today, some 150 years later.

But to the point: We ought not be surprised, then, that the author of the Protocols might envision a situation of Jewish global rule; indeed, it had *already come to pass*, decades before he wrote in the early 1900s. The author was not forecasting the future; he was describing present reality, and extrapolating that into the future. This point has been unappreciated by commentators on the Protocols; it significantly contributes to our understanding of the circumstances in which they were written.

*****

In the remainder of this essay, I will address four main points: (1) the matter of a "forgery"; (2) the political situation in Russia at the time; (3) the writing style of the Protocols; and (4) the question of their veracity. I will then close with a look at some consequences for the present day.

First: As noted by several people, there seems to be no doubt that the text of the Protocols borrows heavily from passages in Joly's 1865 book, to the point of selective plagiarism. Several passages are nearly identical and several others are too similar to be coincidental. But as I stated in the Introduction, the question then is: what follows from this? And the answer is: nothing of significance. If indeed the document was of Jewish origins, it only means that the Jewish speaker, or the Jewish transcriber, borrowed heavily from fellow-Jew Joly. It would be as if

---

[4] *Classic Essays*, pp. 64-65, 80.

some military general laid out a plan of attack on the battlefield and used phrases from Shakespeare without proper citation—perhaps to better 'fire up' his men. The plan could be completely real and effective, and yet it would be utterly unrelated to any "plagiarized" passages from Shakespeare. At worst, we might call the general a poor (or unethical) writer; but that is obviously of no consequence. In the same way, the Jewish plan could, in theory, be completely real and efficacious while simultaneously being a plagiarism.

If, on the other hand, it was written by a non-Jew—perhaps to expose Jewish power, perhaps to promote anti-Semitism, perhaps to further other political goals—then it also comes to nothing. Again, we have, at worst, a poor or unethical writer; but so what? If the writer was looking to maximize impact, or to give the document an impressive sound, it is little surprise that he would borrow from appropriate texts. Who, giving a motivational speech or writing some inspirational text, wouldn't like to throw in a little Shakespeare, or Lincoln, or Voltaire, or Plato?

The question of a "forgery" is different. If a non-Jew wrote it as a Jewish speech or meeting minutes and intended it to be taken as such, then indeed it is a fraud and a deception, in that sense. But we don't know the author, and even if we did, we likely would not know his intentions. We don't know if those early Russian journalists who published it knew its origins, nor do we know if Nilus himself knew. Consequently, the matter of a forgery is an open question that will likely never be answered.

But again, as with the plagiarism question, we can say that, to a large extent, it does not matter. If the document says something real and meaningful about Jewish power and Jewish intentions, and if it leads to actual insight into the Jewish Question, then the document has legitimate value.

Second: There are good reasons to think that the author was a non-Jewish Russian, specifically one concerned about the decline of traditional power structures in Russia and the West, the decay of traditional values (including Christian values), and the rise of a detrimental and licentious form of liberalism. This Russian clearly has no love lost for the Jews, but they may have simply been convenient targets, as Mattogno (present volume) argues.

In this scenario, we need to keep in mind the political context. The Russian system of government, for several centuries, was czarism. The first czar is usually considered to be Ivan the Terrible (reign 1547-1575); the czarist system then ran more-or-less continuously for well over three centuries, until 1917. The four czars in closest proximity to the Protocols were:

- Nicholas I (reign 1825-1855)
- Alexander II (1855-1881)
- Alexander III (1881-1894)
- Nicholas II (1894-1917)

As it happens, all four had conflicts with the Jews. Nicholas I had some 2.5 million Jews under his authority, and early in his reign he implemented a forced military conscription for all Jewish males (the Hebrews have historically been famous draft dodgers, preferring to pay others to fight). Nicholas generally pushed for assimilation into Russian culture, something else that Jews have traditionally opposed in the strongest way. He also instituted special taxes on his many Jewish subjects.

Alexander II lifted the Jew-taxes and increased their freedom of movement; but to no avail. He still earned Jewish enmity. Thus, a radical anarchist group, Narodnaya Volya, which was disproportionately Jewish, made plans to assassinate the czar. (Two leading Jews in the group were Mikhail Zlatopolsky and Aaron Zundelevich.) And they succeeded in 1881, when two hand-thrown bombs took his life.

Upon the assassination, Alexander II's son assumed the title of czar, becoming Alexander III. He implemented the anti-Jewish 'May Laws' and his government inaugurated a series of pogroms against the Jewish population, compelling many to flee to Europe. He died of illness in 1894 at the age of 49, to be succeeded by his son, Nicholas II. Intermittent pogroms continued under his reign, including the widely-known 'Kishinev Massacre' of 1903 in which some 50 Jews were killed. It was just about this time that the Protocols were likely being written.[5]

Thus we see that, as of (say) 1903, a Russian pro-czarist sympathizer would have witnessed at least 75 years of conflicts with Jews, including their role in the killing of Alexander II. If the Protocols were still being

---

[5] Nicholas II would later be executed by a group of Jewish Bolsheviks in 1918, along with his wife and five children.

polished up in 1904, the author might well have been shocked by the assassination of the Russian Minister of the Interior, Vyacheslav von Plehve, in July of that year; the killer was a Jewish radical named Igor Sazonov. Certainly all these events would have played a part in the construction of the Protocols in Russia—if indeed that is what happened.

Third: Consider now the content and the writing style of the document. As I noted in the Introduction, the ideas of the text are subtle and sophisticated but the organization of the text itself is terrible; the writer arbitrarily jumps from one theme to the next, even within a given protocol, and there is no structural coherence to the work as a whole. There is no logical flow from an initial point or opening statements to an end point, and there is no systematic argumentation. I am tempted to say that a decent college writer could compose a better text. This, oddly enough, is actually an argument for its authenticity: no skilled forger would create such a clumsy text! But if a scribe or note-taker was jotting down comments from some fast-talking Jewish rambler, he might well have produced such an incoherent piece of writing.

Another point in favor of authenticity is the idea of the Sovereign. Nowhere else in either philo-Semitic or anti-Semitic literature do we find reference to an individual Jew ruling the world, to my knowledge. This is a case of an idea so preposterous that it just might be true: that is, that some Jews circa 1900 may indeed have resurrected the ancient Messiah concept of the Old Testament and advocated a modern-day Jewish world ruler. Such Jews would likely be ultra-orthodox and, most probably, anti-Zionist; they would believe that any human attempt to return Jews to Palestine circumvents and thus violates God's promise of a divinely-ordained savior. This has the further advantage of explaining why there is so little reference to Zionism in the text—only two passing references (P3 and P5), and there only to the "Zionist blood" of the Sovereign, not to Zionism per se.

A third novelty is the form and style of presentation—that is, of meeting minutes or lecture notes—which leads to the intriguing possibility that they give some sort of direct and unprecedented insight into nefarious Jewish plans. Perhaps a Russian anti-Semite would try this entirely new technique, but it certainly is an unusual choice, the likes of which no other anti-Semite has tried before or since. Either it was a flash of brilliance, or—the document is authentic. (But then we are back to the question of why such a clever anti-Semite would construct such a clumsy document; it makes no sense.)

The text contains other oddities: Neither the Talmud nor the Shulchan Aruch are mentioned, as would be expected from a conventional anti-Semite; writers of that time frequently cited damning passages from those documents in support of their claims. Also, Old Testament passages are almost non-existent (one exception in P5), and the biblical Messiah figure is never defended via Old Testament citation—which argues against my point above. The word 'Jew' appears only twice, both in P8. Christianity is also referenced only twice (P1 and P17). But 'God' appears 20 times, and 'Goy' or 'Goyim' some 130 times. In sum, these facts are neither what we might expect from a Gentile "forgery" nor from a leaked Jewish document; once again, further mysteries.

Fourth: In the end, some might say, all that matters is: Do the Protocols give a true depiction of Jewish intentions and activities? And for Ford, Rosenberg, Hitler and others, the answer is Yes—the document is accurate, therefore it is a reliable guide to Jewish thinking and thus useful in formulating solutions to the Jewish Question. It is 'true' if it gives a true reading of the Jewish mindset and Jewish worldview.

And is it accurate? Do Jews indeed have intentions to dominate or rule the world? This is arguably the central question of the entire Protocols. And here we can say with confidence that the answer is a resounding Yes. For evidence, we need look no further than the Jewish Bible, otherwise known as the Old Testament. The opening book of Genesis includes some infamous passages on how "man" (in reality, Jews, given that this was written by Jews, for Jews) is granted "dominion" over the Earth:

> Then God said, "Let Us make man in Our image, according to Our likeness; let them have *dominion* over the fish of the sea, over the birds of the air, and over the cattle, over all the earth and over every creeping thing that creeps on the earth." ... Then God blessed them [Adam and Eve], and God said to them, "Be fruitful and multiply; *fill the earth and subdue it*; *have dominion* over the fish of the sea, over the birds of the air, and over every living thing that moves on the earth." (1:26-28; emphasis added)

> So God blessed Noah and his sons, and said to them: "Be fruitful and multiply, and fill the earth. And the fear of you and the dread of you shall be on every beast of the earth, on every bird of the air, on all that move on the earth, and on all the fish of the sea. They are given into your hand." (9:1-3)

Later in the same book, God—that is, the Jewish God, Jehovah—says to Abraham:

> To your descendants I will give this land [of Canaan / Palestine]. (12:7)

> I will establish my covenant between me and you and your descendants after you, throughout their generations for an everlasting covenant... And I will give to you, and to your descendants after you, the land of your sojourning, all the land of Canaan, for an everlasting possession. (17:7-8)

Isaac then passes the promise along to his son Jacob, progenitor of the Jewish people: "Let peoples [Gentiles] serve you, and nations bow down to you" (27:29).

Then in Exodus, God says to Moses:

> You [Jews] shall be my own possession among all peoples; for all the earth is mine, and you shall be to me a kingdom of priests and a holy nation. (19:5-6)

Moses later replies to God, "We [Jews] are distinct...from all other people that are upon the face of the earth" (33:16)—because God is "with" the Jews alone, among all humanity. What arrogance.

In Deuteronomy we find God again speaking to Moses:

> I will put the dread and fear of you upon the peoples that are under the whole heaven, [they] shall tremble and be in anguish because of you. (2:25)

Moses then recalls what God promised to the Jews:

> [H]ouses full of all good things, which you [Jews] did not fill, and cisterns hewn out, which you did not hew, and vineyards and olive trees, which you did not plant. (6:11)

Speaking to his fellow Hebrews, Moses cites the fateful words (twice):

> For you are a people holy to the Lord your God; the Lord your God has *chosen you* to be a people for his own possession, out of all the peoples that are on the face of the earth. (7:6 and 14:2)

Lest there be any doubt, Moses adds that "you shall rule over many nations" (15:6), and "they [the Goyim] shall be afraid of you" (28:10).

Then we have the book of Isaiah, which contains several belligerent and world-dominating passages:

> Those who strive against you [Jews] shall be as nothing and shall perish (41:11).

> Kings shall be your foster fathers... With their faces to the ground, they shall bow down to you, and lick the dust of your feet (49:23).

> The wealth of the nations shall come to you (60:5).

> Foreigners shall build up your walls, and their kings shall minister to you...that men may bring you the wealth of the nations (60:10-11).

> You shall suck the milk of nations (60:16).

> [A]liens shall stand and feed your flocks, foreigners shall be your plowmen and vinedressers...you shall eat the wealth of the nations (61:5-6).

The message could hardly be clearer: Jews are destined by God himself to rule the earth. This is perhaps the central component of the Jewish worldview; it has been ingrained in all Jews, religious or secular, almost to the point of a subconscious compulsion: *God promised us that we will rule the world*. The narcissism and megalomania of such a view is impossible to overstate. And when it is attempted to be put into action, disaster ensues for all.

The second main theme of the Protocols is the Jewish contempt for the Goyim—something cited well over 100 times in the document. Again, we must ask: Is this true? Do Jews generally, and as a whole, hold humanity in contempt? Are they misanthropes? Do they 'hate humanity'? If the historical record is any indication, they most certainly do. Without even quoting numerous denigrating passages from the Talmud or Shulchan Aruch,[6] I can cite dozens of observations by famous figures throughout history who made precisely this claim:

- "Moses introduced [to the Jews] a way of life which was, to a certain extent, misanthropic and hostile to foreigners." Hecateus, 300 BC (*On the Jews*).

- "[T]he Jews alone, of all nations, avoid dealings with any other people and look upon all men as their enemies." Diodorus Siculus, 50 BC (*Historical Library* 34, 1).

- Moses instructed the Jews to "show goodwill to no man" and to offer only "the worst advice" to others. Lysimachus, 20 BC.

- Jews distinguish themselves by "their hatred of the human race." Tacitus, 115 (*Annals*).

- "The Jews have long been in revolt...against all humanity... [They] are separated from ourselves by a greater gulf than divides us from Susa or Bactra or the more distant Indies." Philostratus, 230 (*Biography of Apollonius*).

---

[6] For a discussion of such passages, see *The Book of the Shulchan Aruch* (Erich Bischoff; 2023).

- The Jews are "the impious enemies of all nations." Porphyry, 280 (*Against the Christians*).

- "The Jewish nation dares to display an irreconcilable hatred against all nations, and revolts against all masters; always superstitious, always greedy for the good of others, always barbarous—cringing in misfortune, and insolent in prosperity." Voltaire, 1756 (*Essai sur les moeurs*).

- "[The Jews] are, all of them, born with raging fanaticism in their hearts... I would not be in the least bit surprised if these people would not some day become deadly to the human race." Voltaire, 1771.

- "The sullen obstinacy with which [the Jews] maintained their peculiar rites and unsocial manners seemed to mark them out a distinct species of men, who boldly professed, or who faintly disguised, their implacable hatred to the rest of human-kind." Edward Gibbon, historian, 1788 (*Decline and Fall of the Roman Empire*).

- "This widely diffused republic of cunning usurers...have been for thousands of years, nay almost from their beginning, parasitical plants on the trunks of other nations; a race of cunning brokers, almost throughout the whole world..." Johann Herder, philosopher, 1791 (*Reflections*).

- "[Judaism] excludes from its communion the entire human race, on the ground that it was a special people chosen by God for Himself—[an exclusiveness] which showed enmity toward all other peoples and which, therefore, evoked the enmity of all." Immanuel Kant (*Religion within the Limits of Reason Alone*).

- "The only act Moses reserved for the Israelites was...to borrow with deceit and repay confidence with theft." G.W.F. Hegel, 1796 ("Spirit of Christianity").

- "This whole Jewish world which constitutes a single exploiting sect, a sort of bloodsucker people, a collective parasite, voracious, organized in itself, not only across the frontiers of states but even across all the differences of political opinion..." Mikhail Bakunin, 1871 (in Wheen, *Karl Marx*).

- "The Jew has neither to think nor ponder, nor even to calculate, because the hardest calculation lies in his instincts which, closed to any ideality, are perfectly finished in advance. A wonderful, incomparable phenomenon: the plastic demon of decay of humanity, in triumphant security..." Richard Wagner, composer, 1881 ("Know thyself").

- "When Jews step forward as innocence itself, then the danger is great." Friedrich Nietzsche, 1887 (*Will to Power*, sec. 199).

- "The Jews...have a life-interest in making mankind sick, and in inverting the concepts of 'good' and 'evil,' 'true' and 'false' in a mortally dangerous and world-maligning sense." Friedrich Nietzsche, 1888 (*Antichrist*, secs. 24, 44).

- "The Jew is a money-getter...[and] his success has made the whole human race his enemy." Mark Twain, 1899 ("Concerning the Jews").

- Jewish immigrants to America are "moral cripples," "haters of government," and "corrupters of police." "Many of them have developed a monstrous and repulsive love of [financial] gain... When now, they use their Old-World shove and wile and lie in a society like ours, as unprotected as a snail out of its shell, they rapidly push up into a position of prosperous parasitism, leaving scorn and curses in their wake." Edward Ross, sociologist, 1914 (*The Old World in the New*).

- "The Jew is not a good citizen in this sense, that he does not give a whole-hearted allegiance to the institutions, conventions and collective interests and movements of the community in which he finds himself. Neither is he creative in the common interest. He is an alien with an alien mentality… You may repudiate and fight against the clumsy revengefulness, the plunderings, outrages and fantastic intimidations of the Nazi method, but that does not close the Jewish problem for you. It merely brings you back to the fundamental age-long problem of this nation among the nations, this in-and-out mentality, the essential parasitism of the Jewish mycelium upon the social and cultural organisms in which it lives." H. G. Wells, 1936 (*Anatomy of Frustration*).

- "[The Jews are] planetary master criminals of the most modern modernity." Martin Heidegger (in Trawny, *Myth of Jewish World Conspiracy*).[7]

Both main themes are thus proven: Jews indeed have designs on world domination, and they indeed view all of non-Jewish humanity with contempt and hatred. The Protocols are, in this sense, true.

What, then, does all this mean? It means, first of all, that any nation with even 0.1% Jews is in for big trouble; with their disproportionate wealth, massive networks of coreligionists, and with a deeply-ingrained ethic of exploitation and domination, even a tiny Jewish minority can wreak havoc. Consequently, every nation should act in its own self-defense by limiting its Jewish population to no more than a small fraction—and the closer to zero the better. Those Jews that are there must be flagged as Jews, monitored closely, and compelled to pay special income and wealth taxes to offset the financial and social costs that they will certainly impose on the nation. They must also be excluded from leadership roles in large corporations, media, academia, and government.

Secondly, given that there will be countries incapable of resisting Jewish influence, and given that the nation of Israel will continue to exist, this means that Jews globally have a number of safe havens from which to conduct their mayhem. This situation demands that the truly independent nations band together against them, leverage the power of

---

[7] Source details for all the above quotations can be found in *Eternal Strangers* (Dalton 2020).

the UN where possible, and strictly impose boycotts and sanctions on both Israel and on any nation deemed under Jewish control.

Third, there must be a massive and ongoing public education program by which the truth is proclaimed, openly and clearly. People must be made aware of the long history of critical evaluations of Jews, they must realize the damage inflicted on Western society for centuries, and they must understand the cost to their lives and well-being in the present day. Western Jewish media vigorously censors all such information and rabidly condemns anyone who dares to even raise the topic, which ensures that the general public never suspects Jewish perfidy and, at the same time, that they also condemn anyone who might suggest otherwise. Having been well-trained by years of propaganda, the public reflexively dislikes and distrusts anyone whom the Jewish media labels an 'anti-Semite' or a 'Nazi sympathizer' or a 'White supremacist.' The average person has very little ability to think critically, to view social power structures with skepticism, or to speak out against Jewish interests. Thanks to controlled education, stifled dissent, and Hollywood brainwashing, people do, in fact, "serve the Jews": they swallow the Jewish line of thinking, they defend and support Jewish interests, and they—many of them, anyone—act very much like the contemptible Goyim of the Protocols. In some sense, we get what we deserve.

Perhaps, though, things are changing. In can be difficult to gauge public dislike of Jews, but there are a few indicators that are suggestive, and they are moving in the right direction. "Anti-Semitic incidents"—defined as events or actions that Jews don't like—are on the increase in the US and globally. In the US over the past 10 years, the number of occurrences increased from 751 to 3,697.[8] The year 2022 saw an "all-time high," according to the ADL. Secondly, we can compare American attitudes about the Middle East. Over the past decade, the percentage sympathetic with Israel declined from 64% to 55%, while those sympathetic to Palestine rose from 12% to 26%. Americans are still largely pro-Jewish, but the changing trends are significant. Finally, consider the Holocaust. Recent surveys from 2022 in both the US and the Netherlands showed that about 25% of youth believe that the Holocaust is "a myth or the numbers were exaggerated." Around 15% of all Italians say the Hol-

---

[8] Cited from www.statista.com.

ocaust "never happened," and about 13% of all Britons think it either never happened or was exaggerated.[9] Again, these are far from majorities but they represent substantial numbers of people. And they suggest large and growing numbers willing to challenge the standard Jewish narrative.

In the end, perhaps it is fitting that the Protocols are wrapped in so much mystery. Their unknown origin endows them with a certain gravitas, a luster, an aura of something long suspected and perhaps now, finally, revealed. They are accurate on many levels; strikingly so, given that they appeared well before both World War One (1914) and the Russian Bolshevik Revolution (1917)—events that would validate many of their predictions. True, we have no Jewish "Sovereign" running the world, or even any major nation, but we do have potent and wealthy Jewish lobbies steering events and decisions in virtually all Western countries, most notably the United States. Jewish donors corrupt politicians, and activist Jews in Hollywood, academia, and the media work to portray Jews and Israel in as positive a light as possible, and to minimize or censor anything detrimental to their image. And more subtly, all these groups work to project Jewish values and a Jewish worldview on a largely naïve and unsuspecting populace. If the Protocols can serve as even a partial antidote to this global calamity, they will have earned their keep.

---

[9] For more on the Holocaust, see my books *Debating the Holocaust* (4th ed., 2020) or *The Holocaust: An Introduction* (2016).

BIBLIOGRAPHY

Ball, H. 1919/1993. *Critique of the German Intelligentsia*. Columbia University Press.
Bischoff, E. 1929/2023. *The Book of the Shulchan Aruch*. Clemens & Blair.
Cohn, N. 1967. *Warrant for Genocide*. Harper & Row.
Dalton, T. 2019. *The Jewish Hand in the World Wars*. Castle Hill.
Dalton, T. 2020. *Eternal Strangers: Critical Views of Jews and Judaism*. Castle Hill.
Dalton, T. (ed.) 2022. *Classic Essays on the Jewish Question: 1850 to 1945*. Clemens & Blair.
Dalton, T. 2023. *The Steep Climb: Essays on the Jewish Question*. Clemens & Blair.
Evola, J. 1953/2002. *Men Among the Ruins*. Inner Traditions.
Goebbels, J. 2019. *Goebbels on the Jews: The Complete Diary Entries, 1923 to 1945* (T. Dalton, ed.). Castle Hill.
Hitler, A. 1924/2022. *Mein Kampf* (two volumes; T. Dalton, trans.). Clemens & Blair.
Joly, M. 1865/2002. *Dialogue in Hell between Machiavelli and Montesquieu*. Lexington Books.
Roth, S. 1925. *Now and Forever*. R. McBride.

INDEX
(Protocols only)

alcohol 80, 96, 143
America 98
amusements 115
anarchy (anarchists) 78, 80, 86, 96, 111, 143
anti-Semitism 100
aristocracy 81-82, 86, 95, 134
atheism 117
autocracy 79-80, 104-105, 107, 120, 124 (*see also* monarchy)

Bible (Proverbs) 92
Bischoff, Erich 118n12
Bourgeois, Leon 127

Catholicism 92
China 98
"chosen people" ("God's chosen") 92, 109, 116-117
Christianity (Christians) 80, 128
Communism (communists) 86, 100
czarism 120

Damocles, sword of 137
Darwin, Charles 83
David, King 145-146
decomposition of blood 105
despotism 89, 91, 125

economics 87, 99
education 93, 101, 126-127
Elders *see* wise men
elections 103-106
entertainment *see* amusements
equality 80

Fate 145
France 127
free speech 84
Freemasons (Masonry) 86, 89, 100, 109, 113, 117, 119-122
French Revolution 87-88

God 84, 89, 91-92, 109, 116-117, 120, 142-144
gold 78, 84, 87, 90, 92, 137, 142
Goyim as beasts 80, 88, 109, 121-122, 127, 139
greed 82, 100 (*see also* morality)

hatred (racial) 92, 97, 100, 107

Italy 120

Japan 98
Jesuits 91
Jews 99
journalism 85-86, 112 (*see also* press)

Kahal (Qahal) 130
King of Israel 125, 129, 144, 146

liberalism 77-79, 87, 105, 122, 124
liberty 88-89, 110
"liberty, equality, fraternity" 81, 100
luxury 95, 143

Marx, Karl 83
Masonry *see* Freemasons

media *see* press
"might makes right" 79
military 97
miscegenation *see* decomposition of blood
monarchy (monarchists) 80, 100
 (*see also* autocracy)
monopolies (economic) 95
morality (morals) 78
Moses 117

Nietzsche, Friedrich 83

"Patriarch of the International Church" 129
"Patriarch of the World" 125
Per me reges regnant 92
"Pillar of the Cosmos" 146
police force 97, 129, 131
"Pope of the World" 129
population growth 136
pornography 118
poverty 85
"power and hypocrisy" 80
press 83-84, 98, 101, 105, 108, 110-115, 133
progress (social) 93, 116

Qahal *see* Kahal

racial mixing *see* decomposition of blood
revenge 100
revolution 119
rights 86-87, 108
Russia 120

science 86-87
sedition 133
Shulchan Aruch 118n12
socialism (socialists) 86, 100
society women 80

Sovereign 88, 107, 111, 124-127, 131-139, 143-146
 (*see also*: Patriarch of the International Church, Patriarch of the World, Pillar of the Cosmos, Pope of the World, universal ruler, World Ruler)
speculation (economic) 89, 95
string-pullers (wire-pullers) 97
Sulla, Lucius 120
Super-Government 94, 100
Symbolic Serpent 85

United States *see* America
Universal Kingdom 130
universal ruler 86
universities 126

violence 80, 143
Vishnu 112, 129
voting *see* elections

war (world war) 83, 92, 97
wise men (wise counselors) 82-83, 118, 120-121, 145-146
World Ruler 146

Zionism (Zionists) 88, 92

www.ingramcontent.com/pod-product-compliance
Ingram Content Group UK Ltd.
Pitfield, Milton Keynes, MK11 3LW, UK
UKHW020245240426
12048UKWH00026B/1611

9 798987 726327